D1324437

John Stuart Mill and the Pursuit of Virtue

John Stuart Mill and the Pursuit of Virtue

Bernard Semmel

YALE UNIVERSITY PRESS
NEW HAVEN AND LONDON

Published with assistance from the
Mary Cady Tew Memorial Fund.

Designed by James J. Johnson
and set in Monticello Roman type by Grafacon, Inc.
Printed in the United States of America
by BookCrafters, Inc., Ann Arbor, Michigan.

Library of Congress Cataloging in Publication Data

Semmel, Bernard.
John Stuart Mill and the pursuit of virtue.

Bibliography: p.
Includes index.
1. Mill, John Stuart, 1806–1873. I. Title.
B1607.S44 1984 192 83–10215
ISBN 0–300–03006–1

10 9 8 7 6 5 4 3 2 1

TO MAXINE

Contents

Preface

John Stuart Mill has been the subject of hundreds of books and articles for well over a century. Although there is a broad middle ground upon which many writers meet, there have been from the time of his death to the present strong dissenting views. My own opinions belong more or less on this middle ground, though I see Mill as distinctly more conservative than he has generally been depicted. While no one can endow Mill with a "system"—this is one of his excellences—I have attempted a fresh way of understanding and linking his most characteristic opinions. I see these as unfolding from certain closely connected ethical, philosophical, and historical conceptions. While individually these have hardly gone unnoticed, they have not to my knowledge been treated as an interlocking unit with a decisive bearing on Mill's entire thought. Such a perspective makes it possible to read a number of Mill's writings in a substantially different way, among them his best-known essay, *On Liberty*.

While valuing the special methods of analysis and discussion of political theorists and philosophers, from whom I have learned much about Mill and his thought, I have decided to adopt the less-technical approach of the historian of ideas. I hope this will make this essay's argument accessible to a wider readership. Since the University of Toronto Press completed its edition of Mill's letters, there are no unpublished sources. Any claim to fresh materials must therefore lie in my having used extensively the mostly untranslated and until now little-exploited correspondence between Mill and Auguste Comte. The leading subjects of this exchange (on women and the possibility of development) play an important role in my interpretation of Mill's ideas.

I have a number of debts to acknowledge. First of all, I am grateful to the John Simon Guggenheim Memorial Foundation, whose grant of a fellowship for the academic year 1974–75 enabled me to reread Mill and to think through his special contribution to modern liberalism. This was the second such grant I received from the foundation, and I value this mark of its confidence. In the fall of 1975, the department of history at Yale gave me the opportunity of presenting my view of *On Liberty* to a university audience whose questions proved stimulating. I wish to thank the *British Journal of Sociology* for its invitation to contribute to its Fall 1976 special issue on history and sociology; this spurred me to examine at length the ideas of the liberal historian H. T. Buckle, particularly their relationship to Mill's thought. I was also pleased to comply when asked to speak on Mill and the pursuit of happiness before the Anglo-American Historical Conference in London in the summer of 1979. A talk I gave at the American Historical Association's annual meeting in 1979 on the maritime policy and strategy of mid-Victorian liberalism permitted me to discuss the grounds of Mill's opposition to that policy in greater detail than I have found necessary in the present essay.

I should like to thank some friends and colleagues with whom I have discussed certain ideas of the essay or who have read it in whole or in part. These include Martin Albaum, Karl S. Bottigheimer, J. R. Dinwiddy, Oscar A. Haac, Leonard Krasner, Richard A. Levine, Frank Myers, John W. Pratt, Alice and Franklyn Prochaska, Charles E. Staley, David F. Trask, Martin B. Travis, Selwyn Troen, Fred Weinstein, Ruben Weltsch, and John A. Williams. They have made suggestions, a number of which I have followed. I am also grateful to Charles Grench of the Yale University Press for his sympathetic interest and useful counsel, and to Becky Saletan for her editorial assistance and judgment. I have had occasion to call on the generous help of librarians on both sides of the Atlantic and wish particularly to thank those at the British Library, as well as the librarians of Columbia University, the Senate House of the University of London, and the State University of New York at Stony Brook.

Twenty years ago, I dedicated to my wife a book I wrote on the Governor Eyre controversy, in which Mill took a prominent role. In inscribing this essay to her as well, I can only inadequately express how much I owe to her continuing encouragement, to her patience, and to her readiness to comment upon successive drafts of the essay. To say more would be out of place in a preface. I must also mention my son, Stuart, who has proved more helpful than he knows in the course of dinner-table discussions of problems that beset any such work, and who provided an additional, perhaps compelling, motive for its being written.

PROLOGUE

The Choice of Hercules

JOHN STUART MILL RECALLED IN LATER LIFE "THE VERY early age" at which he read with his father the myth of Hercules at the crossroads. Xenophon had included in his memoirs of Socrates this once well-known story first told by the Sophist Prodicus. From his reading of Xenophon's tribute to Socrates, there had come upon the young Mill a lifelong veneration for the Greek philosopher as "a model of ideal excellence." The moral fable of Prodicus would also survive as a confirming and pervading influence. "I well remember," Mill observed in his autobiography, "how my father at that time impressed upon me the lesson of the 'Choice of Hercules.'"[1]

Prodicus had told how young Hercules, as he emerged from boyhood, met two beautiful young women at a crossroads. The first was pure, modest, and sober, and she wore a white robe. The other was "plump and soft," "open-eyed," and "dressed so as to disclose all her charms." The first sought to take Hercules along the road of virtue, and the other, that of sensual and material happiness or vice. When they saw the young hero, Happiness rushed ahead to have the first word. "Hercules," she called out, "I see that you are in doubt which path to take towards life. Make me your friend; follow me, and I will lead you along

1. *The Autobiography of John Stuart Mill*, ed. John Jacob Coss, p. 33. (Hereafter, *Autobiography*.)

the pleasantest and easiest road." She offered Hercules "all the sweets of life." He would not know hardship, worry, or war but would devote himself to gratifying his senses. She would teach him moreover "how to come by all these pleasures with the least trouble," so that he might profit by other men's labors and seize advantage wherever he could. By this time, Virtue had come up alongside and offered a different path. If Hercules took the road to which she pointed, he would perform "high and noble deeds." Rather than deceive him with a tale of "a short and easy road to happiness," she would tell him how the gods had really ordered life. "For of all things good and fair," she declared, "the gods give nothing to man without toil and effort." She urged him to a life of noble exertion and reminded him that Virtue was "first in honour among the gods and among men that are akin to me." Those who followed her path would not live "forgotten and dishonoured" at death but would "live on, sung and remembered for all time." If Hercules chose Virtue, he would possess "the most blessed happiness" and at his death be chosen to live with the immortal gods.[2]

Although as a utilitarian James Mill's "standard of morals was Epicurean" in making happiness life's primary object, his son has told us, "in his personal qualities, the Stoic predominated." James urged the choice of virtue, made by Hercules, upon John Stuart if he were to gain "the most blessed happiness." The elder Mill wished to inculcate the Socratic virtues of

> justice, temperance (to which he gave a very extended application), veracity, perseverance, readiness to encounter pain and especially labour; regard for the public good; estimation of persons according to their merits, and of things according to their intrinsic usefulness; a life of exertion in contradiction to one of self-indulgent sloth.[3]

2. Xenophon, "Memorabilia," in *Memorabilia and Oeconomicus* (Loeb Classical Library, 1953), pp. 20–23.

3. *Autobiography*, p. 33.

The paternal lesson succeeded so well as to shape at the root the character of John Stuart Mill's liberalism.

Mill's reputation as a political thinker has survived almost uniquely among the English writers of the nineteenth century. He remains the almost unchallenged intellectual patron of Anglo-American liberalism. His *Autobiography* succeeds in establishing its bona fides with young men and women to whose personal circumstances, most particularly to whose education, his life offers no obvious similarities. His *On Liberty* is read with enthusiasm and has even become one of the touchstones of our politics. If at the beginning of our century Supreme Court Justice Oliver Wendell Holmes could complain of his fellow justices that they acted as if the laissez-faire sermons of Herbert Spencer were part of the Constitution, we shall see that present-day conservatives might well level this charge against Mill's essay, as it has sometimes been understood. In recent years, his tract on women, which argued for complete equality between the sexes, has made Mill into even more of a cult figure to contemporary liberals.

A number of recent writers have examined Mill's life and thought as if they were the advocates of either God or the Devil at a ceremony of sanctification. Social and political conservatives have come to regard him as their quintessential enemy, and liberals of all shades to see him as the philosopher with whom they share the greatest sympathy. Their praise or damnation of him as man and thinker has been shaped as much by their attitude toward modern liberalism as by their wish to understand Mill. And those who have reviewed these writings about Mill in the popular and scholarly journals have frequently acted on the same principle. Under these conditions an essay in reinterpretation—or perhaps we should say one of restoration—becomes a risky undertaking, particularly if the writer believes that a number of Mill's positions have been seriously misunderstood.

Liberty as a goal for a good society has always been a subject of controversy. The idea of liberty or freedom has a number of ambiguous and sometimes contradictory meanings. Rabelais's Abbey of Thélème had as its motto Do As Thou Wilt, and this is the significance frequently given the concept. Most of the ancient thinkers agreed that liberty meant the freedom to obey the natural laws that governed the universe, society, and our lives in that society, while the eighteenth- and nineteenth-century German philosophers understood liberty as freedom to do what God or reason enjoined. Liberal writers on politics in modern times have stressed the liberty of the individual, the assertion of his rights within wide limits against society's efforts to restrain them. Advocates of more conservative views have denounced these thinkers as being not genuine liberals but libertines.

Mill, like liberty, has proved a subject of contention, and there is a wide range of opinions concerning his position on the political spectrum. A Nobel Prize–winning free-market economist and social theorist, for example, has praised Mill as an advocate of libertarian individualism;[4] in broad agreement with this view, a Marxist political philosopher has denounced him as an exponent of the politics of an amoral, alienating "possessive individualism."[5] Other Marxist and quasi-Marxist writers have defended Mill against such charges, seeing him rather as having tried to restore social values to an egoistic, individualist liberalism.[6] An English

4. See F. A. Hayek, *The Road to Serfdom*, especially pp. 5, 84, 160; and *The Constitution of Liberty*. On a libertarian Mill and modern conservatism, see Frank S. Meyer, "In Defense of John Stuart Mill," *National Review* 1 (28 March 1956): 24.

5. See R. P. Wolff, *The Poverty of Liberalism*, pp. 3–50 passim.

6. This has been the position of C. B. Macpherson, whose *The Political Theory of Possessive Individualism: Hobbes to Locke* (Oxford, 1962) brought the term "possessive individualism" into general discussion. Macpherson has written of Mill's "moral model" in his *Democratic Theory: Essays in Retrieval* (see pp. 4–6 and 174–75 especially), as well as in *The Life and Times of Liberal Democracy*, pp. 44–64. A similar defense of Mill from a perspective on the left, against Wolff's one-sided portrait, may be found in Graeme Duncan, *Marx and Mill: Two Views of Social Conflict and Social Harmony*, pp. 272–76; see also Graeme Duncan and John Gray, "The Left Against Mill," in *New Essays on John Stuart Mill and Utilitarianism*, ed. W. E. Cooper, K. Nielsen, and S. C. Patten.

political theorist has depicted Mill as an authoritarian elitist and has accused him of a "moral totalitarianism."[7] Noting the uses made of Mill's arguments by advocates of a permissive society, a conservative historian of ideas has revised and extended the charges of certain Victorian critics that *On Liberty* bordered on anarchism, while observing that Mill's other writings were substantially different in their emphasis.[8] A conservative political theorist has attacked in all of Mill's thought what he regards as the immoral, liberal concept of an "open society."[9] Of course, a company of liberal defenders continues to portray a moderate Mill—a liberal, a democrat, and a utilitarian, each term variously qualified—a position more or less in harmony with the mainstream of interpretation that has prevailed for over a century.[10]

7. Maurice Cowling, *Mill and Liberalism*, p. 104. Some support for Cowling's position may be found in Shirley Robin Letwin, *The Pursuit of Certainty: David Hume, Jeremy Bentham, John Stuart Mill, Beatrice Webb*, especially pp. 8 and 301. C. L. Ten has seen only one of Mill's writings, *The Spirit of the Age*, in 1831, as substantiating Cowling's view; see his *Mill on Liberty*, pp. 144–51. For other criticisms of Cowling's view, see Duncan, *Marx and Mill*, pp. 276–80; see also J. C. Rees, "Reaction to Cowling on Mill," *The Mill Newsletter* 1 (Spring 1966): 2–11.

8. See Gertrude Himmelfarb's brilliantly argued *On Liberty and Liberalism: The Case of John Stuart Mill*. Himmelfarb has presented a hypothesis of "two Mills," the Mill of *On Liberty* and *The Subjection of Women*, both written under the influence of Harriet Taylor and her overriding interest in the liberation of women, and a second and much sounder Mill. See also her introduction to *John Stuart Mill, Essays on Politics and Culture*. For criticisms of Himmelfarb's position, see J. C. Rees, "The Thesis of the Two Mills," *Political Studies* 25 (September 1977): 369–82; and Ten, *Mill on Liberty*, pp. 151–66.

9. See Willmoore Kendall, "The 'Open Society' and Its Fallacies," *American Political Science Review* 54 (1960): 972–79. The term came into general discussion in Karl R. Popper, *The Open Society and Its Enemies*, though Popper's view of Mill is ambiguous to say the least (see pp. 279–81).

10. See, for example, Albert William Levi, "The Value of Freedom: Mill's *Liberty* (1859–1959)," *Ethics* 70 (1959): 37–46; and David Spitz, "Freedom and Individuality: Mill's Liberty in Retrospect," in *Liberty*, ed. C. J. Friedrich. See also C. L. Ten, "Mill and Liberty," *Journal of the History of Ideas* 30 (January–March 1969): 47–68; and more recently, his *Mill and Liberty*. For a general statement of the moderate position, see John M. Robson, *The Improvement of Mankind: The Social and Political Thought of John Stuart Mill*.

I wish to offer a fresh perspective of this moderate Mill, one who emerges, as we will witness in his letters and essays, from his wrestling with the grand issues of political philosophy. Mill confronted both the ethical problem of choosing between happiness and virtue and, underlying it, the profound, though ultimately unanswerable, philosophical and historical question of free will and necessity—the question of how free we are to choose. In attempting solutions to these problems, Mill had always in mind his foremost political and social objective: the need to maintain liberty as well as progress and order if a good society were to be preserved.

The myth of the choice of Hercules had been used to inculcate a preference for virtue over vice for nearly two millennia by the time the young Mill encountered it.[11] For the ancient philosophers, Prodicus's Hercules, possessing the power to choose, represented man's free will against the *ananke* (necessity) of animal appetites and sloth. Broadly speaking, Hellenistic society had seen two grand divisions among moral thinkers: there were those who praised virtue as the greatest good, and those who assigned that place to pleasure or happiness. The Stoics understood the Herculean labors as representing the efforts of the virtuous to achieve control over themselves and then to employ their moral strength in furthering a society devoted to advancing the common good. Though the Stoic cosmos—both the physical laws which governed the movement of the planets and spheres and the moral laws which bound men—was ruled by necessity, Cicero pointed out in his essay *On Fate* that there was room in their system for a virtue that might alter not merely the apparently irresistible chain of anterior causes leading from one event to another, but even

11. For the uses of the fable of the choice of Hercules in literature, see G. K. Galinsky, *The Herakles Theme*, pp. 101–03, 146–48, 198–99, 213–15; and in art, Erwin Panofsky, *Hercules am Scheidewege* (Leipzig, 1930), pp. 37–196.

the dictates of a divine Providence. The earlier Stoics had seen Hercules as a demigod; the later exponents of the school envisioned him as a man and consequently saw all men as endowed with the free will, the philosophical liberty, to leave behind the road of animal pleasure and necessity and to adopt the path of virtue.[12]

Taking their inspiration from the philosophy of the ancient world, the early modern thinkers of Renaissance Florence saw man at the center of the universe, the effective and responsible shaper of society and of history, in conscious opposition to the medieval religion which had viewed him as passively relying on God's supervisory guidance. There were two principal strands of this Renaissance humanism, one associated with Dante, who urged the responsibility of each individual for the good of the society, and the other a Petrarchan ideal of self-cultivation for an elite. The fifteenth-century Florentine Epicurean writer Poggio delighted in pushing and distorting Petrarch's conception into a public pose of libertine cynicism. But a number of the late fourteenth- and early fifteenth-century Florentine humanists continued to maintain the socially responsible ideal of Dante, and to blend it with that of Petrarch. For the Christian-Stoic thinker and statesman Coluccio Salutati, for example, men, by God's grace, could conceive of a good society and possessed the will to bring it into existence; his was the conception of a "civic humanism," in Hans Baron's phrase, dependent on the moral model of the citizen as a man of virtue. Leonardo Bruni joined to this conception the conviction that a humanist state must rest on the base of political liberty, as did his contemporary, Leon Battista Alberti, who similarly embraced the ideal of social responsibility.

These humanists of the Renaissance revived the cult of the

12. See E. V. Arnold, *Roman Stoicism* (Cambridge, 1911), especially chaps. 4 and 5; and E. Zeller, *The Stoics, Epicureans, and Sceptics* (New York, 1962). When the Stoics wished to single out one of their early leaders, Cleanthes, for special praise, they called him a second Hercules.

hero Hercules: Salutati even composed a monumental though never-completed study of the labors of Hercules, the man of virtue who could overcome fortune. Alberti saw men as engaged in an inner struggle between the irrational forces which drew them toward an animal nature, to an indolent self-indulgence, and those rational forces which urged them to creative activity, which Salutati had named *virtù;* Alberti called the readiness to yield to this passive nature *necessità*. But through reason and creative activity—through the pursuit and practice of virtù—man could triumph over his passivity and animality. In politics, Alberti saw men as capable of creating a society having a stable permanence and yet admitting indefinite improvement. He called upon his fellow citizens to assume their public duties and thereby to secure for themselves the immortality of an honorable fame.

By embracing virtue, Alberti believed, man's human self might triumph over the purely material concerns of his animal self. In this lay humanity's true freedom and dignity. For powerful as necessity and fortune were, and strong as the anterior chain of causation might be, they could be opposed and altered by the man of virtù. The man of moral worth, as well as, in later usage, the man of a powerful and tempestuous will, could overcome necessity. As the men of the Renaissance observed, *Virtù vince Fortuna,* Virtue conquers Fortune.[13]

But the humanist component of this Renaissance philosophy was to come under strong attack in the centuries ahead, principally at the hands of those who called themselves liberals. With the decline of religious faith, science was to replace theology as the

13. See Hans Baron, *The Crisis of the Early Italian Renaissance*, pp. 104–29, 404–11; and Felix Gilbert, *Machiavelli and Guicciardini*, pp. 37–45, 105–52 passim. Quentin Skinner has stressed the importance of Stoicism in Renaissance thinking in *The Foundations of Modern Political Thought* 1, especially pp. xiv, 42–44, 87–88, 162–63. See also R. G. Witt, *Hercules at the Crossroads: The Life, Works, and Thought of Coluccio Salutati* (Durham, N.C., 1983).

chief rival of the humanist spirit. Just as religion had once postulated a system under which man and the universe were subject to divine will, so now the philosophers depicted a world in which all were under the aegis of scientific laws. The philosophy which accompanied the rise of modern science was consequently flawed from the beginning. While liberal rhetoric sounded appeals to freedom, liberal "science," repudiating individual liberty and responsibility, saw men as virtual puppets in the unremitting grip of relentless laws of physics and biology, psychology, history, and economics. What place was there for a deliberately chosen virtue in such an order of things? Yet for much of the nineteenth century liberals preferred to overlook this basic contradiction in their beliefs.

Sooner or later, the philosophical seams of the liberal outlook were bound to show the strains of inner contradiction. Liberals would feel compelled to make a choice between humanism and mechanism, and between virtue and happiness. In our century, most have chosen happiness (sensual satisfaction or material welfare), with which a mechanistic necessity has powerful links. Recent writers, admirers of the ancient philosophers and their ideal of a society living virtuously under the natural law, have reproduced the earlier division between the followers of the Stoics and those of the Epicureans, and have placed Mill in the group of moderns who thought only of entitlements, individual rights, and material happiness.[14] However, despite his hereditary loyalty to a system that stressed both material happiness and necessity, we shall see that Mill moved in another direction.

Since he had received in his formative years a thoroughgoing education in the classics, it should not be surprising that the questions Mill posed were those of the Greek philosophers, as

14. This is particularly the view of students of the University of Chicago political theorist Leo Strauss. See, for example, Hilail Gildin, "Mill's *On Liberty*," in *Ancients and Moderns: Essays on the Tradition of Political Philosophy in Honor of Leo Strauss*, ed. J. Cropsey.

were often enough the answers he painstakingly elaborated.[15] Although rejecting *absolute* free will as contrary to reason, and believing in a necessary chain of causes, in his best-known works his spirit was that of Hercules and the Christian-Stoics of the Renaissance. In every facet of his work, Mill revealed his choice of both virtue and liberty.

For well over a century now—following the example of the French historian and critic Hippolyte Taine—writers have used Mill and the Scottish philosopher and historian Thomas Carlyle to define the extreme poles of Victorian thought. Mill was the positivist thinker, empiricist, and disciple of the French Enlightenment, while Carlyle was the intuitionist and mystic, the spokesman for the German idealism of Hegel and Goethe. Most particularly, these writers have portrayed Mill as a utilitarian, a disciple of Jeremy Bentham's mathematically calculated standard of the greatest material happiness of the greatest number, while a Stoic Carlyle has been depicted as a semisecularized Puritan who sought duty and virtue, not pleasure.

With Carlyle, in Taine's view, "the spiritual and inner man frees himself from the exterior and carnal" and thus he "perceives duty amidst the solicitations of pleasure." The Scotsman's mysticism differed from the German by "its practicality": "he seeks God, but duty also," for "in his eyes the two are but one."[16] Following the German philosophers, Carlyle declared for a free will which made possible individual moral autonomy, against the "scientific" necessity of the Enlightenment, which saw men as creatures of passion and material interest. The utilitarians, Carlyle charged, had dismissed the possibility of a freely chosen response to the call of duty in favor of a mechanistic and "false earthly Fantasm, made-up of Desire and Fear." "Foolish Word-monger and Motive-

15. For Mill's debt to the classics, see H. O. Pappé, "The English Utilitarians and Athenian Democracy," in *Classical Influences on Western Thought: A. D. 1650–1870.*

16. H. A. Taine, *History of English Literature* 4: 323.

grinder," Carlyle wrote of the utilitarian, "who in thy Logic-mill has an earthly mechanism for the Godlike itself, and wouldst fain grind me out Virtue from the husks of pleasure." He decried the England of his time in which "God's Laws are become a Greatest-Happiness Principle, a Parliamentary Expediency" and urged, rather, the love of sacrifice as higher than the love of happiness, and as bringing a more sublime, more holy happiness. For Carlyle, Taine observed, "the idea of duty, the religious spirit, self-government, the authority of an austere conscience, can alone . . . reform a corrupt society."[17]

Mill was a master among philosophers, in Taine's opinion, a Hegel in his powers, though far from the German idealist in his philosophical outlook. Mill was quintessentially English, a logician, one of the "logic-choppers" of whom Carlyle had written, as well as a follower of the utilitarian principle of the greatest happiness that Carlyle had denounced. He was a proponent of induction, the last of a line of English empirical philosophers from Bacon, Hobbes, Locke, and Hume, who had "cleared the human mind of its illusions, presumptions, and fancies"—an enemy of mystics, intuitionists, and idealists.[18]

Taine's approach in sharply contrasting Mill's ideas with those of Carlyle reflected the opinion of the two held by their contemporaries[19] and foreshadowed that of posterity as well. This was the antithesis drawn a half century ago by an American student of Victorian letters, as it was a quarter of a century later in an essay by a noted English literary critic. It predominated in the standard biography of Mill in the 1950s, in which he was depicted as "the Saint of Rationalism." In yet another study of

17. Quoted in ibid., 330; also 349.

18. Ibid., 358, 399–400.

19. See, for example, P. P. Alexander, *Mill and Carlyle: An Examination of J. S. Mill's Doctrine of Causation in Relation to Moral Freedom. With an Occasional Discourse on Sauerteig, by Smelfungus* (Edinburgh, 1866); and, soon after their deaths, Edward Jenks, *Thomas Carlyle and John Stuart Mill* (Kent, 1888).

Mill's thought, a philosopher saw the two as repesenting a division between conflicting systems of belief: Carlyle, the exponent of an organic political theory in the tradition of Rousseau and Hegel, one which stressed free will and the role of history; and Mill, following Hume and Bentham, of a utilitarian theory, which sought individual happiness. If Mill were "the articulate voice of the Liberal revolution," this writer suggested, then Carlyle was "the prophet of the counter-revolution." Similarly, in the 1970s, a historian and critic of Mill's ideas distinguished between the moral and political opinions of *On Liberty* and "alternative systems of thought," noting first of all "the *Weltanschauung* of a Carlyle."[20] Another writer had argued earlier that Matthew Arnold rather than Carlyle was Mill's proper complement because Carlyle "in his substance and spirit" represented "so extreme" a position.[21]

Certainly there were important differences between Mill and Carlyle—on the critical issue of democracy, for example—but I will argue that there was a deep and decisive layer of agreement. While Mill never disavowed his debt to the tradition of the English and French Enlightenment, he, like Carlyle, believed the systems erected on its foundations were fundamentally defective; at bottom Mill was, like the Scotsman, a proponent of virtue and free will, of individual autonomy and responsibility. He was as dedicated to the need for order, which Carlyle apotheosized, as he was to political liberty and the need for improvement. If Carlyle was an English translator of German ideas, Mill transcribed Carlyle's Puritan spiritualism into language acceptable to ma-

20. Emery Neff, *Carlyle and Mill: An Introduction to Victorian Thought*; F. R. Leavis, introduction to *Mill on Bentham and Coleridge* (New York, 1950), pp. 13–15; Michael St. John Packe, *The Life of John Stuart Mill*, bk. 7; R. P. Anschutz, *The Philosophy of J. S. Mill*, pp. 9–10; and Gertrude Himmelfarb, introduction to *On Liberty*, by John Stuart Mill (London, 1974), p. 44. Himmelfarb saw the theology of Cardinal Newman and Matthew Arnold's philosophy as other alternatives.

21. Edward Alexander, *Matthew Arnold and John Stuart Mill*, pp. 6–7.

terialists, rationalists, and empiricists. He thus permitted the liberal descendants of the Puritans, concerned about their duty in this world, to lay claim to their spiritual inheritance by setting it in terms of a Socratic Stoicism. Mill cast his lot with those who spoke of soul and of conscience, and of virtue, duty, and truth as ultimate values.

Mill certainly did not believe the choice between virtue and happiness a simple one. Happiness was not merely sensual pleasure, the gratification of impulse. At the highest level, it conformed to the dictates of morality and reason, and therefore, properly understood, was an entirely desirable good. In his 1832 essay "On Genius," which he began by calling upon the opinions of Carlyle, Mill observed that "whether, according to the ethical theory we adopt, wisdom and virtue be precious in themselves, or there be nothing precious save happiness, it matters little; while we know that where these higher endowments are not, happiness can never be." This was a truth, Mill continued, essential to a correct understanding, and at this point he quoted Carlyle directly on "the significance of man's life."[22]

But if Mill agreed with Carlyle—contrary to the philosophical precepts of the Benthamites and the practical codes of a commercial society—that virtue gave meaning to life and was the basis of true happiness, he was not to agree with the Scottish historian that *entsagen,* sacrifice and the renunciation of happiness, was the necessary road to virtue. This might have been the course for saints or the ascetics who wished to imitate them, but it was not a path most could follow. While virtue insisted that each individual be conscious of the needs of others, men and women ought also to be able to pursue their own happiness, not always to be asked to think first of their duties to society. Increasingly, Carlyle came to see his call for a virtuous self-assertion as directed

22. J. S. Mill, "On Genius," in *Autobiography and Literary Essays*, ed. J. M. Robson and J. Stillinger, *Collected Works* 1: 330.

only to genius, only to the strong. On the other hand, Mill was to see self-realization as the proper goal for all.

Even while he became one of Carlyle's "fervent admirers," his opinions on such matters being animated by the "wonderful power" of Carlyle's writing, Mill was aware that the Scotsman differed with him on such vital questions as "religious scepticism, utilitarianism, the doctrine of circumstances, and the attaching any importance to democracy, logic, or political economy."[23] It had, after all, been a utilitarian James Mill, not Carlyle, who had first instructed John Stuart on the choice of Hercules. Nonetheless, Mill shared with Carlyle a dedication to the common weal, rather than to that yielding to unrestrained individualism prevalent among some sections of the Victorian middle classes. Moreover, unlike Carlyle, Mill was to call for a virtue voluntarily accepted as a guide to life in the Stoic manner, not one imposed by a Savonarola, a Cromwell, or a Robespierre.

There have been certain closely related misunderstandings of Mill's thinking. All the leading commentators have seen the essay *On Liberty* as a plea for the negative freedom of the liberty of the individual against the state and society. I will argue that it was in fact a tract whose major purpose was to advocate the positive freedom of self-development—and of self-control and self-dependence—of the German philosophers, and that this constituted an important part of Mill's conception of virtue.[24] Despite a widely prevalent negative view of German thought, early nineteenth-century liberals on both sides of the Atlantic, among them Ralph Waldo Emerson and George Eliot, acknowledged their intellectual debt to German philosophy, not only to such figures as Kant and Goethe, but to their English disciples, Coleridge and Carlyle.[25] In 1842, Mill observed in a letter to a friend that

23. *Autobiography*, p. 123.

24. See Isaiah Berlin, *Four Essays on Liberty*, pp. 118–72, for a discussion of the distinction between negative and positive liberty.

25. Rosemary Ashton's *The German Idea: Four English Writers and the Reception of German Thought 1800–1860* (Cambridge, 1980) discusses the widely

the English were now more likely to look for new ideas in the writings of the Germans than in those of the French, and he reported that many Englishmen had read not only Kant but even Schelling and Hegel. Mill was among the seekers after this philosophy despite his repeated objections to German intuitionism, as we shall see. His debt to the Germans—particularly to Goethe and his idea of self-perfection—was not incurred directly but, as he was later to confess to the same correspondent, by way of their English and French interpreters,[26] among them Coleridge and, more important, Mill's friend and early mentor Carlyle.

The happiness with which virtue contends in our time is more complex than that implied by Prodicus's moral myth. For Hercules, happiness (or pleasure) was to mean simply a yielding to irrational impulse or instinct—to the animal appetites, to passion, to an agreeable sloth. The Stoic philosophers of the Renaissance, like the ancients, understood that civilization rested on the disciplining of the passions and rejected this happiness of impulse. But happiness might also be thought to be an *interest* pursued by individuals in what Max Weber was to describe as a goal-rational manner, a subordinating of the impulse toward immediate gratification to a long-range material advantage: this was the form most characteristic of nineteenth-century liberalism. Still a third form was the goal of makers of systems, such as Bentham, Comte, and Marx—to organize society so as to promote most efficiently the material interest of all. The Benthamite maxim of "the greatest happiness for the greatest number" more or less

---

held "misinformed and negative idea of the Germans" in nineteenth-century England (p. 1), yet at the same time describes the pervasive influence of German thought not only on Coleridge and Carlyle, but on such liberals as George Eliot, G. H. Lewes, and, less centrally, J. S. Mill. For Mill, see pp. 1–4, 19–21, 25, 126, 177.

26. Mill to Comte, 22 March 1842 and 13 March 1843, *Lettres inédites de J. S. Mill à Auguste Comte*, ed. L. Lévy-Bruhl, pp. 42 and 169. (Hereafter, *Lettres inédites*.)

adequately represents this formulation, one characteristic also of twentieth-century liberalism.

John Stuart Mill was at first to agree with the Benthamite objective, but we shall see that while still a young man, in part because of a personal crisis, he was to disengage himself entirely from the happiness of material interest, whether that of the goal-rational economic man or that of a Benthamite society, as an exclusive end. The pursuit of individual interest in its Weberian form, Mill came to believe, led to heartless competition, made immoral greed seem just, and was fatal to virtue. The efforts of system makers to organize society for happiness would mean not only the crippling of the inward man, upon whose individuality and self-development virtue and genuine happiness depended, but the destruction of liberty. For Mill, a good society required the choice of virtue not only over irrational impulse but also over rational interest, in both the individual case and that of the utopias of the system makers. In Weberian terms, Mill wished to subordinate goal-rational to value-rational behavior; in the phrase of the moral theologian, which Mill in fact was to adopt, he wished to turn to "right reason."

Mill underwent in his lifetime, as we shall observe in the chapters that follow, the full course through which liberals have passed in two centuries. He had at first a faith in Bentham's felicific calculus as a means for achieving a good society and then recognized that the utilitarians had entirely neglected the problems of the inward man, which he came to think the only really important ones. He sought guidance from the Saint-Simonians, largely on sexual questions, and found their views ultimately unsatisfactory for much the same reasons. He then became hopeful that Comte's positivism would provide the answer to social and moral problems, but discovered that Comte, too, had bypassed the vital questions, particularly that of man's freedom to shape his own life. He explored this problem of liberty and necessity, so fundamental to the choice of virtue, first on his own and then as it unfolded in the works of leading historians, notably Tocqueville and Buckle. Like Carlyle, he bemoaned the decline of virtue in contemporary society and developed a view of liberty and utility that he hoped would enable men to resist the ominous tendencies that his prognosis of historical development led him to foresee.

Though Mill longed for a moral code that might be freely adopted and widely shared, he saw that Comte's religion of humanity, with its imposed altruism—or indeed, the scheme of any utopian system maker—was just as repressive as the inflexible codes of the revealed religions, or even more so. Mill's conclusions were not to be cast in the form of rigid social prescriptions, but in terms of his moral ambitions for a mass, democratic society. The apparently practical and "scientific" solutions of such contemporaries of his as Bentham or Saint-Simon, Comte or Marx—solutions that still command numerous disciples, though they are frequently ignorant of their masters—have proved inadequate, as Mill foresaw they would. After the death of James Mill, John Stuart took the opportunity to set aside his father's and Jeremy Bentham's narrow utilitarian creed, which in completely disregarding morals and the inner life, self-dependence and individuality, he had come to believe would have disastrous consequences.

John Stuart Mill was to call for a "neoradicalism" founded on a more complex view of human motivation and needs. "As good may be drawn out of evil," he wrote to a correspondent in 1836, Mill felt his father's death made it "far easier" for him to accomplish what he more and more was to see as his political and philosophical mission: to transform features of his father's creed that "were part of the inheritance of the 18th century" by the introduction of certain central conceptions of German transcendental philosophy. He wished to speak for "not radicalism but neoradicalism," a position which was not "a bigotted adherence" to any doctrinal form "& which is only to be called radicalism inasmuch as it does not falter or compromise with evils but cuts at their roots." Following Carlyle and the German idealists, Mill proposed to hold "in the highest reverence all which the vulgar notion of utilitarians represents them to despise." The new political philosophy would take "into account the whole of human nature not the ratiocinative faculty only," would see "Feeling at least as valuable as Thought," and, as Mill's subsequent writings were to make plain, would make a place in the liberal creed for virtue and not merely material happiness.[27]

What Mill a century and a half ago called "neoradicalism," with, ultimately, its choice of virtue over a potentially liberticide material interest, must be the basis for a present-day liberal reply to the enemies of moral and political freedom on both the left and the right. We live by myths, sometimes without being fully aware that we do so. The choice of Hercules may be seen as Mill's personal myth, about which he formed a complex of interconnected ideas that pervaded and gave a distinctive shape to all his thought. By invoking this complex, he set up a standard of opposition to those forms of liberalism that were becoming dominant, and which he believed were enemies to much that he valued. Mill was to see the translation of his personal myth into a public myth as the necessary basis of a good society.

27. Mill to E. Lytton Bulwer, 23 November 1836, *The Earlier Letters of John Stuart Mill, 1812–1848*, ed. Francis E. Mineka, *Collected Works* 12–13, p. 312. (Hereafter, *EL*.)

ONE

The Burden of John Stuart Mill

THE PHILOSOPHER ALFRED NORTH WHITEHEAD ONCE wrote of the surprise of westerners that orientals could believe in two quite different religions. A Chinese, for example, could be a Confucian and a Buddhist at the same time. Whitehead saw this peculiarity exhibited in the West as well, for he believed that there was a profound inconsistency in the two faiths maintained simultaneously in Europe and America: one displayed a confidence in a "scientific realism, based on mechanism," and the other a contradictory "unwavering belief in the world of men and of the higher animals as being composed of self-determining organisms." "This radical inconsistency at the basis of modern thought accounts for much that is half-hearted and wavering in our civilization," Whitehead declared. It enfeebled all thought.[1]

Within Christianity itself, this fundamental contradiction was also present. Theologians accepted an Augustinianism which saw man as a creature whose every act was divinely predetermined, as well as a quasi Pelagianism which regarded him as an autonomous being, endowed by God with a free will enabling him to choose the path that led to salvation. Christians had debated and had attempted to reconcile these positions for centuries. After Luther, and, in a more thoroughgoing fashion, after Calvin had

1. Alfred North Whitehead, *Science and the Modern World*, pp. 106–07.

revived an Augustinian determinism, the Catholic church renewed its efforts to find an opening for the free will which the early Reformation had so fiercely denied, without entirely undoing the necessitarian logic upon which so much theological argument depended. In Calvinist Holland in the early seventeenth century, the Dutch theologian Arminius worked out a similar compromise for Protestantism, and his example was followed in eighteenth-century England by the Methodist John Wesley's construction of his Evangelical Arminianism.[2]

The Newtonian world view of the seventeenth- and eighteenth-century liberal Enlightenment needed to retain a belief in both free will and determinism as much as did Christian dogmatics. In the mechanical vulgarization of the Deists, the universe was a clock and God was the clockmaker who had set this mechanism in motion. One eighteenth-century Calvinist theologian, the well-known writer of hymns Augustus Toplady, saw in the new science a confirmation of theological determinism. Toplady declared that there was "no such thing as causality, or accident, even in matters of temporal concern, much less in matters spiritual and everlasting." To believe that God would create the universe and then "turn us adrift, to shift for ourselves, like a huge vessel without a pilot" was "a supposition, that subverts every notion of Deity." What appeared certain to Toplady was that "the whole creation, from the seraph down to the indivisible atom, ministers to the supreme will, and is under the special observation, government and direction of the omnipotent mind." Toplady was delighted with the defense of necessity by contemporary scientists. Without the law of gravity, "one happy effect of physical necessity," there would be chaos in the physical world, the Calvinist theologian observed, even as there would be anarchy in the moral world but for the principle of determinism.[3]

2. See Bernard Semmel, *The Methodist Revolution*, pp. 3–22 especially.

3. A. M. Toplady, *The Works of Augustus M. Toplady* (London, 1825), 5: 160–66 and 6: 67.

Toplady corresponded with the scientist Joseph Priestley, who was also a leading liberal political thinker and a founder of English Unitarianism. Priestley had ingenuously noted the similarity of his scientific belief in determinism to Calvinist predestination and called it "a strange phenomenon." Toplady, not finding it strange at all, observed that, after all, "what is Calvinism, but a scriptural expansion of the philosophic principle of necessity?" On the other hand, Toplady observed, Arminian free will was "no less incompatible with the religion of reason, than with the religion of the Bible." Although put off by Priestley's materialism, which he thought "atheistical in its tendency," Toplady was friendly to a fellow determinist, even chidingly suggesting to Priestley that "having set your foot in the Lemaine Lake"—Calvin's Lake Geneva—you may "plunge in." "Seriously," Toplady concluded, "I think you have admitted a Trojan horse into your gates."[4]

The Unitarian Richard Price agreed that a "scientific" determinism was a Trojan horse. In politics a liberal and a democrat like his friend Priestley, Price saw the contradiction between his faith in the possibility of universal redemption and the retention of necessity in any form. He became an early advocate of free will within the Unitarian movement.[5] A liberal age which believed that all men were created equal could only reject a theology in which all men did not have an equal opportunity to achieve salvation. This had been the heart of Wesley's exhilarating evangel to the common people of England in the eighteenth century. While never denying the reality of original sin, Wesley saw men

4. Ibid., 6: 240–43, 291, and 240–41.

5. See, for example, Richard Price, "Additional Observations on the Nature and Value of Civil Liberty and the War with America," in *Richard Price and the Ethical Foundations of the American Revolution*, ed. Bernard Peach (Durham, N.C., 1979), pp. 136–43; also "Observations on the Importance of the American Revolution and the Means of Making It a Benefit to the World," in ibid., pp. 193–94.

as capable, largely by their own efforts, of attaining a Christian perfection.[6]

By the early nineteenth century, the spirit of a liberal and egalitarian theology had virtually driven necessity out of Christian doctrine, and the principle, so long the hallmark of the Reformation creed, had become the almost exclusive possession of science and, to a lesser extent, of liberalism. Christianity was to turn to the intuitionist philosophy of the German idealists of the late eighteenth and early nineteenth centuries—Kant, Goethe, Fichte—and their doctrine of a divinely installed, innate moral sense which guided men's consciences, leaving them free to decide whether to act well or sinfully. Secular liberalism, on the other hand, was poised uncertainly between the liberty enjoined by its social and political theory and the necessity of the new science; it insisted that men were self-determining organisms even as it illogically maintained its faith in a scientific determinism.

John Stuart Mill's philosophy was marked by this ambivalence. That Mill's thought was composed of disparate elements is hardly news. He boasted of his Goethean "many-sidedness," as opposed to the narrowness of the rival positions of Bentham and Coleridge. In recent years, a number of scholars have attempted to find a unifying principle in Mill's ideas that would make consistent what on the surface has appeared a series of contradictions, or at least to provide some means of making these inconsistencies comprehensible.[7] Others have been content to dismiss Mill as an eclectic who proved unable to meet the challenge of system building,[8] although one may argue that it is a theological

6. See Semmel, *Methodist Revolution*, pp. 96–99; also pp. 187 and 23–55 passim.

7. See, for example, Robson, *Improvement of Mankind*, in which Mill is seen as "an unqualified utilitarian" (p. 271).

8. One writer, R. P. Anschutz, in *The Philosophy of J. S. Mill*, has described Mill as "the arch-eclectic" who like his architect contemporaries designed one part of his philosophic edifice in the Renaissance style, another in the Gothic, and still another in the Moorish (p. 59); John Plamenatz, in *The English Utilitarians*,

artifact to expect that truth will prove amenable to any system. Mill was too devoted to truth not to try to make room for apparently divergent truths. But a number of Mill's difficulties grew out of his attempts to create a balance between philosophical liberty and necessity, and between political liberty and order—antinomies which he increasingly saw as linked.

Writing as a historian of ideas in one of his later essays, Mill described three stages of modern intellectual development: the Protestant Reformation, the eighteenth-century Enlightenment, and the late eighteenth- and early nineteenth-century German transcendentalism.[9] The first two represented what Mill had inherited from his father; the last he acquired on his own. The Enlightenment philosophy of reason and science became Mill's lifelong base and embodied the necessitarian strand of his thought. The transcendentalism of the German idealist philosophers provided the ideas of free will and self-development with which he attempted to modify this determinism. In Protestantism, with its links to both liberty and necessity, he found a model for the union of these opposites: "Such is the facility with which mankind believe at one and the same time things inconsistent with one another," he observed in later life of the general body of Christians, without perceiving its application to himself.[10]

The most far-reaching of the intellectual legacies of the elder Mill was the necessitarian Benthamite philosophy upon whose psychological insights he had raised his son, and upon which almost all his ethical, socioeconomic, and metaphysical views

---

has dismissed Mill as "bewildered by the intricacies of his own thought" (p. 122). A political philosopher, A. D. Lindsay, observed that "Mill's openmindedness was too large for the system he inherited; his power of system-making too small for him to construct a new one"; see his introduction to J. S. Mill, *Utilitarianism, Liberty, and Representative Government*, p. viii.

9. J. S. Mill, *On Liberty*, in *Essays on Politics and Society*, ed. J. M. Robson, *Collected Works* 18: 243.

10. Mill, *Autobiography*, p. 29.

were founded. In 1824, when the first issue of their quarterly *Westminster Review* appeared, the Benthamites emerged as a new school, and John Stuart spoke of their "air of strong conviction" when almost no one else appeared to have a "strong faith in as definite a creed." James Mill exercised the chief ascendancy over the talented group of young Benthamites, which included the banker and future historian of Greece George Grote, the lawyer and political theorist John Austin, and, of course, Mill's son, already widely respected as the remarkably successful product of an unusual education. What made James the chief of the school was not merely his powers of intellect and persuasion, but his possession, as his son put it, of "the extreme rarity: that exalted public spirit, and regard above all things to the good of the whole."[11] The doctrine over which he presided included Bentham's utilitarianism, the new political economy of Malthus and Ricardo, and Hartley's metaphysics.

Jeremy Bentham had applied his principle of utility by asking of every proposal, and of every law and institution no matter how well established, whether it contributed to the greatest happiness of the greatest number in society. Nor did he leave the answer to this question in the hazy terms which allowed easy distortion by interested observers. Bentham had quite early in his life determined to give himself up entirely to his "genius" for legislation and had constructed a "felicific calculus" to determine as precisely as possible the amount of pleasure and pain (in degree, duration, and so on) produced by a particular action. Only when all the sums were done could one know whether an action ought or ought not to be undertaken.

In the early years of the nineteenth century, the young James Mill had met the older Bentham, had become persuaded by the new principle, and had formed a party to advance the utilitarian program. Bentham's eccentric genius had long been known, and he had produced a good number of what he saw as eminently

11. Ibid., pp. 70, 71.

practical inventions in the moral field, which much to his surprise had been overlooked. James Mill persuaded the inventor that if sound schemes of reform were to be adopted, government must be removed from the hands of the aristocracy and placed in those of the people generally. The greatest happiness of the greatest number would only be achieved if the greatest number governed.[12]

The disciple was taken up by the master, who had formerly lacked not merely a party but appropriate recognition in England. (A French follower, Etienne Dumont, had edited and translated Bentham's sometimes rough, almost indecipherable notes and had published them in France.) For a time James Mill and his family lived in a cottage attached to the utilitarian philosopher's London house, and Bentham, interested in a successor, observed the talents of the young John Stuart and anxiously asked to adopt the youngster in the event of his father's death. James, too, intended his son to take over the leadership of the Benthamite party, a calling toward which his most unusual education was adapted. Greek at four years old, then Latin, mathematics, history, political economy, psychology—Mill's early training is too well known to bear repetition. Then, at the age of fourteen, John Stuart was sent for a year to live as a member of the family of Bentham's brother in France. The year proved a partial release from the strain of an unremitting education. The Bentham family persuaded him to relax and engage in some of the nonintellectual activities suitable for a teen-aged boy.

Upon his return to England, Mill had a remarkable intellectual and emotional experience. James gave his son certain of Bentham's legal writings to read for the first time. Mill was immediately overwhelmed by the conviction that the usual manner of reasoning on questions of morals and legislation was nothing but a disguised dogmatism. Utility was revealed as an impartial standard which expelled from philosophy such high-sounding but at bottom

12. For the best treatment of Bentham and his thought, see Elie Halévy's magisterial *The Growth of Philosophic Radicalism.*

meaningless sentiments as natural law or conscience. The scientific form of Bentham's classification of offenses and their punishments in accordance with the standard of utility was especially impressive. The logic and the dialectics of Plato had given Mill "a strong relish for accurate classification," a passion confirmed by his having taken up botany as a hobby during his stay in France. The logical form of Bentham's argument as much as its substance completed Mill's conversion.[13]

Though Mill had previously known Bentham's philosophy from his conversations with his father, "in the first pages of Bentham it burst upon me with all the force of a novelty," producing an emotional experience that transformed his life. He wrote:

> When I found scientific classification applied to the great and complex subject of Punishable Acts, under the guidance of the ethical principle of Pleasurable and Painful Consequences, followed out in the method of detail introduced into those subjects by Bentham, I felt taken up to an eminence from which I could survey a vast mental domain, and see stretching out into the distance intellectual results beyond all computation.

The reader of the literature of religious conversion—the sudden coming of the Christian's intense conviction of his faith and salvation—will recognize the mood and the metaphors, though he might well be surprised at the occasion! Mill continued:

> When I laid down the last volume . . . I had become a different being. The "principle of utility" understood as Bentham understood it, and applied in the manner in which he applied it through these three volumes, fell exactly into its place as the Keystone which held together the detached and fragmentary component parts of my knowledge and beliefs. It gave unity to my conception of things. I now had opinions; a creed, a doctrine, a philosophy.

Bentham's vision of a future society operating under the aegis of the principle of utility served "to give a definite shape" to

13. *Autobiography*, p. 46.

John Stuart's aspirations. He now had "in one among the best senses of the word, a religion; the inculcation and diffusion of which could be made the principal outward purpose of a life."[14]

The Benthamite creed extended beyond the principle of utility. "Malthus' population principle was quite as much a banner, and point of union among us, as any opinion specially belonging to Bentham," Mill observed in later life. "This great doctrine, originally brought forward as an argument against the indefinite improvability of human affairs, we took up with ardent zeal in the contrary sense."[15] What had begun as a fatalistic doctrine was altered, in a liberal age, into one that made room for improvement.

Malthus had originally presented his principle of population in 1798 as a rejoinder to optimistic forecasts of a new golden age made by the philosophers of the Enlightenment. Shaken by the events of the French Revolution, and, as an Anglican clergyman, conscious of the essentially sinful nature of all creatures, Malthus was unable to accept this view of inevitable progress. The general outlines of the Malthusian hypothesis are well known: the geometrical rate of increase of population must always exceed the merely arithmetical rate of increase of the means of subsistence. When the numbers of people went beyond the supplies of food available to feed them, nature would seek its remedy in death, starvation, disease, and wars. All efforts to counter the force of this principle, Malthus held, would prove unavailing. If the productivity of the land were increased, for example, or new land brought under the plow, the immediate crisis might be somewhat postponed, but the increase in available food would only encourage a further disastrous increase in population.

Malthus's principle lent itself to a translation into theological terms. The mood of the first edition of Malthus's essay was Augustinian: the doom of an ineradicable original sin had made

14. Ibid., pp. 45–46, 48, 47.
15. Ibid., pp. 73–74.

the realization of a terrestrial paradise impossible. David Ricardo was to base his "iron law of wages" on Malthusian population theory. Wages would necessarily tend to remain at a subsistence level, Ricardo maintained, for were they raised, workers would produce more children, which could only have the result of lowering the price of labor until population and wages were again in balance.[16] Mill saw the "voluntary restriction of the increase of their numbers" as "the sole means" by which the working class could secure "full employment at high wages."[17] Yet despite the scriptural tone of Malthus's views, for some decades devoted Christians vociferously opposed them, for Malthus had not only dismissed as futile the charity that the Church enjoined, but envisioned a providential system more cruel and pitiless than eighteenth- and nineteenth-century Anglicans cared to assign to the Creator.

In 1803, a second, expanded edition of the essay announced a way of escape from overpopulation and disaster. The answer lay in "moral restraint." There was to be a place for voluntary action in the scheme of things. If men and women unable to support a family would refrain from marrying; if others chose to marry later in life, thus cutting short the years of fertility; and if after marriage they limited their sexual intercourse to keep the family small, it might be possible to avert the disastrous cycle. The author of the essay did not, however, appear convinced that sufficient numbers of people would of their own will undertake such behavior.[18]

It remained for the Benthamites to fill the loophole of moral restraint that Malthus had uncovered and to provide a realistic instrument for making choice effective. As a young man, Mill

16. See discussion in Halévy, *Growth of Philosophic Radicalism*, pp. 331–32.

17. *Autobiography*, p. 74.

18. See introduction to T. R. Malthus, *On Population*, ed. and introd. Gertrude Himmelfarb (New York, 1960), pp. xiii–xxxvi; also Patricia James, *Population Malthus* (London, 1979), chaps. 2–4, 11.

was to spend a night in jail for distributing birth-control pamphlets to working people in St. James's Park.[19]

Equally fundamental to James Mill's view of society, his son observed, were the metaphysics of the eighteenth-century Anglican clergyman David Hartley, which described the formation of individual character by circumstances through association.[20] Like other English empirical philosophers, the philosophic Radicals dismissed the Cartesian belief in innate qualities in favor of the Lockean formulation. Man as he emerged from the womb was a tabula rasa upon which experience, operating through the laws of association discovered by Hartley, would write the "program" which would make him different from other men. Quite literally, all men were born equal.

During Mill's lifetime, though well before the work of Mendel and Weismann on heredity, there was to be an increasing inclination to see inherent variations in physical and mental capacities. Most Continental writers generally accepted the reality of racial differences, between, for example, the black man and the white, and the German, the Frenchman, and the Russian. Mill's close friend and biographer, Alexander Bain, noted his unwillingness to accept even the possibility of such innate differences, though Bain, also a steadfast associationalist psychologist, patiently pointed out to Mill the difficulties of a starkly environmentalist position.[21]

While there were certainly scientific grounds for accepting Lockean and associationalist doctrine, we can only see Mill's unwillingness to entertain any doubts as a species of faith. Only if this position were correct could he maintain the vision of the "unlimited possibility of improving the moral and intellectual condition of mankind by education" upon which he based his

19. See Pedro Schwartz, *The New Political Economy of J. S. Mill*, pp. 26–30, 245–50.

20. *Autobiography*, p. 75.

21. Alexander Bain, *John Stuart Mill, a Criticism: With Personal Recollections*, p. 84; also pp. 131, 146–48.

hopes for the future.[22] If people were predestined to occupy a lowly position from the time of birth, if they were not capable of improvement because they were Negroes, or Russians, or proletarians, or women, Mill's view of the world would be shaken. Yet, though a man's character was *determined* by the experiences of his life, largely by forms imposed upon him by others and by social conditions, Mill was to insist that a person was still sufficiently free, by acting on himself, to improve his own moral and intellectual lot.

There were other, more personal grounds for Mill's Hartleian faith: his modesty, which at times bordered on a surprising lack of self-confidence, and his filial piety. The egalitarianism of the tabula rasa and Hartleian associationalism had been the creed of his father, and the basis of the very unusual education that Mill had undergone. He described the success of his father's educational experiment as demonstrating the ease with which the early years of childhood might be constructively employed, rather than as they generally were:

> If I had been by nature extremely quick of apprehension, or had possessed a very accurate and retentive memory, or were of a remarkably active and energetic character, the trial would not be conclusive; but in all these natural gifts I am rather below than above par; what I could do, could assuredly be done by any boy or girl of average capacity and healthy physical constitution: and if I have accomplished anything, I owe it, among other fortunate circumstances, to the fact that through the early training bestowed on me by my father, I started, I may fairly say, with an advantage of a quarter of a century over my contemporaries.[23]

The elder Mill carefully refrained from praising his son and wished also to protect him against hearing himself praised, lest John Stuart "make self-flattering comparisons" between himself

22. *Autobiography*, p. 75.
23. Ibid., p. 21.

and others. "If I thought anything about myself," Mill continued, "it was that I was rather backward in my studies, since I always found myself so, in comparison with what my father expected from me."[24]

Mill's father had instilled in him the feeling that "whatever I knew more than others, could not be ascribed to any merit in me, but to the very unusual advantage which had fallen to my lot, of having a father who was able to teach me, and willing to give the necessary trouble and time." "Oh God," a seventeenth-century Puritan might have said, "well do I know that I have within me no merit whatsoever but that which is due to the free gift of Thy grace." But John Stuart was told that his debt was to his natural father, not his heavenly one. Mill's critics were even to suggest that he was a "made man," as if he had been constructed in the manner of Mary Shelley's monster. Mill concluded that his father's view was "exactly the truth and common sense of the matter."[25] However, in the late 1820s, when he encountered his well-known "crisis," he did have some second thoughts.

Mill's mental breakdown in 1826 was in its most important aspect a religious crisis from which the philosopher never fully recovered. He himself understood this. We recall the evangelical mode which he employed in proclaiming his conversion to Benthamism. Mill described his crisis, similarly, as "the state, I should think, in which converts to Methodism usually are, when smitten by their first 'conviction of sin.'"[26] This was Mill's *accidie*, little different at core from those experienced by Abelard, Luther, or Wesley.

Up to the autumn of 1826, Mill had been content with his life's goal to be "a reformer of the world." But quite suddenly

24. Ibid., p. 23.
25. Ibid., p. 24.
26. Ibid., p. 94.

this happiness dissolved. Mill found himself in "a dull state of nerves," indifferent to what had formerly been pleasurable. He asked himself whether he would be happy if all his hopes for the reform of society were to be realized. When he perceived that the answer was no, his heart sank, and "the whole foundation on which my life was constructed fell down." "I seemed to have nothing left to live for," he wrote. Nor did this dismal mood pass away; indeed it became more grim and more pervasive. Mill quoted lines from Coleridge's "Dejection," which he was not to read till later, as describing his condition at that time:

> A grief without a pang, void, dark and drear,
> A drowsy, stifled, unimpassioned grief,
> Which finds no natural outlet or relief
> In word, or sigh, or tear.

There was no one to whom he could turn. He was convinced that his father would not have the smallest conception of his problem. In any event, his father would be pained to think that John Stuart's education—"which was wholly his work"—had had so doleful an outcome.[27]

Mill was now persuaded, much against his earlier view of the matter, "that the habit of analysis has a tendency to wear away the feelings." The relentless quest for certainty had exacted a wounding emotional penalty. In his own case, as he now understood, only his powers of analysis had been cultivated. He might be intellectually convinced that sympathy and altruistic feelings produced genuine happiness, but to know this did not bring happiness. His education had failed to create those sentiments and had made a "precocious and premature analysis the inveterate habit" of his mind. He had been "left stranded" with "a well-equipped ship and a rudder, but no sail." The negative thrust of the enlightenment doctrine had proved unsatisfying. Mill found "no delight in virtue or the general good"; his ambition had

27. Ibid., pp. 93–95.

entirely "dried up." He felt the need but not the power "to begin the formation of my character anew."[28]

Mill was later to defend Benthamites as a group against the charge that they were "mere reasoning machine[s]," but he admitted that for two or three years of his life such a description was "not altogether untrue of me." The years were those that preceded his breakdown. Young men, Mill explained, can hardly be expected to be more than one thing, and he was a logician. What he lacked was "poetical culture"—though, he wrote, "I was imaginatively very susceptible" of such feelings—which might have provided sentiments of "genuine benevolence, or sympathy with mankind" and a "high enthusiasm for ideal nobleness."[29] Bentham himself had looked down upon the imagination and upon feelings in general and has been quoted as describing the child's game of push-pin to be as good as poetry, if it produced as much pleasure.

What Mill called poetical culture, a previous generation might have called religious sensibility. Certainly the great seers of the nineteenth century, poets like Wordsworth and Coleridge and writers of poetical prose like Carlyle, filled roles more similar to those of William Law, John Wesley, and George Whitefield in the preceding century than to those of Pope and Dryden. Poetry in the early nineteenth century, like religion earlier, supplied its devotees with sentiments of benevolence and nobleness and provided the urn in which the spontaneous feelings of youth might be stored. Without the instilling of such sentiments, there would be breakdown, Mill concluded at the time of his crisis. It is well known that Mill turned for relief to Wordsworth and to Carlyle. Readers of the *Autobiography* will also recollect that after six months of this gloom, Mill chanced to read the passage in Marmontel's *Mémoires* that told of the death of the hero's

28. Ibid., pp. 96, 97–98.
29. Ibid., pp. 76–77.

father and the son's sudden realization that he could now fill his father's place in the family's affections. Mill began to cry and his "burthen grew lighter" as he perceived that he still possessed feelings. Once more, he could find pleasure in everyday affairs and in his work for the public good. His condition gradually improved, and though he had several relapses, he reported that "I never again was as miserable as I had been."[30]

But in his diagnosis of the crisis, Mill perceived a philosophical cause clearly allied to his partly suppressed resentment of his father. He had been a ship "carefully fitted out," but without a sail. Mill saw the depressions to which he was subject as the consequence of "the doctrine of what is called Philosophical Necessity [which] weighed on my existence like an incubus." "I felt as if I was scientifically proved to be the helpless slave of antecedent circumstances"; "I often said to myself, what a relief it would be if I could disbelieve the doctrine of the formation of character by circumstances." Mill sought and believed he had found a way out from under this burden. "I saw that though our character is formed by circumstances, our own desires can do much to shape those circumstances." "What is really inspiriting and ennobling in the doctrine of free-will," he concluded, "is the conviction that we have real power over the formation of our character."[31]

In the late 1820s and in the 1830s, Mill renounced his Benthamite sectarianism. From the time of his intellectual and emotional crisis, the necessitarian creed of his father and Bentham was no longer sufficient for him. It had to be supplemented by portions of the free-will faith of the German romantics. The former doctrine, when held alone, had produced breakdown. The latter, alone, could not be acceptable to an adherent of science and reason, raised in the doctrines of Hartley, Bentham, and Ricardo. Yet Mill saw some truth in both. He was to take up

30. Ibid., p. 99.
31. Ibid., pp. 118–19.

the idealist Carlyle as his friend, and Coleridge and Wordsworth as his poetical guides. Nonetheless, convinced that philosophical idealism was in the ascendancy in Britain and in Europe, Mill identified himself most prominently with the truths he had received from his father and Bentham, and against the doctrines of intuitionism and revealed religion. But since he held on to his newfound faith as well, George Grote and others of his former circle saw themselves abandoned in favor of their enemies, meaning, above all, Carlyle.[32]

Thomas Carlyle was born in Scotland in 1795 to poor parents who helped to educate him to be a minister of the Kirk. But Carlyle had lost his faith and set off for London, where he determined to earn his livelihood as a writer. A self-proclaimed mystic, he became a great admirer of the German idealist philosophers and, in consequence, a severe critic of a materialistic and mechanistic liberalism.

Not only the German idealists but a group of French socialists, the Saint-Simonians, exercised an early influence on the Scotsman. These socialists had established a new religion on the basis of the later ideas of their master, Comte Henri de Saint-Simon, whose *Nouveau Christianisme*, first published in 1824, had impressed Carlyle. The Saint-Simonians' influence upon Carlyle has been discussed by scholars, who have noted the appearance of their views of historical progress in his works. Goethe, whom Carlyle much admired and with whom he corresponded, had even felt compelled in 1830 to warn the Scotsman to steer clear of the sect.[33] There were important points of agreement between the German philosophers and the Saint-Simonians; both sought a spiritual regeneration and saw individual rights as an aberration

32. Bain, *Mill*, pp. 55–57, 83–84n.

33. See Thomas Carlyle, *The Collected Letters of Thomas and Jane Welsh Carlyle*, ed. C. R. Sanders and K. J. Fielding, 5: 191n. (Hereafter, *Collected Letters*.)

that must give way to a nobler ideal of duties to the state. It was, then, under the joint influence of the Germans and the Saint-Simonians that Carlyle proceeded to attack materialistic individualism.

"Men are grown mechanical in head and in heart, as well as in hand," Carlyle complained in "Signs of the Times" in 1829, an essay that foreshadowed a number of Mill's later ideas. The philosophers of the age were no longer Socrates or Plato, who had praised the pursuit of virtue and the happiness obtained from its practice, but Adam Smith and Jeremy Bentham, who taught that our happiness and, indeed, all "our sentiments" depended entirely on external conditions. Carlyle charged the Benthamites in particular with seeing good government as a machine fueled by the "appetite for self-interest" and requiring "no virtue in any quarter."[34]

Invoking truth and virtue, the ideals of a heroic and moral age, Carlyle declared war on the philosophies of "the Mechanical Age." Materialistic doctrines like those of the associationalist Hartley and the determinist Priestley had led "into bottomless abysses of Atheism and Fatalism." These philosophers had denied the very existence of any inward sentiments that could not be perceived or measured mechanically. There was no room for the passions, for poetry or religion, for enthusiasm or wonder.[35] All actions, even such historical events as the Crusades or the Puritan Revolution, were seen as motivated by an interest in securing profits and avoiding losses, rather than (as was in fact the case) by religious sentiment. Men ascribed events not to the ideas and emotions, embedded "in the mystic depths of man's soul," that moved people to act, but to the "force of circumstances." While civil liberty seemed secure, "our moral liberty is all but lost," Carlyle declared. Men were prisoners of a fatalistic creed, "shackled

34. Thomas Carlyle, "Signs of the Times" (1829), in *The Works of Thomas Carlyle* 27: 63, 67.

35. Ibid., pp. 65–66.

in heart and soul with far straiter than feudal chains."[36] In all this, the Scotsman appeared to be speaking precisely of Mill's condition during his psychological crisis.

Carlyle passionately defended the creed of humanism, in which man was not "the creature and product of Mechanism" but its creator, and invoked the Stoic faith in virtue. It was not the *forms* of government that made a virtuous people, as "the Code-maker" (Carlyle's name for Bentham) had asserted, but a virtuous people that formed a good government. Unfortunately, the present age was not a spiritual but a material one:

> The infinite, absolute character of Virtue has passed into a finite, conditional one; it is no longer a worship of the Beautiful and Good; but a calculation of the Profitable. Worship, indeed, in any sense, is not recognised among us, or is mechanically explained into Fear of pain, or Hope of pleasure. Our true Deity is Mechanism.

The reputed superior morality of the age was produced "not by a greater love of Virtue," but by the superiority of the police and of "that far subtler and stronger Police called Public Opinion." It was an age in which self-denial, "the parent of all virtue," was but rarely encountered, in which no one loved truth "with an infinite love," in which "Virtue is Pleasure, is Profit," making of it "no celestial, but an earthly thing."[37]

Yet Carlyle understood the need to interweave the spiritual (poetry, religion, morality) and the mechanical. Both had to be forwarded if the vices of each, advanced separately, were to be avoided. An imbalanced concentration on the inward sentiments might lead to superstition and fanaticism; an inordinate stress on the outward and mechanical would destroy "Moral Force," which fathered all other powers. The Scottish writer complained that "in true dignity of soul and character" the present might well be inferior to past civilizations. But Carlyle did not despair,

36. Ibid., pp. 70–71, 75, 79.
37. Ibid., pp. 73–74, 78–79.

for he had "a faith in the imperishable dignity of man" and in his "high vocation." If mechanism imprisoned man as in a glass bell, by drawing on their spiritual resources men could shatter that bell and recover the heroic wisdom and nobility of the past. Men might secure not merely political liberty but a "higher, heavenly freedom." Only a fool would attempt to reform the world before he had undertaken "the only solid, though a far slower reformation," that of himself, Carlyle concluded.[38]

When Carlyle read several historical articles written by Mill in 1831, he proclaimed, somewhat surprisingly, "Here is a new Mystic." Carlyle recognized Mill's themes to be similar to those set down a quarter of a century earlier by the German idealist philosopher Fichte, and more recently by the Saint-Simonians.[39] Mill was at this time relatively innocent of German philosophy; he had become intimate with the followers of Saint-Simon and was sympathetic not only to their views on historical development, as we shall see, but also to certain of their other opinions. Certainly, as Carlyle had seen, the Saint-Simonian philosophy of history had helped to stimulate and to shape Mill's 1831 articles. Still, it was remarkable to have discovered a mystic in the son whom James Mill had educated so as to minimize any effect the imagination and the emotions might have on the rational faculties. Carlyle made inquiries concerning the author of the articles, and the two men met and became fast friends, despite their differing intellectual styles. In a letter to his wife, Jane, in late August 1831, Carlyle referred to Mill as "a converted Utilitarian, who is studying German." After meeting Mill in early September, Carlyle was entirely won over: "A slender rather tall and elegant youth," he wrote Jane, with "two small earnestly-smiling eyes: modest, remarkably gifted with precision of utterance; enthusiastic, yet lucid, calm. . . . We had almost four hours of the best talk I have mingled in for long: The youth walked home with me

38. Ibid., pp. 73, 81–82.
39. *Autobiography*, p. 122; also p. 115.

almost to the door" and "seemed to profess almost as plainly as modesty would allow that he had been converted by the Head of the Mystic School, to whom personally he testified every heart-looking regard."[40]

Mill had been trained as a rationalist and a logician, while Carlyle's conversation and writings were, as Mill later correctly described them, "a haze of poetry and German metaphysics." Carlyle, moreover, was opposed to virtually all the liberal doctrines to which Mill, despite his rebellion from the narrow utilitarian creed, continued to adhere. But Mill was moved by what he called Carlyle's "wonderful power." "I was during a long period one of his most fervent admirers," he was later to write, "but the good his writings did me, was not as philosophy to instruct, but as poetry to animate."[41] To the horror of his old friends, Mill had been won over, and his ensuing correspondence with Carlyle testifies to a considerable intimacy.

Mill determined to be the instrument by means of which Carlyle might become better known to the public, "unless," as he wrote to the Scotsman, "an iron Necessity, insuperable by the free will of man should . . . prevent"—a pregnant phrase. These early letters of the 1830s display Mill as "a logical expounder," admiring from his "humbler sphere" Carlyle as an "artist." Mill saw his role as that of "an auxiliary" to Carlyle; he would translate the intuitive truths which Carlyle had declaimed as a poet into "the metaphysical and logical form, which would make the Truth accessible to a *greater* number of persons." In one letter to Carlyle, he observed that "if I have any *vocation,* I think it is exactly this, to translate the mysticism of others into the language of Argument."[42] This Mill succeeded in doing in a number of his major essays.

40. Thomas to Jane Carlyle, 29 August and 4 September 1831, *Collected Letters* 5: 379, 398.

41. *Autobiography*, pp. 122–23.

42. Mill to Carlyle, 29 May and 17 July 1832, 5 July 1833, and 2 March 1834, *EL*, pp. 104, 113, 169, 219.

Like Mill, many English Unitarians were also to make the journey from an Enlightenment determinism to a German transcendentalism. Among the first was Coleridge, who had begun his career as a Unitarian minister and a great admirer of the associationalist philosopher Hartley. "I am a complete necessitarian, and understand the subject as well as Hartley himself," he wrote to the poet Robert Southey in late 1794.[43] Coleridge had even persuaded his friends Southey and Wordsworth to join him in these views. A "practical faith in the doctrine of philosophical necessity," a belief "that vice is the effect of error and the offspring of surrounding circumstances, the object therefore of condolence not of anger," was essential if men would "erect the edifice of Freedom" and not "the Temple of Despotism," he declared.[44] When his first son was christened in 1796, Coleridge gave him the name of Hartley, "that great master of Christian philosophy."[45]

By 1801, however, Coleridge had cast aside the doctrine of association and "with it all the irreligious metaphysics of modern infidels—especially the doctrine of necessity." He had come to this new position through his reading of the German philosophers, though his growing distaste for the French Revolution, founded, he thought, on the necessitarian views of the philosophes, played an important role in his conversion. By 1804, Coleridge was denouncing "the pernicious doctrine of Necessity" as a "labyrinth-den of sophistry" and was pleased that he had been able to rescue both Wordsworth and Southey from the false view.[46]

Coleridge had been the first of the English Unitarians to turn to the German philosophers; in the United States, similar views were championed by a number of New England Unitarians

43. Coleridge to Southey, 11 December 1794, in *Letters of Samuel Taylor Coleridge*, ed. E. H. Coleridge, 1: 113. (Hereafter, *Letters*.)

44. Coleridge, "Conciones ad Populum" (February 1795), in *Collected Works of Samuel Taylor Coleridge* 1: 48–49.

45. Coleridge to T. Poole, 24 September 1796, *Letters* 1: 169.

46. Coleridge to Poole, 16 March 1801 and 15 January 1804, *Letters* 1: 348–49, 2: 454.

under the influence of Coleridge, the German thinkers, and, somewhat later, Carlyle. Among these transcendentalists, as they called themselves, were the Unitarian theologian William Ellery Channing and his disciple Ralph Waldo Emerson.[47] The young Emerson had read and admired Carlyle's early writings and journeyed to Scotland in 1833 to meet him. By chance, it had been Mill who provided Emerson with a letter of introduction to the Scotsman, though he did not think the American "a very hopeful subject." Greatly to Mill's surprise, Carlyle was enthusiastic after speaking to Emerson.[48] The Scottish seer, as is well known, was to remain an intellectual hero of Emerson's and an idol of this New England circle.[49] Emerson arranged for the American publication of Carlyle's *Sartor Resartus,* which called for a heroic self-assertion against middle-class conformity and was to become a volume of inspiration for the New England transcendentalists.

Though the conversion of the main body of English Unitarians from necessity to free will was somewhat delayed, by the late 1820s such a move was underway. The British Unitarian organ, the *Monthly Repository,* edited by William Johnson Fox, included two articles on Hartley in 1828. While not prepared to condemn him entirely, as Coleridge had done, the authors of these pieces reinterpreted Hartley's writings to make room for free will. The *Repository* defended Hartley against the misrepresentation of his views "as degrading man into a mere machine"; on the contrary, the philosophy of association served "to raise our views of the dignity of human nature" by demonstrating how men, from being originally "mere masses of material observation . . . capable of

47. For a general survey of American transcendentalism, see F. O. Matthiesen, *American Renaissance* (New York, 1941), and Van Wyck Brooks, *The Flowering of New England, 1815–1865* (New York, 1941).

48. Mill to Carlyle, late July, 2 August, and 5 October 1833, *EL*, pp. 169, 171, 183.

49. See, for example, J. F. Clark, "The Influence of Carlyle," in *The Transcendentalists: An Anthology*, ed. Perry Miller (Cambridge, Mass., 1950), pp. 43–44; and, in the same volume, N. L. Frothingham, "*Sartor Resartus*," pp. 103–05. Thoreau also wrote an adulatory essay on Carlyle.

none but earthly and sensual pleasures," might be "gradually emancipated from this slavish dependence," being "capable of indefinite degrees of intellectual and moral improvement."[50] This defense of Hartley from the standpoint of the German philosophers, at core antinecessitarian in its denunciation of "slavish dependence" and in its appeal for "intellectual and moral improvement," has an extraordinary resemblance to what was becoming Mill's position on the subject. In the years following, Fox made the *Repository* a vehicle for enlightening England on the new German philosophy. Goethe and Schiller were the subjects of enthusiastic articles,[51] and Herder was defended against the charge that he was a historical fatalist; on the contrary, the *Repository* suggested approvingly, the German historian, faithful to the spirit of his nation's philosophy, believed "the advancement of society to depend on the free choice and voluntary cooperation of individual men."[52]

The *Repository* in 1831 also found "much . . . both to admire and imitate" in the Saint-Simonians. The Unitarian journal praised the principal aim of their "system," the battle against selfishness and for brotherly love. "Nothing has occurred since the Reformation in which the interests of Christianity, that is, of humanity, have been so deeply involved as in the development of this new doctrine," the *Repository* declared, though it cautioned against "some enthusiastic extravagances" and observed that the kind of hierarchy the Saint-Simonians proposed "would not be a little dangerous." The Unitarian organ approved also of the Saint-Simonian view of historical development.[53]

50. [W. T.], "Hartley's Rule of Life," *Monthly Repository* 2 (May 1828): 293–94, 297–98; continued in ibid. (September 1828): 595–601.

51. See "On the State of Religious Opinion and Religious Liberty in Germany," *Monthly Repository* 4 (1830): 585–89; [J. M.], "Letter from Germany," ibid. 5 (April 1831):281; and the series of monthly articles on "Goethe and His Works," ibid. 6 (May through November 1832): 289–308, 361–71, 460–69, 505–20, 595–603, 681–89, 742–56.

52. [T.], "Herder's Thoughts on the Philosophy of the History of Mankind," *Monthly Repository* 6 (April 1832): 38–42, 223.

53. See "The French Sect of Saint Simonites and the New Christianity

Fox was an intimate of the young Mill, who was to become a contributor to the *Repository* and a member of the editor's circle of friends. The *Repository* remained the official organ of the denomination until 1832, but more orthodox Unitarians lost confidence in the periodical because of Fox's unconventional views, particularly on marriage and divorce. Mill clearly shared these views, as did Harriet Taylor, the wife of a Unitarian wholesale druggist whom Mill met one evening at Fox's table, and with whom he was to fall in love and, after her husband's death, to marry. Members of Fox's circle were also to join Mill in his special admiration for Carlyle and his opinions.[54]

By the late 1830s, the mainstream of English Unitarianism had turned decisively against necessity. James Martineau, who was to be the leading theologian of the denomination for over half a century, had long been a follower of Hartley, Priestley, and Bentham. At this time, he came under the influence of Coleridge, Channing, and Carlyle. Discarding determinism and embracing free will, Martineau created a place in his doctrine, as he saw it, for both soul and conscience. The "sense of individual accountability," he observed in a sermon in 1839 in which he proclaimed his new views, "notwithstanding the ingenuity of orthodox divines on the one hand, and necessitarian philosophers on the other," was "impaired by all reference of the evil that is in us to any source *beyond ourselves*." It was consequently impossible for Christians to defend the doctrine of philosophical necessity, "which presents God to us as the author of sin and suffering."[55] When a copy of Martineau's sermon reached Boston, Channing wrote with delight at this lifting of "a mill-stone around the neck of Unitarianism in England." For his own part, Martineau

of Its Founders," *Monthly Repository* 5 (February 1831): 82, 88; "The Saint Simonites," ibid. (March 1831): 189; review of "De la Religion Saint-Simonienne," ibid. (April 1831): 279–81.

54. See Packe, *Life of Mill*, pp. 120–45, 179, 288.

55. Quoted in J. Drummond and C. B. Upton, *The Life and Letters of James Martineau* 2: 272.

declared that he had experienced a sense of deliverance, "an escape from a logical cage into the open air."[56]

In later years the Unitarian theologian was to single out certain figures as having exerted a special influence on his views. Martineau kept in his "gallery of *theologians*" "a niche for the author of *Hero-Worship*," an 1841 work in which Carlyle argued that greatness lay in the practice of the heroic virtues. Carlyle, like Coleridge, had had a "vast influence" on "the inmost faith of our generation"; but it had been Carlyle particularly who had "touched with a strange devoutness many a class, which book and surplice had ceased to move." Martineau meant the "academics, artists, litterateurs, 'strong-minded' women, 'debating' youths, Scotchmen of the phrenological grade."[57] He was speaking, in fact, of people like John Stuart Mill, Harriet Taylor, and their friends.

One may reasonably argue that one of the attractions which Mrs. Taylor possessed for Mill at their first meeting in 1831 was that she, like other Unitarian liberals, and like Mill himself, was troubled by a repressive, necessitarian past and had sought solace in a Carlylean transcendentalism. As late as 1840, Mill and Harriet Taylor were regular visitors to Carlyle's household; Bain was to describe Mrs. Taylor as "one of his [Carlyle's] great admirers."[58] Another admirer of Carlyle was Mill's close friend John Sterling, the Coleridgian whose article eulogizing the Scotsman Mill published in his *London and Westminster Review* in 1839. After Sterling's death, Carlyle wrote his biography. Harriet Taylor may well have served as a storer of Carlylean influence after Mill's break with the Scottish philosopher and the death of Sterling—as the personification of the necessary

56. Quoted in ibid., 272–73.

57. James Martineau, "Personal Influence on Present Theology," in *Essays, Reviews, and Addresses* 1 (London, 1891): 224–26, 271.

58. Bain, *Mill*, p. 163; see also R. P. Anschutz, "J. S. Mill, Carlyle, and Mrs. Taylor," *Political Science* 7 (1955): 65–75.

other half of thought which Mill sought to merge with his Benthamite inheritance.[59]

We recall that Mill had discovered a fundamental philosophical conflict at the root of the crisis which faced him in the autumn of 1826—that between free will and determinism. In the next several years, he was to succeed in resolving this antagonism, to his own satisfaction at least. When in 1843 Mill published his first major work, his classic *System of Logic,* he undertook a formal treatment of the problem. This may be found in the chapter titled "Of Liberty and Necessity," which he described at the time to a friend as "the best chapter in the two volumes."[60]

Mill's solution to the metaphysical difficulty drew heavily on the conclusions of the German philosophers. In this chapter of the *Logic* Mill insisted that the believers in necessity had attributed a meaning to the term which it ought not properly to bear, that of an irreversible fatalism. "A necessitarian believing our actions follow from our characters, and that our characters follow from our organization, our education, and our circumstances, is apt to be with more or less of consciousness on his part, a fatalist": this was the faith in which Mill himself had been raised, and which he had come to find an intolerable burden. Such a view "revolts our feelings," Mill declared, and caused its advocates to suffer "depressing consequences." The "feeling of moral freedom" of which we were conscious was the feeling that we could "modify our own character" if we chose; by keeping this sentiment clearly in view, the free-will doctrine had given those who adhered to it "a practical feeling much nearer to the truth" than had the doctrine of the necessitarians. If the Owenites were cited by Mill

59. The close personal and intellectual relationship between Mill and Sterling was discussed in Carlyle, *The Life of John Sterling* (1851), in *Works* 2: 71, 78, 88, 151, 160, 167; see also William Leonard Courtney, *Life of John Stuart Mill*, pp. 59, 73, 101, 173.

60. Mill to R. B. Fox, 14 February 1843, *EL*, p. 569.

on the side of necessity, the German writer Novalis was quoted on the side which accepted "a power of self-formation." "The Free-will doctrine has, I believe, fastened in its supporters a much stronger spirit of self-culture," Mill concluded.[61]

The solution that Mill had devised was designed to serve more a psychological and a religious purpose than a philosophical one, if we are to credit Mill's description of it in a letter to James Martineau in 1841. Writing to the Unitarian minister, Mill referred to a passage in one of Martineau's lectures in which the theologian had observed that "it is probable that in the secret history of every noble and inquisitive mind there is a passage darkened by the awful shadow of the conception of Necessity." "I shall never forget the time," Mill observed, "when I was myself under that awful shadow you speak of, nor how I got from under it." But all this would be "written down in my book," he noted, referring to the forthcoming *Logic*.[62]

The same subject came up in Mill's correspondence with the French liberal thinker Alexis de Tocqueville in 1843. After Tocqueville had read the *Logic,* he wrote to tell its author that he had been especially pleased by Mill's treatment of "that eternal and frightening question of human liberty, the solution to which affects not only morals but politics." He described Mill's distinction between "necessity, as you understand it, and *irresistibleness,* fatalism," as "a gleam of light." "It seems to me," Tocqueville concluded, "that you are opening a neutral terrain upon which the two opposed schools, or at least reasonable men from the two schools, would easily be able to meet and to understand each other."[63] In reply, Mill described Tocqueville's "approval of the point-of-view from which I treated the question of human

61. J. S. Mill, *A System of Logic, Ratiocinative and Inductive*, ed. J. M. Robson, *Collected Works* 7–8, pp. 840, 839, 841–42.

62. Mill to Martineau, 21 May 1841, *EL*, p. 477.

63. Tocqueville to Mill, 27 October 1843, *Correspondance anglaise, Oeuvres complètes*, ed. J.-P. Mayer, 2: 345.

liberty" as "very precious to me." Mill saw this "most important [chapter] of the book" as representing a conclusion he had come to some fifteen years earlier as he had emerged from his mental illness. "I had found peace in these ideas," he wrote to Tocqueville, since "they alone had entirely satisifed my need to put intellect and conscience into harmony"—terms, we should note, more congenial to German idealism than to Benthamite philosophy.[64]

Mill had attempted to place "the idea of human responsibility on a solid intellectual foundation." Revealing more explicitly the religious underpinning of his crisis, he continued: "I do not believe any thinker, the least bit serious, can enjoy true peace of mind and of soul until he has achieved some kind of satisfactory solution to this great problem" of free will and determinism. Most curiously, Mill concluded his letter with the hope that his solution would satisfy the psychological needs—not the interest in truth, a more proper end for a philosopher—of those who could find no other answer to the question: "I do not wish to impose my solution upon those who are content with their own," he observed, "but I believe that there are many men for whom it will be, as it has been for me, a veritable anchor of salvation."[65]

While a student at Edinburgh University, James Mill had fallen under the influence of the philosopher Dugald Stewart

64. Mill to Tocqueville, 3 November 1843, *EL*, p. 612.

65. Ibid. Mill's letter to Tocqueville was in French, and its quasi-religious sentiments and phrases are not an accident of my translation:

> ce chapitre-là . . . est l'expression fidèle des idées . . . dans lesquelles je puis dire que j'avais trouvé la paix, puisqu'elles seules avait satisfait pleinement chez moi au besoin de mettre en harmonie l'intelligence et la conscience, en posant sur des bases intellectuelles solides le sentiment de la responsibilité humaine. Je ne crois pas qu'aucun penseur un peu sérieux puisse jouir d'une vraie tranquillité d'esprit et d'âme, jusqu'à ce qu'il ait accompli quelque solution satisfaisante de ce grand problème. Je ne désire pas imposer ma propre solution à ceux qui sont satisfaits de la leur, mais je crois qu'il y a beaucoup d'hommes pour qui elle sera, comme elle a été pour moi, une véritable ancre de salut.

and thought himself an adherent of the Scottish intuitionist school that included Francis Hutcheson, Thomas Reid, and Stewart. In articles written in 1802 and 1806, before becoming a convert to the Benthamite creed, James Mill had denounced Hartley's deterministic associationalism in favor of the views of the intuitionist philosophers.[66] The elder Mill's high regard for the moral fable of the choice of Hercules probably owed a good deal to the persistent interest of these Scottish thinkers in what might be called the mechanics of virtue. Hutcheson had written of the existence of an innate "moral sense," and his disciple Reid saw man as a social being whose perceptions were formed by a communal "common sense." Reid and his followers, who became known as the common sense school, defined virtue as a preference for the common over the private good. They saw men as moved by feelings of sympathy and benevolence, a view Adam Smith, following Hutcheson and Reid, was to stress in his 1759 *Theory of Moral Sentiments*, and not merely by a rational consideration of self-interest, Smith's focus in his later tract on economics.[67]

After adopting a Hartleian Benthamism, James Mill bitterly criticized the Scottish school, but his son was rather more sympathetic to its position. Though it would not do for Benthamites to speak of an innate moral sense, so foreign to their view of the Lockean tabula rasa, we find the young Mill suggesting as early as 1833 that such concepts as "moral sense" or "common sense," major themes of the Scottish school, were something more than "covers for dogmatism." Not only did he find that Bentham had not convincingly refuted "the ethical doctrines either of the Reid and Stewart school, or of the German metaphysicians," but he also observed that the utilitarian had failed to see the importance

66. See Halévy, *Growth of Philosophic Radicalism*, pp. 438–39.

67. See discussion in Dugald Stewart, "Account of the Life and Writings of Thomas Reid, D.D., F.R.S.E." (1802), in *Collected Works* 10 (Edinburgh, 1858): 304–08; see also Adam Smith, *The Theory of Moral Sentiments* (1759; reprint, London, 1853), part 6, particularly pp. 349–84.

of love, a sense of beauty, or a moral sense as motives for virtuous action.[68]

At this time, Mill saw the Scottish common sense school as occupying a middle ground between the two great philosophical rivals, empirical associationalism and German transcendentalism, and as endeavoring to save intuitionism from the excesses of the latter. By the 1860s, however, he had become convinced that the intuitionism of the Scottish school's last great representative, Sir William Hamilton, was closer to transcendentalism than he had previously thought. By ignoring the "irresistible proofs" that individual, racial, or sexual differences were not innate but produced by external circumstances, the Scottish school was an obstacle to "the rational treatment of great social questions."[69] Such opinions merely supported the position of enemies of reform, hence Mill's shattering attack on Hamilton in the 1860s.

That Mill continued to regard himself as the advocate of English empiricism against both Scottish and German philosophy was clear in his highly polemical *Examination of Sir William Hamilton's Philosophy* in 1862. Nonetheless, in opposing the doctrines of Hamilton, who had died in 1856, and his disciple, the Anglican clergyman H. L. Mansel, Mill once more took up the case of the German philosophers for self-development. In his chapter "On Freedom of the Will," Mill's chief target seemed to be not so much Hamilton and his school, but, as in his *Logic* twenty years earlier, the absolute necessitarianism of the Owenites. Mill's friend Alexander Bain felt, indeed, that there were passages in this critique of Hamilton's idealist philosophy that made Mill appear "a transcendentalist . . . differing only in degree" from those he criticized.[70]

68. J. S. Mill, "Remarks on Bentham's Philosophy" (1833), in *Essays on Ethics, Religion and Society*, ed. J. M. Robson, *Collected Works* 10: 5–6; see also pp. 13, 15, and "Bentham" (1838), in ibid., pp. 85–86, 95–96.

69. *Autobiography*, pp. 191–92.

70. Bain, *Mill*, p. 121.

The opinions of the Owenites had led them "to deny human responsibility," Mill observed, since they believed a man's character was "made *for* him, not *by* him." The Owenites had even rejected the right of society to inflict punishment. On the other hand, Mill argued that punishment acted to form the will and therefore was not only permissible but needful. "By counterbalancing the influence of present temptations or acquired bad habits," punishment "restores the mind to normal preponderance of the love of right, which many moralists and theologians consider to constitute the true definition of our freedom."[71] In this, Mill clearly referred to the German philosophers.

The theologian Mansel had written a critique of the chapter "On Liberty and Necessity" in Mill's *Logic*, in which he had charged Mill with constructing "a system of fatalism as rigid as any Asiatic could desire." Mansel had pointed particularly to Mill's view that if a person "thoroughly knew his own character," he "could predict how he would act in any supposable case." In reply, Mill enlisted the support of the German philosopher Kant, whom Mansel admired, and who, Mill argued, had found the possibility of such prediction entirely compatible with freedom of will. Was Kant therefore a necessitarian? Not at all. The German philosopher had changed "the *venue* of free will, from our actions generally, to the formation of our character." "It is in that," Mill continued, that Kant thought "we are free, and he is almost willing to admit that while our character is what it is, our actions are necessitated by it."[72] This, at core, was also Mill's position.

For Mill, necessity was first of all "this abstract possibility of being foreseen," a simple "invariability of sequence"; if it meant "any mysterious compulsion," he declared, "I deny it as strenuously

71. John Stuart Mill, "On the Freedom of the Will," in *An Examination of Sir William Hamilton's Philosophy*, ed. J. M. Robson, *Collected Works* 9: 453, 458.

72. Ibid., pp. 465, 467.

as any one in the case of human volitions."[73] Like Kant, Mill insisted that our character was in part formed by our will and that "we are under a moral obligation to seek the improvement of our moral character." Such a view, Mill maintained, was very different from the "system of fatalism" of which he had been accused by Mansel. There were for Mill two kinds of fatalism: pure or Asiatic fatalism, "the fatalism of Oedipus," which maintained that "our actions do not depend on our desires" but are under the control of an overruling "abstract destiny"; and a modified fatalism that Mill attributed to the Owenites, which maintained that our actions were at bottom determined by "the motives presented to us," and by our individual character, for which we were not responsible since we had no part in its formation.[74] The "true doctrine" opposed both these varieties of fatalism, for "not only our conduct but our character is in part amenable to our will"; therefore, "we can, by employing the proper means, improve our character." But to do this, we must "voluntarily exert ourselves," as indeed, "it is our duty to do."[75]

Mill concluded by considering predestination, the belief that our actions were "divinely preordained." A belief in predestination sometimes had "a paralyzing effect on conduct," as witnessed among Mohammedans when a man believed he could "infer what God has predestined" by "particular signs" or from "the general aspect of things" and therefore believed "useless any attempt to defeat it." "Because something will certainly happen if nothing is done to prevent it, they think it will certainly happen whatever may be done to prevent it." If God worked according to general laws—and Mill was to envision such a God in his essay on theism—then, he argued, "whatever he may have preordained, he has preordained that it shall take place through the causes on which experience shows it to be consequent." If God had

73. Ibid., p. 467.
74. Ibid., p. 465.
75. Ibid., pp. 466–67.

predestined that Mill would achieve his goals, he had also predestined that this would happen by Mill's "studying and putting into practice the means which lead to their attainment."[76]

In his rectorial address to the students of St. Andrews in 1867, Mill enjoined the active pursuit of virtue. He wished to instruct undergraduates in the leading systems of moral philosophy, not merely those of Judaism and Christianity, he noted, but also those of the Epicureans and of the Stoics; he sought also to clarify for students the chief points that divided metaphysicians, in particular the enormous question whether man's will was free or determined. Only if men learned to distinguish between laws which must be obeyed and free human action, could virtue play its necessary role in creating a stable and progressive society.[77]

Universities must teach both laws and values. Those who decried the study of the principles of political economy as unfeeling had better learn that they operated as necessarily as did the law of gravitation. Gravitation was "the most unfeeling thing I know of," Mill observed, as unfeeling as the winds and the waves: all three broke the necks of persons who did not take their measure. "Would you advise those who go to sea to deny the winds and waves—or to make use of them and find the means of guarding against their dangers?" But it would still be an imperfect education that trained only the intellect. A study of international law, for example, must teach men how to make the foreign policy of their nation "enlightened, just and noble" rather than "selfish, corrupt and tyrannical." When men understood what was best, conscience would make it difficult for them to act on selfish and false principles.[78]

Education should direct itself to "exalting and dignifying" the characters of individuals and of the species by the inculcation

76. Ibid., p. 469.

77. J. S. Mill, *Inaugural Address Delivered to the University of St. Andrews, Feb. 1, 1867* (London, 1867), pp. 78, 64.

78. Ibid., pp. 70, 73–74.

of virtue, Mill declared. In England, men pursued virtue as duty, not as pleasure. Mill held "commercial money-getting business" and Puritanism responsible for this defect. A commercial society regarded any activity other than business a waste of time, while Puritanism saw the cultivation of other than religious feelings as sinful. While continentals generally thought virtue belonged to the realm of the sentiments, Englishmen placed it in that of moral obligation. As a result, Mill suggested, the English possessed a "greater tenderness of conscience." This had had the effect of keeping them from undue wickedness but had not impelled them to a positive pursuit of virtue. If we wish "men to practice virtue," Mill urged, we must try "to make them love virtue" as "an object in itself," and not merely as hard-wrung duty that left them otherwise free to follow self-indulgent material and sensual pleasure.[79] Mill's goal was to bridge the gap between the necessitarianism of scientific law and the inward faith of the German idealist philosophers by calling upon all to pursue virtue as a counter to the forces impeding the formation of a good society.

79. Ibid., pp. 89–90, 90–91.

TWO

The Innocent Magdalen

ONE NIGHT IN 1857 WHILE TRAVELING IN THE NORTH of England, Mill had two dreams about which he wrote to his wife. The first speculated about animal nature and, considered with the second, about the unknown depths of man's sexual being. The second, a lighter-hearted affair, had Mill sitting at a restaurant table with a woman on his left and a young man opposite. The young man, as if delivering a quotation, remarked that "there are two excellent & rare things to find in a woman, a sincere friend & a sincere Magdalen." Mill replied that "the best would be to find both in one," with the woman observing, "no, that would be *too* vain." Defending himself against the charge of vanity, Mill concluded by asking, "Do you suppose when one speaks of what is good in itself, one must be thinking of one's paltry self interest? No, I spoke of what is abstractedly good & admirable." In his dream, Mill thought the young man had erred in the quotation, and that the correct words were "an innocent Magdalen." With the "usual oddity of dreams," Mill wrote, he had not perceived the contradiction.[1]

In his dream, we may speculate, Mill like Hercules was at

1. John Stuart to Harriet Mill, 17 February 1857, *The Later Letters of John Stuart Mill*, ed. F. E. Mineka and D. N. Lindley, *Collected Works* 14–17, pp. 523–24. (Hereafter, *LL*.)

a crossroads, faced with a choice between virtue and sensual happiness. He wished to resolve the dilemma—as who would not—by uniting the two. But in the dream, he was reminded (by philosophy, conscience, his wife?) that it would be "*too* vain"—in the sense of expecting more than he deserved, one may ask, or in that of having unrealistic expectations, that is, in vain? Mill defended himself against both suggestions. He was not thinking of "paltry self interest," he had replied in the dream, but of what was "abstractedly [and hence without corporeal reality?] good & admirable." Even in his dream, Mill understood the difficulty, if not the impossibility, in achieving a highly desirable ("what is good in itself") amalgam of the innocent Magdalen, in making virtue and sensual happiness one. "How queer to dream stupid mock mots, & of a kind totally unlike one's own ways or character," Mill concluded.[2]

Philosophers have often employed women (and sex) to represent this theme, central to Mill's life and thought, as did Prodicus and Xenophon in having Hercules choose between beautiful women who embodied virtue and pleasure. The symbols invoked in Mill's dream can hardly be considered alien to his "ways or character." In this instance, in fact, the apparent contradiction of the "innocent Magdalen" was no mere symbol for a philosophical abstraction but a specific ideal; nearly thirty years earlier Mill had known and greatly sympathized with a sect of Saint-Simonians in search of just such a woman. This association had led Mill in the 1840s into a vigorous controversy over the role of women, which had created an irreparable breach between him and Auguste Comte, under whose special influence he had thought himself at that time.

We must remind ourselves that James Mill, according to

2. Ibid., p. 524. Another view of this dream may be found in Bruce Mazlish, *James and John Stuart Mill: Father and Son in the Nineteenth Century*, pp. 302–03.

his son, saw the future as bringing "a considerable increase of freedom in the relations between the sexes." While the puritanical James was not prepared to say exactly what he meant by this, it was not necessary to do so. In the 1790s, William Godwin and his circle which later included his son-in-law, Shelley, had already preached the new morality of free love. John Stuart insisted that this opinion of his father's was free of "sensuality" whether of "a theoretical or of a practical kind." Raised a Calvinist, painfully aware of the strong impulses to sin which helped no doubt to lead him to an early and clearly inappropriate marriage, the elder Mill suggested that among the fortunate consequences of this increased sexual freedom of the future would be that the imagination of young men would no longer dwell upon sex. Far from seeking to ennoble the sexual act, James believed that making sex into one of the central concerns of life was "a perversion" of true feelings and "one of the deepest seated and most pervading evils in the human mind."[3] Greater freedom was to be given in the short run so that in the long run men might achieve an even greater repression of the passions than the old religion, in its wisdom, would have thought possible.

The problems of the role of women and those of sex and marriage confronted Mill very early in his manhood because of the Saint-Simonians. Comte Henri de Saint-Simon exercised a powerful influence on European intellectual life when he called for a positive reorganization of society based upon science and founded a mystical "nouveau Christianisme."[4] In 1828, Gustave d'Eichthal, the son of a wealthy Jewish banking family of Paris, came to London as a missionary of this new religion. Eichthal himself had been converted to Saint-Simonianism by his former tutor in mathematics, Auguste Comte, who had served as the master's secretary before Saint-Simon's death in 1825. Upon

3. *Autobiography*, p. 75.

4. The definitive work on Saint-Simon's ideas is Frank Manuel, *The New World of Henri Saint-Simon*.

meeting Mill and observing the high regard in which the young Englishman was held, Eichthal determined to convert him to the new doctrine. Trying to free himself from a rigid Benthamism and wishing to avoid similar entanglements, Mill at first resisted Eichthal's attempts, despite his attraction to the sect's historical views and to its interest in the emancipation of women.

As early as 1828, one of the two leaders of the sect with the title of Père, B. P. Enfantin, proclaimed that the Saint-Simonian era would be memorable because it would achieve equality for the sex that had for millennia seemed fated to subordination. But it became increasingly clear that among Enfantin's first objectives was the release of women from the imposition of eternal sexual fidelity. Enfantin denounced the legal prostitution of marriage that forged chains with such dreadful words as faithfulness and eternity and led one partner to a veritable martyrdom. The Christian mortification of the flesh had resulted in the burden of guilt of adultery and the practice of prostitution, he argued. Saint-Simonianism would liberate mankind from such evils. Men and women were divided by Enfantin into two sexual types, one of *mobiles,* who needed to move from one sexual relationship to another, and the other of *immobiles,* who were constant and required monogamy. He urged easier rules of divorce and marriage to suit the mobiles. His followers, including Eichthal, fervently sang the Père's praises, considering him sent by heaven to proclaim the new relationship between the sexes which would inaugurate an era of happiness.

The movement displayed a special sympathy for women "forced" by the circumstances of their lives and the imperfections of social arrangements into a life of prostitution. Enfantin foretold the coming of a woman who would sit by his side (both of them serving as earthly symbols of an androgynous Deity), and who would be the "Messie de son sexe." This female messiah would save the world from prostitution as Jesus had saved it from slavery. He also called for a revival of the medieval chivalry in which a knight was inspired by his lady, who possessed for him the divine character of the Virgin while being a sexually active woman—his mistress, his "châtelaine respectée, bénie, adorée." These two aspects of the châtelaine—her virginity and sexual experience—were for Enfantin embodied in the prostitute. What was this image but that of the innocent Magdalen?

Led by the second Père, Amand Bazard, a number of Saint-Simonians accepted the need for female emancipation, but denounced Enfantin's incitement to free love. For Bazard, such legalized promiscuity would be not a progressive step but a return to the more barbarous conditions of the past, with women more exposed to exploitation than ever. Although divorce was at times a sad necessity, he conceded, the institution of indissoluble marriage had been an important stage in female liberation. By substituting instinctive impulse for moral judgment, moreover, Enfantin would trample on individuality. Bazard reminded the Saint-Simonians that marriage was still a privileged institution to which the great majority of people had yet to raise themselves. A man or woman could acquire a necessary sense of personality and enjoy a genuine freedom only if he or she could choose a marriage partner—of course, he added, with the approval of a superior in the Saint-Simonian society.

In late January 1832, the government began prosecution of the Saint-Simonians for holding illegal meetings and promulgating doctrines subversive to the state, private property, and morals. Enfantin and forty of his disciples retired to a monastic retreat at his Paris estate of Ménilmontant, where they took up a celibate life, awaiting the arrival of the female messiah who would emancipate womankind. The Père Suprême, Enfantin's new title, gave up at this time a three-year relationship with his châtelaine, an ex-prostitute. In late August 1832, the Saint-Simonians underwent a public trial at which both Enfantin and Michel Chevalier, the editor of the sect's publication, the *Globe*, were sentenced to a year's imprisonment and a nominal fine. But the faith of the sect in Enfantin and his mission was unshaken. Before beginning his prison sentence, Enfantin urged his followers to exact from converts adherence to a creed of faith in a God who had "raised up the Father to summon the Female Messiah, who will consecrate a union of perfect equality between man and woman, between humanity and the world."[5]

Both Mill and Carlyle, also a target of Eichthal's evangelical efforts, had been sympathetic to the Saint-Simonians, but as the activities of the sect took a ludicrous turn, they became increasingly hostile.[6] Mill was particularly uncomfortable with the way in which Père Enfantin's followers appeared to worship him. In their exchange of letters concerning "our friends the St. Simonians," it is clear that Mill was also upset by the "charlatanerie" of Enfantin at his trial, evident in his refusal to take the oath, his peculiar costume, and his long pauses "pour attendre des inspirations." Mill's patience was exhausted by the following April, when he learned that the still-loyal members of the society had set off to Constantinople "pour chercher la femme libre," the female messiah, and to announce Enfantin's doctrine of emancipation to the women of the East. The Saint-Simonians were convinced that this new messiah would be found in a Turkish

5. There are a number of treatments of the Saint-Simonians and the woman question. See particularly A. J. Booth, *Saint-Simon and Saint-Simonism: A Chapter in the History of Socialism in France* (London, 1871), pp. 119–217; Sebastien Charléty, *Histoire du saint-simonisme (1825–1864)* (Paris, 1931), especially pp. 126–34, 148, 153, and 205–17; and H. R. D'Allemagne, *Les Saint-Simoniens, 1827–37* (Paris, 1930). Enfantin saw his new sexual dispensation as an illumination, a union of politics and morals, a universal synthesis between thought and deed, theory and practice. In uniting the spirit and the body, he was joining "the burning flesh which teems in the lands of the South, with the spirit which raises itself in the clouds of the North." He was unifying "les deux mondes": the Orient, which represented the spirit and stood for constancy, and whose moral symbol was the jealous Moor Othello, and the Occident, whose symbol was Don Juan and his pursuit of the joys of the flesh.

6. See R. K. P. Pankhurst, *The Saint Simonians, Mill and Carlyle*; Hill Shine, *Carlyle and the Saint Simonians*; and Dwight N. Lindley, "The Saint Simonians, Carlyle and Mill: A Study in the History of Ideas."

harem. "This seems greater madness than I had imputed to them," Mill declared. "It is among the inmates of a harem that they expect to find a woman capable of laying down or as they say *revealing* the new moral law which is to regulate the relations between the sexes! It will be lucky for them if the search is attended with no disagreeable personal consequences to them except only that of not finding."[7]

Some months earlier, though far from "entirely agreeing" with the sect, Mill had regarded it "as the greatest enterprise now in progress, for the regeneration of society."[8] Years later, Mill was to declare that he honored the Saint-Simonians "most of all for what they have been most cried down for—the boldness and freedom from prejudice with which they treated the subject of family." But Mill was neither a defender of sexual promiscuity nor an opponent of marriage, as were the followers of Enfantin. He wished, rather, for the reestablishment of the family on the basis of sexual equality. It was "in proclaiming the perfect equality of men and women, and an entirely new order of things in regard to their relations with one another," Mill was to conclude, that the Saint-Simonians had earned "the grateful remembrance of future generations."[9]

But why had everything come to so awkward a pass? In his analysis of the last days of Saint-Simonianism, Mill could suggest only that such was the inevitable consequence of a good idea fallen into the hands of Frenchmen. "These Saint Simonians have done so much good, that one regrets they were not capable of doing more," he observed, adding that the "excessive avidity & barrenness of the French mind has never been so strikingly displayed."[10]

7. Mill to Carlyle, 29 May and 17 September 1832, 11 and 12 April 1833, *EL*, pp. 106, 119–20, 150.

8. Mill to Eichthal, 30 November 1831, *EL*, p. 88.

9. *Autobiography*, pp. 117–18.

10. Mill to Carlyle, 11 and 12 April 1833, *EL*, pp. 150–51.

After the fall of Enfantin, Mill turned his attention to the writings of the former Saint-Simonian Auguste Comte. In his early letters to Eichthal in the fall of 1829, Mill had praised Comte's tracts on the Saint-Simonian view of history.[11] But Comte had then dropped from his view, for the French thinker had cut himself off from any connection with the sect during the Enfantin period, when it stood at the height of its influence. Comte had little sympathy with Père Enfantin's opinions on the emancipation of women. Having abandoned Saint-Simon in revulsion against the master's efforts to create a religion, he might well have regarded the unhappy fate of the followers of the Père Suprême as confirming his worst presentiments. In the 1830s, Comte devoted himself to writing what was to become the six-volume *Cours de philosophie positive*, a first elaboration of the philosophy of positivism.

Comte's *Cours* was a work that Mill admired enormously. In a letter to the astronomer John Pringle Nichol in late 1837, when only the early volumes had been published, Mill described it as "one of the most profound books ever written on the philosophy of the sciences." Four years later, he told Alexander Bain that although there were some errors, Comte's *Cours* was on the whole "very nearly the grandest work of this age." In the fall of 1841, Mill wrote to Comte to tell of his "intellectual debt." His reading of one of Comte's earlier works in 1828, Mill observed, had given all his ideas "a decided jolt" and had helped to bring about his final withdrawal from Benthamism. (Mill described the Benthamism in which he had been raised, though far from "the essential spirit" of positivism, as the "best preparation we have today" for positivist social doctrine, thanks to its logical character and its opposition to metaphysics.) Now Mill wished to acknowledge his debt to Comte's *Cours*, which had inspired him to undertake the work on logic in which he was then engaged.[12]

11. See chap. 4, below.
12. Mill to John Pringle Nichol, 21 December 1837, *EL*, p. 363; Mill

The Enlightenment tradition to which both Mill and Comte belonged saw the possibility of a genuine "science" of society. Condorcet, the eighteenth-century thinker to whom Comte felt the closest ties, had developed a "calculus of probabilities" which he had sought to apply to social life, and the philosophes of the period strove to make a science of morals, as well as of the philosophy of history. Bentham's "felicific calculus," following the ideas of Hutcheson, Helvétius, and Beccaria, was in the mainstream of the quest for a moral science. The new social science, which Comte called "sociology," would provide the solutions for problems that had baffled generations. Comte, like the Saint-Simonians, looked to the scientists and engineers as an elite who would set aside the prescriptions of a retrograde theology and an anarchic metaphysics and bring a positivist utopia into being. Similarly, both Comte and the Saint-Simonians believed that by understanding the laws of historical development, one might predict the course of future progress and consequently determine how it might be directed and accelerated. This was the spirit of the *Cours* to which Mill, in line with this Enlightenment stream of his thinking, had enthusiastically responded.

Far from well known in France, Comte was not accustomed to receiving such flattering letters, and he was eager to reciprocate Mill's friendly overtures. The French thinker saw himself as beleaguered "by all kinds of natural enemies" in his own country and consequently found it all the more delightful to learn that "the most advanced minds vibrate essentially in unison with mine." Mill's earlier Benthamism was "clear proof of the natural conformity of our intellectual tendencies," the Frenchman agreed, for political economy was a direct precursor of positivist sociology.

---

to Bain, Autumn 1841, *EL*, p. 487; Mill to Comte, 8 November 1841, *Lettres inédites*, pp. 1–2; see also p. 12. Brief sections of the Comte-Mill correspondence have been translated by Kenneth Thompson, *Auguste Comte: The Foundation of Sociology* (New York, 1975), pp. 191–210; however, I have used my own translations.

In reply, Mill somewhat apologetically noted that his belief in the possibility of a scientific psychology, about which he had written in his yet-unpublished *System of Logic*, was in sharp contrast to Comte's emphasis on a positivist phrenology. This would make him guilty of what the Frenchman had denounced as "metaphysical tendencies," but if his views were to be acceptable to his countrymen, Mill observed, he had to make concessions to their metaphysical bent. For his part, Comte was prepared to welcome Mill's views despite their "metaphysical formulas and theological precautions," for he well understood the backwardness of English opinion.[13]

But from the beginning it was clear that Mill was unsympathetic to phrenology and condescending to its pretensions. True to his paternal inheritance, he could not believe that the contours of the skull held a candle to Hartley's laws of association. Nonetheless, in early 1842 Mill asked Comte for a list of books that would provide him with a sound knowledge of phrenology, a subject, he wrote, studied in England only by men of below average intelligence, by the evidence of their writings. In fact, until his discovery of Comte's devotion to the subject, Mill had thought phrenology beneath a true thinker. Pleased at the Englishman's readiness to undertake the phrenological studies "indispensable for the fullest development of philosophic competency," Comte suggested F. J. Gall's work, while warning Mill that circumstances had at times compelled Gall to go beyond his evidence in locating the various moral and intellectual functions in specific parts of the brain. This had undoubtedly had the effect of drawing into the field charlatans who profited from analyzing the bumps on the skulls of their clients, rather than serious scholars.[14]

13. Comte to Mill, 20 November 1841, *Lettres inédites*, pp. 6–7; Mill to Comte, 18 December 1841, ibid., pp. 13–14; Comte to Mill, 17 January 1842, ibid., p. 24.

14. Mill to Comte, 25 February 1842, ibid., pp. 31–32; Comte to Mill, 4 March 1842, ibid., pp. 38–39.

Mill's study of phrenology, however, was to leave his long-held views undisturbed. Although in May he was able to report Gall "a man of superior mind," by June Mill had reverted to his earlier, less favorable, judgment. He was almost persuaded that there was some truth in the view that propensities and capacities were connected to particular parts of the brain. But there were difficulties. For example, though Mill had been assured by phrenologists that his own "organ of constructiveness" was prominent in his cranium, he possessed absolutely no manual dexterity. Nor could he agree with Comte that even the basic threefold division of the brain into animal, moral, and intellectual faculties had been sufficiently well established, let alone the location of more specific capacities. Contrary to the phrenologists, Mill had not observed that persons with small heads and receding foreheads were less intelligent than those with large heads and protruding foreheads.[15]

Gall's great fault, Mill argued, was in not giving sufficient attention to the role of education. Though philosophers like Helvétius may have exaggerated the importance of education, it had been unduly neglected in nineteenth century theories. Mill wished to persuade Comte that by the operation of the laws of mental physiology external circumstances could not only modify character but even determine its form. Moreover, he believed that by their own efforts individuals could modify the qualities the phrenologists thought unalterable.[16]

Both Mill and Comte shared the same dream: they wished to construct a genuine social science on the model of the natural sciences.[17] For Comte, the acceptance of phrenological physiology

15. Mill to Comte, 6 May and 9 June 1842, ibid., pp. 56, 66–67.

16. Mill to Comte, 9 June 1842, ibid., pp. 67–68.

17. Mill to Comte, 22 March 1842, ibid., pp. 43–44. Mill intended to establish a science of ethology which would investigate how external circumstances helped to shape individual and national character; see Mill to Comte, 8 December 1843, ibid., pp. 283–85. A stimulating speculative account of why the work

was vital to this goal. Comte had hoped, he wrote, that Mill might initially have reacted more sympathetically to Gall's fundamental conception, but he was still confident that, quite spontaneously and without further argument, the Englishman's view of Gall would soon become more favorable. Certainly, some of Gall's ideas were in error, and such errors could so shock thinkers that they would at first be unable to grasp the eminent scientific, and especially the logical, value of phrenology. Like the French metaphysicians, Comte suggested, Mill might not be able to bring himself to believe that intellectual and moral studies could be based on biology.[18] In a word, he believed that after Mill had come to identify more entirely with Comte's social and political objectives, he would recognize, by a kind of intellectual *raison d'état,* that Gall's theory had a logical value independent of its truth.

We see that Mill, with some small qualifications, persisted in the views of the psychologists and in the theories of Locke, Hartley, and his father; despite his apologies to Comte for the metaphysical tendencies of his forthcoming work on logic, he was convinced of the superiority of that part of the system he had inherited to Comte's positivism. One might argue that the differences between Comte's *Cours* and Mill's *Logic* were those between the respective roots and styles of the French and English schools of philosophy. Comte had described his *Cours* as the contemporary equivalent of Descartes's *Discours sur la méthode*, a classic of the deductive method; when English opinion took Mill's *Logic* to its bosom, it was because it saw the work as the nineteenth-century equivalent of Bacon's *Novum Organum*, the

---

on ethology was never produced may be found in L. S. Feuer, "John Stuart Mill as a Sociologist: The Unwritten Ethology," in *James and John Stuart Mill: Papers of the Centenary Conference*, ed. J. M. Robson and M. Laine, pp. 86–110. Feuer also appreciated the importance of the issue of voluntarism and determinism for Mill's thought; see pp. 93–94. (Hereafter, *Centenary Conference*.)

18. Comte to Mill, 19 June 1842, *Lettres inédites*, pp. 73–76.

pioneer work of inductive logic. Moreover, physiological phrenology was an analogue of Descartes's theory of innate ideas, just as Mill's theory of education was descended from Locke's tabula rasa.

Mill persuaded Comte that he only wished to maintain "the quasi-metaphysical turn" of the early chapters of his *Logic* because it connected his ideas to the school of Hobbes and Locke at the moment "being trampled underfoot" by the German and Scottish philosophers. Somewhat reluctantly, Comte agreed that the philosophy of Hobbes and Locke, which he noted had been extended in France by Condilliac and Destutt de Tracy, was "much more progressive" than that of the German school, at core a product of "*l'esprit protestant.*" But Comte warned that the basis of his approval was his confidence in Mill's wholehearted adherence to positivism. Otherwise, the Frenchman might be concerned lest Mill so commit himself that a position begun as an expedient might become final.[19]

It is worth noting that Comte's physiological phrenology and Mill's associationalism were both determinist, but in a decisively different way. Cartesian innate ideas and phrenological necessity were unalterable. Lockean or Hartleian determinism, on the other hand, accounted for present behavior along lines of cause and effect while it granted to society, the family, or the individual the opportunity to modify future behavior. Phrenology was fatalistic, while associationalism left open an avenue for education and individual self-development.

Comte read Mill's *Logic* on its publication in 1843 and was particularly moved by Mill's generous tributes to him in its pages. The Englishman had successfully achieved his principal objective, Comte declared, that of providing a transition from "the least backward form of the metaphysical spirit to the true positive spirit." Mill was delighted at this praise: he was now confident,

19. Mill to Comte, 11 July 1842, ibid., pp. 77–78; Comte to Mill, 22 July 1842, ibid., p. 85.

he wrote to Comte, that he could play a role not only in the diffusion but in the formulation of positivism.[20] Having exulted in their agreement on matters of method, Mill went on to discuss certain differences in social doctrine.

While Mill approved of Comte's view of historical development, his "social dynamics," he had important reservations concerning his "social statics," particularly the positivist philosopher's view of the role of women. While recognizing the social necessity of such fundamental institutions as property and marriage—noting that he was not an adherent of utopian thinking in these matters—Mill was persuaded that these institutions would undergo changes more serious than Comte appeared to think. For one thing, Mill was uncertain about divorce, of which Comte strongly disapproved. But Mill confessed that he stood guilty of "a still more fundamental heresy, since I do not, in principle, acknowledge the necessary subordination of one sex to the other."[21]

Mill's disavowal of utopian thinking could only remind Comte of the questions that had divided the Saint-Simonians ten years earlier. Was Mill planning to play Enfantin to Comte's Bazard? In a tone that Mill could only find patronizing, Comte observed that he, too, had passed through such a stage of entanglement in contemporary aberrations. A careful study of biology as well as eight years' seniority had, however, enabled him to transcend the position in which Mill was apparently still trapped.

The Frenchman took on the threatening tone of the inquisitor as well as the patient one of the father confessor. "Heresies" of this order, however "enormous they might seem," he intoned, were "incurable only in those whose hearts had been won over by intellectual deviations." In reply, Mill announced that his disagreement with Comte had deep roots, and that he was very likely among those of whom Comte had spoken. Though Mill

20. Comte to Mill, 16 May 1843, ibid., pp. 190–91; Mill to Comte, 15 June 1843, ibid., pp. 206–07.

21. Mill to Comte, 15 June 1843, ibid., pp. 208–09.

had no wish to take up "the anarchical doctrine of revolutionary times" which rejected all authority, he was still convinced that there was a place for equality in human affections.[22]

While acknowledging that the state of biological science was imperfect, Comte nonetheless insisted, in outlining his case against sexual equality, that it was sufficiently far advanced to establish a hierarchy of the sexes. Both anatomically and physiologically, in all animal species including humans, the female possessed an undeveloped, primitive structure akin to that of childhood and organically inferior to that of the male. Just as the ancients had excluded women from both military and religious spheres because of this physical inferiority, so would modern life be obliged to restrict women to certain pursuits. The idea of a queen in modern times had become almost ridiculous, Comte wrote to his English friend in the sixth year of the reign of Victoria.[23]

People like Mill had put much too much emphasis on training, Comte continued, neglecting the need for a physical constitution suitable to receive such training. Women, like young children, simply did not possess the cerebral structure to perform the complex reasonings of the adult, masculine brain. This was an "inborn inferiority," and was confirmed by the general inability of women to free their reasonings from the passions or to subordinate individual or family interests to those of society. Not even in the home were they competent to perform more than lower-level administrative duties. Women had accomplished nothing of any importance, not only in science and philosophy but even in the fine arts, where their training had been more considerable. Their primary role was that of mother. In a future positivist society, they would also have a spiritual and moral function as judicious moderators. Were women to enter the field

22. Comte to Mill, 29 June 1843, ibid., pp. 217–18; Mill to Comte, 13 July 1843, ibid., pp. 221–22.

23. Comte to Mill, 16 July 1843, ibid., p. 231.

of action and become men's equals rather than their companions, they could not properly fulfill such a function.[24]

Comte called Mill's attention to the inferior social status of women throughout history. While other social classes had risen from a state of inferiority, women had not. The whole of past development had confirmed the natural superiority of men. The verdict of both anatomy and history was clear and could not be altered by theatrical denunciations of the abuse of women by masculine society which the anarchical tendencies of this period of transition had made so common. Certainly "since the establishment of monogamy, and particularly under modern social conditions, the term 'servitude,'" so often employed by feminists, "would be entirely inappropriate for characterizing the social status of our sweet companions."[25]

Though nineteenth-century thinkers like the phrenologist Gall had possibly exaggerated the influence of the primordial organism, in reaction to the eighteenth century's overwhelming insistence on the importance of education, Comte continued, the modern view was much closer to the truth. Since it was obviously easier to change the environment than the organism, the eighteenth century had concerned itself with the environment. But organic questions were obviously more significant: "It is the organism not the environment that makes us men rather than monkeys or dogs, and which even determines our particular type of humanity to a much more circumscribed extent than is often believed." In biological science, Comte observed, the proper method was to attribute to environment only what could not be explained by organism, not vice versa.[26]

Comte refused to acknowledge that women made any real progress toward emancipation in the preceding generation. George

24. Comte to Mill, 5 October 1843, ibid., pp. 246–49.

25. Comte to Mill, 5 October and 14 November 1843, ibid., pp. 249–51, 278.

26. Comte to Mill, 14 November 1843, ibid., pp. 275–76.

Sand had made herself notorious, but she was the inferior in originality as well as in propriety to such seventeenth-century writers as Mmes. de Sévigné, de Lafayette, and de Motteville. The woman's movement consisted of a growing profligacy, providing a further impetus to the strengthening of sexual passions that had accompanied the decline of religion. Spurred on by this "impassioned anarchy," the present uprising of women, or rather of a few women, would only confirm experimentally the necessity of the subordination of their sex. This, however, would be accomplished only after much suffering on the part of individuals and society as a whole. If the social equality of the sexes were ever truly attempted and carried to its "furthest natural limits," Comte warned, it would "turn out to be in direct opposition to the reproduction of our species."[27]

"The more I think of our serious sociological and biological differences on the condition and social destiny of women," Comte concluded, "the more profoundly characteristic it seems to me of the deplorable mental anarchy of our time." That thinkers as closely in sympathy with each other's views as he and Mill were still so divided on what must be the fundamental basis of any hierarchical society would cause him to despair, did he not believe such differences merely temporary. But he, too, he repeated, had gone through such a phase after he had read Mary Wollstonecraft's *Vindication of the Rights of Women*, and he had transcended it; so would Mill. The disorder that followed the French Revolution had called women from their homes to other concerns; the coming social regeneration would restore them to domestic life. Men must remain "the protectors of women," not become their competitors, as the projectors of "anarchical utopias" preferred.[28]

Personal circumstances no doubt colored the views of both philosophers, although Comte protested throughout that he was free of such influences. Yet how could he help being affected

27. Comte to Mill, 14 November 1843, ibid., pp. 279–80.
28. Comte to Mill, 5 October 1843, ibid., pp. 245–46, 250–51.

when in mid-1842, a few months before this discussion of the relationship between the sexes, his wife of seventeen years had left him? Her departure ended what Comte then described as an incompatible relationship with a woman "educated upon vicious principles, and pursuing a false conception of the necessary status of her sex" in human society. She had had no real affection for him, he complained, and possessed an " indisciplinable and despotic" nature. She was an example of the "fatal effects of present-day anarchy on the increasing dissolution of familial ties."[29] Comte announced that despite the fact that he would personally benefit from the possibility of "this Protestant solution" of divorce, he continued to believe that marriage had to be indissoluble if monogamy were to survive.[30]

Shortly afterward, however, Comte met and fell in unrequited love with a woman whose husband was a prisoner rowing in the Mediterranean fleet. Then he qualified his opposition to divorce to make it a possibility for someone precisely in her position. He adored, he worshipped Clothilde de Vaux, and although (or because) he was denied sexual satisfaction, he made her the châtelaine for whom he would wage all his battles and to whom he would dedicate his life. Comte's lyrical effusions on Clothilde were followed after her sudden death by beatification and sanctification; she became the Madonna of the new "religion of humanity" which he was constructing.

Mill's feminism has frequently been attributed to the influence of his friend Harriet Taylor, later his wife. In fact it predated their meeting, and their views on the subject were common currency among those who wrote for the Unitarian *Monthly Repository*. There is every reason to think that Mill was welcomed

29. Comte to Mill, 24 August 1842, ibid., pp. 102–04. Curiously, Mme. Comte is supposed to have been a part-time prostitute before her marriage, which would suggest that Comte had conducted his own search for the innocent Magdalen!

30. Comte to Mill, 30 September 1842, ibid., p. 115.

into this group because he already possessed "correct" opinions. Mrs. Taylor was married to a man who was apparently prepared to permit his wife the company of the young Mill even on unchaperoned trips, and the couple courted scandal by their close association. The extent of Mill's sexual intimacy with Mrs. Taylor—both before and after their marriage in 1854, following her husband's death—has been a frequent subject of speculation. Obviously, we do not and never can know for certain. Their friends, however, were convinced that the relationship was platonic, at least until their marriage.[31] Might Mill's dream described at the beginning of this chapter be understood as a reflection on this earlier situation—while public opinion had seen Harriet's behavior as that of a brazen Magdalen, he knew her to have been chaste?

Mill's replies to Comte, more treatises than letters, displayed his long-time absorption with the problem and his deep commitment to it. Like Comte, Mill declared he was free of the prejudices of both the revolutionists and the conservatives; moreover, he agreed with the positivist that the solution to the problem ultimately depended on research in biology. But Mill insisted that biological science had not yet advanced to the point where any solution was clearly indicated.[32] Many physiologists had indeed compared the muscular and nervous systems as well as the cerebral structure of the female to those of children, but, Mill argued, the inferiority of children to adults depended not on anatomical differences but on lack of training. Certain physiologists had suggested that the smaller, less-powerful feminine brain made women incapable of prolonged investigation, but capable of a certain mental agility—less fit for science, more fit for poetry and practical life. However, there had been nothing

31. For a discussion of Mill's relationship with Harriet Taylor see F. A. Hayek, *John Stuart Mill and Harriet Taylor* (Chicago, 1951); see also H. O. Pappé, *John Stuart Mill and the Harriet Taylor Myth*. Josephine Kamm's *John Stuart Mill in Love* (London, 1977) is a popular account.

32. Mill to Comte, 13 July 1843, *Lettres inédites*, pp. 221–22.

in female education to develop the former capacity, while such training formed an important part of the education of men. The daily petty and distracting pursuits of domestic life certainly did not help to develop this capacity. Nor should women be blamed if they had not been trained to prefer the general interest over that of their families.[33]

With Mill insisting on the greater importance of training in the production of the female stereotype and Comte asserting the primacy of anatomical structure, the pair seemed to be returning to their earlier differences over phrenology. Mill understood that Comte regarded his knowledge of biology and more particularly of cerebral physiology as inadequate. He reminded Comte that he had tried to repair this deficiency. Nonetheless, after studying Gall's volumes on phrenology, he was persuaded that nothing had been genuinely established, that all was vague and uncertain. He therefore wished to set anatomy aside as a basis for discussion.[34]

Replying to Comte's contention that since other classes had risen from slavery to equality, the continued social subordination of women was proof of their organic inferiority, Mill argued that there had never been a case in which domestic slaves had emancipated themselves. They had merely profited by the freedom others had acquired, and consequently their underlying state of dependency had persisted. A serf had been virtually independent from the beginning, responsible for supporting himself and his family, and master of his own household, and it was therefore easier for him to secure his freedom. Although the status of women in Europe in the nineteenth century was superior to that of the medieval serfs, it lacked their "demi-independence," the "habit of directing, within certain limits, their own interests, without any intervention from above." This quasi-autonomy of the serfs had provided the impetus to make themselves free. Women, on the other hand, raised from birth as subordinates

33. Mill to Comte, 30 August 1843, ibid., pp. 237–39.
34. Mill to Comte, 30 October 1843, ibid., pp. 260–62.

whose happiness hinged on the favor of men, were completely dependent, in "a state of pampered slavery" suited to the laziness and cowardice of our species and prolonged indefinitely by the ties of intimacy established between men and women. This was the explanation for "the almost endless delay" in the social emancipation of women.[35]

There was no justification for Comte's absolute verdict on women's incapacity, Mill continued. English households were better conducted than those of other countries, yet in England the wife had the exclusive management of such affairs. Women, certainly Englishwomen, were not fickle, as had been charged, in those matters that affected their permanent interests, though they sometimes used fickleness in dealing with men who thought them only "charming play-things." Nor were women greater creatures of impulse than men. Most Englishmen, Mill observed, no doubt having sexual impulses particularly in mind, thought men incapable of the moral restraint displayed by women and saw women as possessing consciences more scrupulous than those of men. "What is conscience," Mill inquired, "if not the submission of the passions to reason?"[36]

Unlike the utopians, Mill assured Comte, he too wished customs rather than laws to prevail but was convinced that before this great question could be properly settled, it was necessary to tap the experience of women. While this view resembled one put forward years earlier by the Saint-Simonians, Mill observed that that group had "proclaimed their own incompetence to decide the great social questions which they raised" but nonetheless "had the lunacy or charlatanery to offer a supposed solution to them." In all this, Mill reassured the positivist that he merely wished to submit to Comte, in bits and pieces, certain of his views on the subject, "as I would to my older brother in philosophy, not to say more."[37]

35. Mill to Comte, 30 October 1843, ibid., pp. 266–69.
36. Mill to Comte, 30 October 1843, ibid., pp. 263–66.
37. Mill to Comte, 13 July 1843, ibid., pp. 221–24.

In reply, the French philosopher observed that both Mill and he were sufficiently high-minded to restrain "any serious impulse to rivalry" and concluded by dismissing as too abstract the concept of equality as the basis for personal relationships. He preferred fraternity, a term associated with "hierarchical sentiments."[38] What could Mill have made of this appeal to rise above rivalry, couched in terms that stressed a hierarchical fraternity in the relationship between Mill and his "older brother in philosophy"?

Although he had modified or abandoned other opinions he had taken over from "the negative philosophy of my times," Mill wrote to a worried Comte some months later, he had remained and would remain firm in his view on women. "This discussion has left with me," he concluded, "some permanent traces, and I think it will have a definite effect on the direction of my works to come."[39] Mill's letters, or perhaps Comte's continued brooding on the affair, brought the positivist in late December to describe Mill's views in such severe terms as "erroneous and dangerous." The Frenchman was anxious lest Mill publish some statement of their disagreement on the question of women before there had been time for Mill to reconsider. Comte still hoped that future work on positivist politics would deliver his English friend from "such a heresy" as now possessed him.[40]

In all this, Mill was very close to the Saint-Simonian "heretics," not only in his view of a future equality of the sexes, but in his agreement with their underlying belief in the individual's capacity for self-realization. Saint-Simon had described his doctrine as intended most particularly "to afford all members of the society the greatest possible opportunity for the development of their faculties."[41] This goal of self-development was taken up and extended by the Saint-Simonians, who in the romantic mode of

38. Comte to Mill, 16 July 1843, ibid., p. 232.
39. Mill to Comte, 8 December 1843, ibid., p. 284.
40. Comte to Mill, 23 December 1843, ibid., pp. 288–89.
41. Quoted in Frank E. Manuel, *The Prophets of Paris*, p. 126.

the day proclaimed man's vast, virtually unlimited potentialities. Along with their interest in the "rehabilitation of the flesh," the Saint-Simonians celebrated the sanctity of the personality, though not the other liberal principles, which they agreed with their master were anarchic forces. Comte, on the other hand, following the opinions of such phrenologists as Broussais and Gall, saw man's capacities as relatively fixed. For Comte, as we have seen, men and women could find genuine fulfillment only by accepting their traditional roles and submerging their individual personalities in a grander unity, in which like bees in a hive, one individual could readily be substituted for another.

In 1848, after this discouraging exchange with Comte, Mill wrote to his friend Nichol, to whom he had enthusiastically recommended the *Cours de philosophie positive* a decade earlier, that the positivist philosopher was "characteristically and resolutely ignorant of the laws of the formation of character." Comte had assumed that the differences between women and men, philosophers and men of action, or rich people and proletarians were "ultimate, or at least necessary facts," and upon this foundation he had erected the principles of his sociology. If such principles were put into practice, Mill declared, the result would be a system "the most contrary to human liberty of any now taught or professed." Comte would close everyone's way of life against "all change of destination or purpose," just as he wished to make the contract of marriage indissoluble. The Frenchman was in all these questions—and most particularly in his doctrine concerning women—on "a radically wrong road." His political writings as opposed to his "admirable historical views," Mill concluded, were "likely to be mischievous rather than useful."[42]

In his tract *The Subjection of Women*, written in the 1850s but not published until 1869, Mill continued the argument he

42. Mill to J. P. Nichol, 30 September 1848, *EL*, p. 739.

had begun with Comte in the early 1840s. He decried the "legal subordination of one sex to the other" as not only "wrong in itself" but also as "one of the chief hindrances to human improvement." It was of the highest urgency that something be done to elevate a woman's status within marriage and to grant women the right to exercise the franchise and to hold public office. Mill believed that women had a special talent for government. The leading theme of this tract, as in his correspondence with Comte, was that the position into which a person was born ought no longer to constitute "an inexorable bond." It was wrong "to ordain that to be born a girl instead of a boy, any more than to be born black instead of white, or a commoner instead of a nobleman, shall decide the person's position through all life." What was widely regarded as "the nature of women," Mill argued, was "an eminently artificial thing," the consequence of "forced repression" and "unnatural stimulation." Women did not yet possess what all creatures were entitled to, the right to "liberty of development."[43]

A longtime impediment to progress, Mill observed in this tract as he had many times before, was our ignorance of "the influences which form human character." From this stemmed our belief that what now exists had a "natural tendency" to be so. "Because a cotter deeply in arrears to his landlord is not industrious, there are people who think the Irish are naturally idle." "History," Mill continued, "which is now so much better understood than formerly, teaches another lesson: if only by showing the extraordinary susceptibility of human nature to external influences, and the extreme variableness of those of its manifestations which are supposed to be most universal and uniform." Mill remained convinced that the "mental differences" which existed between women and men were "but the natural effect of the differences in their education and circumstances"

43. J. S. Mill, *The Subjection of Women*, pp. 1, 53–59, 97–100, 29, 33, 38–39.

and indicated "no radical differences, far less radical inferiority of nature." He once again dismissed the arguments of phrenologists that women had smaller brains than men; not only was this far from proven, but it was also doubtful that the mere size of the brain determined its quality.[44]

In modern Europe, Mill noted, women exhibited an "addiction to philanthropy." Because of their faulty education, one of sentiments and not of understanding, women were "unable to see, and unwilling to admit" what the political economist readily perceived as "the ultimate evil tendency" of any charity. By "taking the care of people's lives out of their own hands, and relieving them from the disagreeable consequences of their own acts," Mill warned, we sapped "the very foundation of the self-respect, self-help, and self-control which are the essential conditions both of individual prosperity and of social virtue." Instead of doing good, the women philanthropists did great harm. But such women should not be judged too harshly, for how could "a woman born to the present lot of women" appreciate "the value of self-dependence?" If women were liberated from "a life of subjection to the will of others" and permitted one of "rational freedom," it would mean an "unspeakable gain in private happiness" that in Mill's view would come from "the consciousness of working out their own destiny under their own moral responsibility." Persons deprived of freedom sought power to manipulate others; possessing it, they could turn toward improving themselves.[45]

Unlike the ethos of a fatalistic Islam or Brahminism, the spirit of Christianity was believed by Mill to be progressive, not stationary. There had been many people through the centuries who had attempted "to convert us into a sort of Christian Mussulmans," by denying the possibility of human improvement, but they had failed. Such fatalists would similarly fail in their efforts to maintain the subordination of women.[46]

44. Ibid., pp. 40–41, 98, 119–21.
45. Ibid., pp. 162–64, 178–82.
46. Ibid., pp. 85–86.

In a work published in 1869, the historian W. E. H. Lecky shocked Mill by describing the prostitute as a necessary part of civilized society. She was "the most efficient guardian of virtue," but for whom "the unchallenged purity of countless happy homes would be polluted"; "while creeds and civilizations rise and fall," the prostitute remained "the eternal priestess of humanity." Such a position, despite the final phrase, was hardly the Saint-Simonian idealization of the prostitute forty years earlier. Mill saw Lecky's view as typically conservative and tending to the subversion of a good society. Far from seeing the prostitute as a "guardian of virtue," Mill considered prostitution not "consistent with the personal freedom and safety of women" and corrupting to both sexes in making women "a mere thing used simply as a means." Moreover, prostitution inhibited a "frank confidence" within a marriage.[47]

Of course, Mill was ready to defend prostitutes against ill treatment by the state. In the last few years of his life, he participated in a campaign to protect women suspected of being prostitutes in towns with military establishments against compulsory medical examinations. Such a system, based on a double standard, Mill believed to be inherently vicious and subject to inevitable abuse, since it entrusted the police "with power over women which no men are fit to have."[48]

The great problem, Mill wrote to a friend in 1870—invoking both elements of Hercules' choice—was "how to obtain the greatest amount of chastity and Happiness for men, women and children." Society must give marriage "with equality of rights on both sides" a "fair trial," he observed. Noting that the sexual "propensity" had been fostered by a male-dominated society and by the Catholic church, both of which "exaggerate the force of the natural passions,"

47. W. E. H. Lecky, *History of European Morals* (New York, 1869), 2: 289–91; Mill to Lord Amberley, 2 February 1870, *LL*, pp. 1692–93. It may be of interest that in 1873 Lord Amberley was to ask Mill to serve as godfather to his newborn son, Bertrand Russell; Mill agreed.

48. Mill to unidentified correspondent, 11 January 1870, *LL*, p. 1681.

Mill prophesied that sexual passion would become "completely under the control of reason" with men as it already had with many women. These women had brought their passions under control "because its becoming so has been the condition upon which women hoped to obtain the strongest love and admiration of men." "The gratification of this passion in its highest form" would consequently be "conditional upon restraining it in its lowest."[49] Men and women must consequently choose chastity, that is, virtue over carnal pleasure and the animal passions, if they were to secure genuine happiness.

The so-called Bloomsbury group has proved of great interest to our own time, when its view of morals has been widely diffused. The group included such writers and critics as Leonard and Virginia Woolf, Lytton Strachey, and E. M. Forster, as well as the economist John Maynard Keynes. In a remarkable memoir, Keynes described his own moral outlook and that of Bloomsbury liberalism as one of an "unsurpassable individualism." Following what they mistakenly believed to be Mill's view of individual liberty, as well as certain ethical dicta of the Cambridge philosopher G. E. Moore, the members of the circle idealized intense self-absorption, particularly the state of being in love. Keynes properly described this narcissistic self-centeredness as both amoral and asocial. These aesthetes and intellectuals, recognizing neither "inner sanction" nor moral obligation and believing they had the wisdom to judge each case on its merits, were "in the strict sense of the term, immoralists." Despite his later opinion that this philosophy had been based on a "disastrously mistaken" view of human nature, Keynes confessed that "I remain, and always will remain, an immoralist."[50] It is narcissistic Bloomsbury liberalism that critics often have in mind when they complain about the consequences of Mill's teachings.[51]

49. Mill to Lord Amberley, 2 and 12 February 1870, *LL*, pp. 1693–95.

50. J. M. Keynes, *Two Memoirs*, pp. 97, 83–84, 98.

51. For the use of Mill's *On Liberty* as a defense of nonconformist standards of sexual conduct, see H. L. A. Hart, *Law, Liberty, and Morality* (New York,

Although Bloomsbury might have argued that Mill's views were one of the sources of its lifestyle, the writings of the philosopher do not justify hailing him as its patron. In his 1857 dream, Mill had confronted the choice between carnal pleasure and virtue. Though it would be "abstractedly good & admirable" to be able to find both in union, the woman in Mill's dream assured him that this would be "*too* vain." The dreamer when awake could not fully endorse such a view. Mill did not advocate an ascetic's denial of pleasure. On this question, he seemed prepared to accept not the one-sided, rather priggish Hercules of Prodicus but perhaps the hero depicted by Goethe in 1773: "If I had really met those two ladies, you see," his Hercules declared, "I would have grabbed one under this arm, the other under that arm, and forced both of them to come along."[52] But this may be too earthy a translation of Mill's wish "to obtain the greatest amount of chastity and happiness" for both sexes!

Mill wished first of all to stress the potentialities of a freely willed self-development. The abolition of the legal subordination of women would lead to a blossoming of talents, not, as Comte thought, to libertinism and anarchy. Virtue would triumph over what seemed a physiological fatalism. By self-assertion and self-development, women could raise themselves to equal status and thereby become both the sexual and intellectual companions of men.

1963). Hart used Mill to support the recommendations of the Wolfenden Committee to repeal laws making homosexual behavior between consenting adults in private a punishable offense; he also noted the similarity of the views of Lord Devlin, an opponent of the committee's recommendations, to those of J. F. Stephen, a nineteenth-century critic of Mill's tract (see pp. 14–16).

52. Quoted in Galinsky, *The Herakles Theme*, p. 215.

THREE

The Theory and Practice of Virtue

MILL SURVEYED THE COMMERCIAL AND INCREASINGLY egalitarian society of nineteenth-century England and saw it as inherently hostile to virtue. He agreed with the ancient philosophers that the materialistic and self-seeking ethos of a commercial society was inimical to honor and personal dignity, truth telling, and moral or physical heroism, qualities without which a good society could not exist. An egalitarian society, moreover, threatened to subordinate the individual to the mass, and thereby to suppress liberty and diversity in favor of an oppressive conformity. Mill's interest in bringing society "nearer to some ideal standard" caused him to sympathize with the Saint-Simonians and to speak of himself as a socialist.[1]

In a world of fierce economic competition and moral anarchy, the Saint-Simonians had called for a reassertion of virtue. In 1850, the Unitarian and Comtist sympathizer Harriet Martineau described "the system called St. Simonism" as preaching "a new law of love and human equality," as well as a regime of virtue in which all were to enjoy "the free use of their best powers, and [to] reap their natural reward": "Work was to be worship, and affectionate co-operation was to be piety." The rulers of the new society would be "persons of virtue and genius." Was it

1. *Autobiography*, p. 117.

remarkable, she asked, that "some of the best hearts" and "some of the noblest minds of the time" were attracted to the new philosophy? Yet the Saint-Simonian system was based on "a scheme of hierarchy" which "might easily, and would probably become an intolerable despotism . . . a locked frame-work, in which individual freedom might become impossible."[2]

Was it feasible to establish a regime of virtue—not only for an elite but for all—and still to preserve and even enlarge the sphere of individual liberty? This was to be a critical question for Mill. While determined to preserve "the greatest individual liberty of action," he looked forward to a "change of character" in both laborers and employers that would lead them to associate for the sake of "public and social purposes, and not, as hitherto, solely for narrowly interested ones." Men might gradually be brought to such a virtuous state, though Mill warned against "premature attempts to dispense with the inducements of private interest in social affairs" whose very precipitousness might undermine liberty.[3]

When the Civil War broke out in America in 1861, Mill saw it as "a turning point, for good or evil," and he became a strong partisan of the North, whose success he believed would be a victory for virtue. The triumph of the Confederacy, on the other hand, would disseminate vicious principles everywhere and would undermine the prestige of democratic government. Mill could not but be disturbed that not only the aristocracy but almost all of the upper and middle classes, even those who called themselves liberals, had become supporters of the South. This was proof of "how little permanent improvement" had taken place in "our influential classes."[4] Not even liberal principles could overcome feelings of malicious pleasure at the misfortunes of a

2. Harriet Martineau, *The History of England during the Thirty Years' Peace: 1816–1846* (London, 1850) 2: 141.

3. *Autobiography*, pp. 162–63.

4. Ibid., p. 188.

rival or, more practically, expectations of profit as a consequence of a Southern free-trade policy. Virtue had yielded to the cruder sentiments of a commercial society.

Much to Mill's surprise, his long-time intellectual antagonist William Whewell, professor of moral philosophy at Cambridge, had also become a keen sympathizer with the antislavery cause. Some ten years earlier, Mill had criticized Whewell's doctrine of virtue, that what was legally correct was also morally good. Not only must we not violate the legal rights of others, the Cambridge intuitionist had argued, but we should not even wish to do so: "And thus we rise . . . from legality to virtue." By this standard, Mill countered, Americans who found slavery vicious were wicked men; in fact, Whewell had specifically asserted that "the laws of the state are to be observed even when they enact slavery." But with the coming of war, Whewell emerged as so fervent a defender of the North that he offended his Cambridge colleagues with his rejoinders to their arguments. He even refused to allow the pro-Southern *Times* into his home.[5]

On learning all this, Mill happily welcomed his philosophical rival into his camp. He wrote to tell Whewell "how strongly I have felt drawn to you by what I have heard of your sentiments" concerning the war "between freedom & slavery." "No question of our time has been such a touchstone of men," he declared. Whewell's practice had diverged from the strict definition of his theory of virtue. Most of the English middle class, however, had responded during the American war only to the materialist ethos of modern society and to the demands of a crass expediency. Mill felt "a special tie," his letter to Whewell concluded, to those who had proved "faithful when so many were faithless."[6]

How was it that the utilitarian and empiricist Mill could so

5. Quoted in J. S. Mill, "Whewell on Moral Philosophy" (1852), in *Essays on Ethics, Religion, and Society*, ed. J. M. Robson, *Collected Works* 10: 188, 200; Mill to J. L. Motley, 26 January 1863, *LL*, p. 828.

6. Mill to William Whewell, 24 May 1865, *LL*, pp. 1056–57.

identify his practical views on public morals with those of his philosophical opponent? Whewell's position on the Civil War, it may be argued, was more compatible than his previous legalistic definition with an intuitionist's view of virtue. On the other hand, we shall see that Mill had constructed a theory of virtue that, though apparently based on utility, took the "inward man" (whom the intuitionists charged Benthamites with ignoring) strictly into account. This non-Benthamite view of virtue pervaded all Mill's philosophical writings, as it did his various positions on practical politics.

Mill had first clashed with Whewell's intuitionism in the *System of Logic* in 1843,[7] and he returned to the attack in 1852 in an article on Whewell's moral philosophy that he was to describe some years later as one of "not many defences extant of the ethics of utility."[8] There was something spurious, however, about Mill's "defence" of Benthamite utility against the Cambridge professor. Mill certainly had no sympathy with the a priori, intuitionist basis of Whewell's ethics, nor did he fail to demonstrate the faulty method and careless logic of his opponent. But he seemed more interested in disputing the claim of the intuitionists to a monopoly on such virtues as conscience, duty, and rectitude than in defending Bentham's moral system. Utilitarians no less than a priori moralists, Mill replied, declined to lie, steal, or murder on grounds of expediency. Such worthy sentiments belonged equally to a properly conceived utilitarian ethics, he argued, though he felt compelled to admit that Bentham himself had not conceived it properly.[9]

Whewell had chosen to attack the principle of utility in the form in which it had appeared in the writings of both Paley and

7. Mill, *System of Logic*, p. 263; also pp. 645–48; Whewell replied in "Mr. Mill's Logic" (1849), in *William Whewell's Theory of Scientific Method*, ed. R. E. Butts (Pittsburgh, 1968), pp. 265–308. See also Mill to Sir William Molesworth, 19 November 1840, *LL*, p. 1995.

8. Mill to Theodore Gomperz, 30 August 1858, *LL*, p. 570.

9. Mill, "Whewell," p. 194.

Bentham, but Mill argued that a utilitarian need not burden himself with either of these philosophers. Though Mill found Bentham's method eminently more praiseworthy than Paley's, there were still "large deficiencies and hiatuses" in the former's view of human nature. Whewell had, however, attacked Bentham on his method, where he was strong, not where he was "really vulnerable." Any system of morality formed on intuitionist grounds, Mill was convinced, must be circular and therefore faulty. Where Whewell had come to sound conclusions, it was because he had enlisted the principle of utility without knowing it. Like other intuitionists, he drew "from a double fountain—utility and internal conviction," whereas a utilitarian could shape his views on the one principle alone.[10]

This principle, for Mill in any event, was not the Benthamite one of individual self-interest, narrowly conceived to include only material happiness. In fact, in an essay written some twenty years earlier Mill had criticized Bentham's neglect of the "inward man" and virtue as severely as had the intuitionist opponents of the utilitarian thinker. Since James Mill had still been alive at the time this piece was written, Mill had arranged for its anonymous publication.[11]

Mill observed in his 1852 essay on Whewell that the eighteenth-century thinkers had divided on the subject of utility rather differently than their nineteenth-century successors. Since those who questioned the established morality—philosophers like Shaftesbury and Hume—had done so on the basis of "instinctive feelings of virtue," the defenders of commonly accepted opinions had turned to utility. This orthodox group included Dr. Johnson and William Paley, both of whom advocated a morality in which the chief criterion of virtue was expediency and the motive force self-interest. By the end of the century, however, in the hands of such men as Helvétius, Godwin, and Bentham, utility had

10. Ibid.
11. *Autobiography*, pp. 138–39.

become the basis for the radical critique of the prevailing morality. It was at this point that orthodoxy turned against utility and took up the doctrines of an "*à priori* or self-evident morality, an end in itself, independent of all consequences." Its adherents had found what they required to accomplish this, Mill observed, in the doctrines of the German idealists.[12]

Mill was also to turn from a Benthamite view of utility. He was to defend his position, however, on the basis not of an "*à priori,* or self-evident morality," but of a virtue that embodied the highest concerns of social utility. This first became clear in his 1833 anonymous "Remarks on Bentham's Philosophy."

Owing to his ignorance of other men's opinions, Bentham had failed to give a satisfactory answer to the frequently justified criticisms of his views by the disciples of the German philosophers, Mill declared in this essay. Most importantly, Bentham had failed to understand the connection between an act and the state of mind that had produced it. This was a considerable deficiency in a moralist. For example, the utilitarian philosopher understood lying or theft entirely in terms of the consequences of a particular act. He did not consider that such acts, widely practiced, would destroy the confidence necessary to a good society, since they suggested the presence of "habits of mind and heart" that would bring about greater evils than might be the consequence of isolated incidents. To condemn such vices on general principles was therefore not a display of "prejudice and superstition," as orthodox Benthamites would have it; such vicious conduct reflected a "*character* essentially pernicious" to the greatest happiness.[13]

The proper application of the standard of happiness required "a much deeper insight into the formation of character" and human nature than the utilitarian philosopher possessed, Mill observed. Bentham's narrow view of utility might readily serve as the basis for ordinary legislation, but it would fail if one used

12. Mill, "Whewell," pp. 170–71.

13. J. S. Mill, "Remarks on Bentham's Philosophy" (1833), pp. 6–8.

it to advance the interest of virtue, to improve "the national character," to carry "forward the members of the community towards perfection," or to preserve them "from degeneracy." But Bentham had rarely concerned himself with such goals, and Mill saw this as one of his greatest faults.[14]

Bentham erred in believing that our acts were designed to secure the most pleasure and the least pain as a *consequence* of their performance. Mill argued that the *prospect* of pleasure or pain before undertaking a course of conduct might well be the more critical motive. The very thought of performing a vicious act might be so abhorrent as to make action impossible. Indeed, he observed, unless this were the case, "the man is not really virtuous." The virtuous man shrinks from vice not because he has carefully deliberated its consequences but because of a deep "*impulse,* that is, by a feeling (call it an association if you think of it) which has no ulterior end." The practice of virtue or the avoidance of vice was "an end in itself."[15]

But Bentham had seen physical happiness as the only goal of human conduct. He had been oblivious to virtue and had omitted from his list of motives "conscience, or the feeling of duty": "one would never imagine from reading him that any human being ever did an act merely because it is right, or abstained from it merely because it is wrong." This was an error that pervaded all Bentham's thinking. His use of the term "interest," moreover, suggested that man was limited to his purely selfish concerns, and that he could not rise to a consideration of the interests that he shared with the rest of society.[16]

In Bentham's neglect of concern for the public interest as an effective motive in human nature, in his ignoring of virtue, Mill saw the utilitarian's writings "to have done and to be doing very serious evil." Because of this grave defect, "the more en-

14. Ibid., pp. 8–9.
15. Ibid., pp. 12–13.
16. Ibid., p. 13.

thusiastic and generous" spirits had turned against not only Bentham's opinions but all efforts to put morals on a sound philosophical basis. But even more dangerous were the distortions that Benthamite views imposed on those who accepted them. They were "perverting to their whole moral nature" and, moreover, contradicted "all rational hope of good for the human species."[17] In making these accusations, Mill found himself agreeing with the view of Benthamism presented by the intuitionist, idealist philosophers.

Unless we accepted the undoubted fact that mankind was capable of disinterested virtue, Mill declared, we could not attain "one tenth part of the happiness which our nature is susceptible of." In opposition to prevailing middle-class opinion, and following the arguments of the German philosophers, Mill saw no significant increase of happiness through changes in outward conditions alone. "Our hopes of happiness or moral perfection" were founded on inward improvement and on a faith in the possibility of "virtuous exertion" in favor of social interests. The writer on ethics, if he were to perform his task usefully, must demonstrate "in every sentence and in every line, a firm unwavering confidence in man's capability of virtue." Socrates, Plato, and Christ had been such moralists; Bentham, on the other hand, had proclaimed the hopeless view that men were inherently and unalterably dedicated to selfishness. But man was not condemned by the necessity of his nature to a "miserable self-seeking," Mill insisted; he could freely choose virtue and thereby secure the greatest happiness.[18]

Mill and the Saint-Simonians differed sharply in their estimate of the new industrial system. The Saint-Simonians eulogized English progress, convinced that industrial growth would inaugurate an era of peace and plenty in place of the feudal regime of war and scarcity. They celebrated the leading *industriels,* the

17. Ibid., p. 15.
18. Ibid., pp. 15–16.

English captains of industry and financiers, to whom they gave credit for the economic miracle of the Industrial Revolution and wished to entrust the future leadership of their society. Mill, on the other hand, was more persuaded by Carlyle's denunciation of the materialistic credo of commercial society than by the Saint-Simonian adulation of the industriels. He connected England's economic superiority, he wrote in 1829 to the Saint-Simonian Eichthal, with "the very worst point in our national character, the disposition to sacrifice every thing to accumulation, & that exclusive & engrossing selfishness which accompanies it." The selfishness bred by the commercial spirit carried over into every part of English life, Mill maintained, producing an "indifference" and "moral insensibility" which made men unwilling to learn to do good.[19]

In 1836, Mill wrote an article entitled "Civilization," in which he discussed the defects of modern commercial society. In a commercial society men concentrated their energies on "money getting," and success depended "not upon what a person is, but upon what he seems." An individual became "lost in the crowd." Those who wished to influence public opinion were obliged to cultivate the arts of charlatanry in order to reach an audience inundated with books and articles. Not only was the individual made "impotent in the crowd," but individual character became "enervated." "The spectacle, and even the very idea of pain"—of "harshness, rudeness, and violence," of "the struggle of one indomitable will against another"—had been removed from the sight of the middle classes. Thus, while "the refined classes" of modern society possessed more of the "amiable and humane" qualities, they had "much less of the heroic." There had descended upon them "a moral effeminacy, an inaptitude for every kind of struggle."[20]

In order to counter these tendencies of a commercial society,

19. Mill to Eichthal, 15 May and 8 October 1829, *EL*, pp. 31–32.

20. J. S. Mill, "Civilization" (1836), *Collected Works* 18: 129, 133, 132, 133, 130–31.

it was necessary to discover ways "to invigorate the individual character," to revive the dormant virtue of the refined classes. Modeling his views on Coleridge's vision of a clerisy, Mill called for a transformation of the churches and universities that would produce individuals both "determined and qualified to seek Truth ardently, vigorously, and disinterestedly." Through a university education founded not on dogmatic religion but on ancient literature, history, and the philosophy of the mind, students might learn the principles governing the progress of man and society and understand "the astonishing pliability" of human nature and how best to improve it. The chief purpose of education should be to evoke "the greatest possible quantity of intellectual power, and to inspire the intensest *love of* truth," regardless of where they led. This was how to form "great minds" able to maintain "a victorious struggle with the debilitating influences of the age" and how to strengthen "the weak side of Civilization by the support of a higher Cultivation." Next, Mill urged that positions of "honour and ascendancy" be filled by virtuous men.[21]

Four years later, in his essay on Coleridge, Mill wrote that while he was cheered by the increase of physical comforts and knowledge in the new civilization, nonetheless, in the authentic Christian-Stoic vein, he preferred the position of Coleridge, Carlyle, and the German philosophers, whom he called "worshippers of independence." To these thinkers, the advantages of civilization had been purchased by the repression of the virtues of individual courage and "self-relying independence." Mill agreed that this was too high a price to pay and joined the conservatives in denouncing the "effeminate shrinking from the shadow of pain," the subordination of the denizens of mass civilization to artificial, monotonous, passionless lives, the destruction of any clear individuality, and the demoralization produced by the "great inequalities in wealth and social rank" of commercial society.[22]

21. Ibid., pp. 136, 141, 145, 144, 140, 143, 147.
22. J. S. Mill, "Coleridge" (1840), *Collected Works* 10: 123–25.

In an 1840 article, Mill observed that Tocqueville, in his study of American government, had at times confused the effects of democracy with those of commercial civilization. The unhappy characteristics that Mill had described in his article on civilization and that Tocqueville had seen as the product of the conditions of equality in America were not to be found in economically backward Quebec, where a rough equality existed; but they were present in bustling, commercial England, where there was no equality. In Quebec, there was no "go-ahead spirit—that restless, impatient eagerness for improvement . . . that mobility, that shifting and fluctuating . . . that jealousy of superior attainments" which existed in England and the United States. The evil was a product not of equality but of the predominance of commercial classes who imposed their image upon all of society.[23]

Mill denounced this "yoke of *bourgeois* opinion," holding it responsible for the mediocrity of intellectual life as characterized by the wider diffusion of superficial knowledge, the dominance of a "matter-of-fact spirit," and the "dogmatism of common sense." These were among the results of progress in a society that prided itself on its wealth. This was true of England, whose institutions rested on prescription, and even more true of America, whose government had only recently been constructed on abstract principles. These characteristics, then, were "quite compatible" with the existence of both "peers and proletaires."[24]

Was it then inevitable that a modern commercial society beget alienation, rootlessness, an imposed conformity, and intellectual mediocrity? Fortunately, human affairs were "not entirely governed by mechanical laws, nor men's characters wholly and irrevocably formed by their situation in life." Economic and social changes, "though among the greatest," were "not the only forces which shape the course of our species." Ideas were "not always

23. J. S. Mill, "De Tocqueville on Democracy in America" (1840), *Collected Works* 18: 191–92, 196.

24. Ibid., pp. 194, 196.

the mere signs and effects of social circumstances"; rather they themselves were "a power in history." A virtue independent of purely economic pressures might alter the seemingly necessary course of events. If men were made to understand the dangers of the "unbalanced influence of the commercial spirit," and if the "wiser and better-hearted politicians and public teachers" acted to erect a "salutary check" on this influence, there was yet hope.[25]

But there had to be a social base for opinions different from those of the mass of people. In a commercial country, where the military spirit was no more, such a base might be found in "an agricultural class, a leisured class" of independent gentlemen, "and a learned class." Mill now placed his hope for England in the counterinfluence of the agricultural class, with its "local attachments" and "greater willingness to look up to, and accept of, guidance" from its social superiors. This class would exert the force of the preindustrial community and serve as "the counterbalancing element in our national character," representing "the type opposite to the commercial,—that of moderate wishes, tranquil tastes, cultivation of the excitements and enjoyments near at hand." In America, unfortunately, the farmers had no local attachments and were as mobile as the commercial class. Nor did America have either a leisured or a learned class, additional advantages that England possessed.[26]

Mill returned to these themes in 1848 in the *Principles of Political Economy*. Once more he condemned the widespread acceptance of the ideal of the commercial classes in which the normal and desirable state of human society was "struggling to get on" by "trampling, crushing, elbowing, and treading on each other's heels." This was certainly the present state, "the disagreeable symptoms of one of the phases of industrial progress," even, as a later edition of the *Principles* maintained, possibly a "necessary stage." In 1848, Mill saw the United States as embodying not

25. Ibid., pp. 197–98.
26. Ibid., pp. 198–200.

only the most desirable aspects of a democratic and commercial society, but also the least. In America, one sex was "devoted to dollar-hunting" and the other "to breeding dollar-hunters." Mill eliminated this jibe in the 1871 edition and observed with evident surprise that the American Civil War had proved that this disagreeable stage of industrial development was not "necessarily destructive of the higher aspirations and the heroic virtues." While it was perhaps better to have a commercial society urging men to struggle for wealth than a military society seeking to employ them in war, Mill believed that only in backward nations was it still useful to increase production.[27]

Mill envisioned, then, an ideal state on the model of the ancient philosophers, stationary in population and wealth but progressive in virtue. While one may argue that his society was impracticable, Mill's ideal confirmed his choice of virtue over mere material happiness. There would be in this society no slowing down for "mental culture, and moral and social progress," "no stationary state of human improvement." Relieved from studying "the art of getting on," Mill declared, men could turn their attention to "the Art of Living." He depicted a state living under law, like that postulated by the ancients, with all classes content with their relative conditions, but with the producing classes prepared to support a class "with sufficient leisure, both physical and mental," to serve as a model for all in furthering "the graces of life."[28]

A leading theme of the *Principles* was the use of freely willed virtue to secure economic justice in commercial society. This conception was the basis for Mill's somewhat overdrawn distinction between the laws of production and those of distribution. The laws of production, he declared, were, indeed, "laws," with "nothing optional or arbitrary" about them. Whatever men willed, the

27. J. S. Mill, *Principles of Political Economy*, ed. J. M. Robson, *Collected Works* 2–3, pp. 754n and 754–55.

28. Ibid., pp. 755–56.

production of a society would always be dependent on and limited by its capital, industriousness, skill, technological advance, and ability to organize its labor force. Similarly, savings and investment, that is, "productive expenditure," would always tend to enrich a community, while in the long run "the unproductive expenditure of individuals will *pro tanto* tend to impoverish" it. But if the laws of production were unalterable, they did not determine the way a society distributed its products. That was "a matter of human institution solely" and differed from age to age and from country to country. Men could freely decide on patterns of distribution and even make experiments to achieve the best practical consequences.[29] Mill proposed as a device worth testing, for example, a restriction on the amount a person might inherit, to oblige every person to be socially useful; he cautioned, however, that to do away with inheritance entirely would eliminate an important incentive in the process of production, as well as limit the usefulness of private property in diffusing power and thus protecting liberty.[30]

Karl Marx had a substantial doctrinal stake in arguing, contrary to Mill, that the laws of distribution could not be altered at will. In the preface to the 1873 edition of *Capital,* Marx denounced the attempt in Mill's *Principles* to distinguish between laws of capitalist production and voluntary decisions concerning distribution as "a shallow syncretism": Mill was attempting "to reconcile irreconcilables," the communist economist declared.[31] In a later volume of his magnum opus, Marx returned to the attack on Mill, observing that the laws of distribution were entirely determined by and "essentially coincident" with those of production—were, indeed "their opposite side."[32] For Marx,

29. Ibid., pp. 199–200. See also *Autobiography*, pp. 174–76; for a critique of Mill's strict separation of the laws of production and distribution, see Schwartz, *New Political Economy of J. S. Mill*, pp. 64–66.

30. Mill, *Principles of Political Economy*, pp. 810–12, 887–95.

31. Karl Marx, *Capital* (New York, 1936), pp. 19–20.

32. Karl Marx, *Capital* (Moscow, 1959), 3: 856, 861.

the laws of capitalist production had made necessary the accumulation of surplus value by a small class at the expense of a growing and increasingly impoverished proletariat. The result would be the inevitable social revolution toward which all his efforts were directed. The failure of Marx's prophecy can in good part be attributed to the peaceful alteration of the patterns of distribution in industrial societies.

Mill saw the widespread paternalism of the 1840s as inspired by a fear of a Chartist revolt as well as by the sentimentality of a reinvigorated Christianity. This development was particularly worrying to him because of the imminent arrival of democratic politics. The "superficial philanthropy" of the upper classes had occupied itself with sanitary and housing reform or with anti-poor-law agitation rather than with the underlying problem, he observed in an 1844 letter to a friend. No one now spoke of the need for foresight or self-control on the part of the poor, or even of the usefulness of Malthusian restraint. The frantic activities of the rich, dreading social upheaval and anxious to buy off the poor, could only instill in the lower classes "the faith that it is other people's business to take care of them." It was necessary to encourage the poor to attain independence rather than to habituate them to dependence, he wrote to another friend three years later. Instead, a mindless and fearful aristocracy, as well as a guilt-ridden middle class, had lost "the moral dignity of the past" and had forgotten that merely passive qualities could not secure well-being. Mill was especially unhappy that the aristocracy, which had once possessed a sense of honor and both will and character, now "bend with a willing submission to the yoke of bourgeois opinion."[33]

In a letter to Comte in 1847, Mill assailed the "system of charitable government" which sought to give to the poor more

33. Mill to R. B. Fox, 9 September 1842, *EL*, p. 544; Mill to Chapman, 8 November 1844, *EL*, pp. 640–41; Mill to John Austin, 13 April 1847, *EL*, pp. 712–13.

money, shorter hours, or sanitary improvements. Though not doubting the goodwill of the upper classes, he saw paternal government as "setting aside the moral dignity of the poor." "What one does for people," he argued, "is only useful to them if it merely supports what they do for themselves." The upper classes foolishly believed "that the happiness of the proletariat depends on the wealthy"; they did not see "that in the last analysis it depends on the energy, the good sense, and the foresight of the proletarians themselves." Of such matters, Mill groaned, "our would-be philanthropists have not the slightest idea."[34] Comte, of course, was of this number. For him a good society depended on stimulating the altruistic feelings of the rich on behalf of the poor.

The following year, in his *Principles,* Mill dismissed what he called "the theory of dependence and protection" in favor of a proletarian "self-dependence." "The future well-being of the labouring classes," he declared, "is principally dependent on their own mental cultivation." This proletarian self-development would bring about the "improved intelligence" of the working class and would thereby restrain population growth, consequently undermining the working of the "iron law of wages." In this way, the working classes might escape the gloom of both Comtian and Ricardian necessity.[35]

Virtue was the quality that would stir the working class to exert themselves and to overcome their dependence. By self-cultivation, the working classes, like women, would shatter the bonds that had kept them merely the servants of others. In the future, none but "the least valuable work-people"—those with "too little understanding, or too little virtue"—would consent to work all their lives for wages."[36] Some would go into association

34. Mill to Comte, 17 May 1847, *Lettres inédites*, pp. 549–50.

35. This was the theme of Mill's "On the Probable Futurity of the Labouring Classes," in *Principles of Political Economy*, bk. 4, chap. 7. Mill, *Principles of Political Economy*, pp. 759–60, 763–65.

36. Ibid., pp. 765–66, 793.

with capitalists on a profit-sharing basis; some already had. Others would associate among themselves along cooperative patterns. The participation of workingmen in cooperatives was essential if they were to achieve self-dependence, Mill argued.[37] He concluded by espousing the usefulness, indeed the indispensability, of competition, very much in opposition to contemporary socialist opinion.[38]

Like Tocqueville in his study of America, Mill worried about the dangers that democracy posed to virtue. In the 1830s, the commercial middle class was in the ascendancy, but the future would see the working class prevail, he was convinced. But if a class were "most powerful," it need not be "all-powerful": the grand political problem of the future must be "to prevent the strongest from becoming the only power," he observed. It was necessary to "repress the natural tendency" of the most powerful class "to sweep away" all resistance. Since "any counter-balancing power" needed "the sufferance of the commercial class" in order to exist, it was first necessary to persuade that class to "tolerate some such limitation." For if the growing middle class were abandoned to "the mere habits and instincts of a commercial community," the result must be what Tocqueville had described as the "tyranny of the majority." Tocqueville had observed that it had in the past been necessary to compel aristocracies to bend their private interests to accommodate those of the people as a whole, but had argued that "other perils and other cures await the men of our age." Diversity had characterized the former aristocratic societies, while uniformity was the rule in the new democracies. While previously the privileged classes had exaggerated the need to respect private rights, modern society insisted too much that individual interest yield to that of the majority. "It would seem as if the rulers of our time sought only to use men in order to effect great things," Tocqueville concluded; I

37. See discussion in ibid., pp. 769–94.
38. Ibid., pp. 794–96.

wish that they would try a little more to make great men." Nothing "comparable in profundity," Mill proclaimed, had yet been written on democracy.[39]

The great danger of democracy, in Mill's view, was "not of too great liberty, but of too ready submission; not of anarchy but of servility." The peril was a conformity imposed by a central power, supposedly to protect citizens, but in fact "trampling . . . with considerable recklessness, as often as convenient, upon the rights of individuals, in the name of society and the public good." How could this danger be averted? By popular education and the nourishing of the spirit of liberty, Mill and Tocqueville agreed. The "superior spirits" in a democracy ought to bend their efforts, in Mill's words, "to vindicate and protect the unfettered exercise of reason, and the moral freedom of the individuals."[40] While ultimate control of government must rest with the people, the best government was that of "the wisest, and these must always be a few," Mill declared. He saw "the one and only danger of democracy" to be that of making legislators mere delegates for putting the wishes of the majority into effect.[41] How to create a place for virtue in the political process was a critical problem. Unless it were solved, the egalitarian democratic state would have no place for liberty.

In the early years of his life, John Stuart Mill favored the secret ballot; from his middle years to his death, he opposed it. In his early support, Mill took it as given, like any English Radical of his time, that only the ballot could protect the elector against intimidation by his social and economic betters.[42] Opposition to the ballot was widely understood as opposition to the

39. Mill, "Tocqueville on Democracy" (1840), pp. 200, 189–90.

40. Ibid., pp. 188–89.

41. J. S. Mill, "De Tocqueville on Democracy in America" (1835), *Collected Works* 18: 74.

42. Mill to Tocqueville, 7 January 1837, *EL,* p. 317; see Mill to Albany Fonblanque, 13 February 1837, *EL,* p. 327. See also B. L. Kinzer, "J. S. Mill and the Secret Ballot," *Historical Reflections* 5 (Summer 1978): 19–39.

entire Radical agenda, as Mill himself observed at the time. By the late 1830s, although he continued to believe the ballot "necessary, & but little objectionable," Mill felt the issue had become entirely domesticated: it was no longer a strictly Radical doctrine but a Whig, "juste milieu, middle class doctrine."[43]

A decade and a half later, Mill had changed his mind about the ballot. He now saw it as "a step backward," and referred to Montesquieu's and Cicero's view that the secret ballot in the last years of the Roman republic had been responsible in part for its fall. A number of Whigs, including Lord Palmerston, shared this position. Mill's old friend George Grote remained one of the ballot's defenders, as did the new generation of Radicals who followed Cobden and Bright. In a dream in 1855, Mill saw himself in a debate with the American statesman John C. Calhoun: to Mill's view that the ballot was no longer necessary, Calhoun—no doubt expressing the dreamer's own doubts—replied that "it will not be necessary in Heaven, but it will always be necessary on earth."[44]

Mill explained his revised view of the ballot both privately and publicly. Intimidation by social superiors was no longer the coercive force it had been, he argued in a letter to an Australian correspondent. Society now needed protection from the voter's selfish personal or class interests and worst instincts. The obligation to make his vote public would induce the elector to place the general good of the community above other considerations. If an elector had to defend his vote to others, he would be obliged to become more certain of his grounds. The "mere obligation of preserving decency" was a restraint on the abuse of electoral power, Mill observed in a tract on parliamentary reform: "People will give dishonest or mean votes from lucre, from malice, from

43. Mill to J. M. Kemble, 14 October 1839, *EL*, p. 410.

44. Mill to Lord Monteagle, 20 March 1853, *LL*, p. 103; Mill to Harriet Mill, 2 February, 24 January, and 30 June 1854, 13 January 1855, *LL*, pp. 147, 218, 221, 289.

pique, from personal rivalry, from the interests or prejudices of class or sect, far more readily in secret than in public."[45]

An honest public vote, moreover, would help to form the ethical characters of both the elector and his community. To cast a vote was for Mill a moral act. He strongly dissented from the view that suffrage was a right: such a doctrine "would be enough to corrupt and destroy the purest democracy conceivable." It was a trust, and there would "never be honest or self-restraining government unless each individual participant feels himself a trustee for all his fellow citizens and for posterity"; Mill noted that "no Athenian voter thought otherwise."[46] This was the way to a virtuous polity.

One of the chief objects of education was "to foster courage and the public spirit." The "virtues of freemen" did not include concealment; why should freemen choose to have "the soul of a slave" and insist upon the secrecy of the ballot? The ballot merely encouraged electors to lie about their vote to those who asked, a consequence particularly corrupting among the English, who for all their faults had this grand virtue: their "higher classes do not lie," and their lower classes "though mostly habitual liars, are ashamed of lying." England ought not "to run any risk of weakening this feeling, a difficult one to create, or, when once gone, to restore." The secret ballot would thus produce "a permanent evil" for merely transitory benefits.[47]

Curiously, Mill did not sufficiently consider in this connection his long-held fear that public opinion in a democracy would insist on conformity to its views—that a secret ballot might be necessary to protect the voter from the tyranny of the majority. Writing to his Australian friend in 1858, Mill fleetingly observed that

45. Mill to H. S. Chapman, 8 July 1858, *LL*, pp. 558–59; J. S. Mill, "Thoughts on Parliamentary Reform" (1859), *Collected Works* 19: 335–36.

46. Mill to G. C. Lewis, 20 March 1859, *LL*, pp. 607–08.

47. Mill, "Parliamentary Reform," pp. 337–38; see also J. S. Mill, "Considerations on Representative Government" (1861), *Collected Works* 19: 488–91.

the public sanction he sought to bring into play by his opposition to the ballot might have a coercive force,[48] but he avoided further discussion of the issue. Mill appears to have expected those citizens who were both courageous and good to oppose the worst instincts of public opinion, and thereby to educate all in the pursuit of virtue.

But until such time as the democracy would become virtuous, it was necessary to find a political mechanism to rid universal suffrage of its drawbacks. Mill was convinced that this could only be accomplished by providing a special political role for minorities, who could counterbalance the working-class majority and the self-seeking, materialist ethos which it shared with the bourgeoisie. In 1838 he had seen Tocqueville as the Montesquieu of the nineteenth century, a man who might well devise a system for making the democracy of the future safe for liberty. Some twenty years later, Mill believed that he had discovered how this might be done. He became the leading advocate of a plan for proportional representation devised by the liberal writer Thomas Hare. To deter tyranny of the working-class majority, it would be necessary to make certain that the votes of minorities, particularly those of the "highly educated and public spirited persons" scattered through the country, would not be submerged in constituency after constituency. Such a "virtual blotting-out" of minorities was at bottom undemocratic. Hare's system would permit electors anywhere in the country to vote for candidates of whom they approved, and any candidate obtaining a certain quota of votes would gain a seat. An elector would cast a list of preferences, and if his first candidate were defeated or had already gained a minimal quota, his vote would be given to the second person on his list, and so on. Such a system would not only assure minorities of representation, but would allow "able men of independent thought" who had made themselves "honourably dis-

48. Mill to Chapman, 8 July 1858, *LL*, p. 559.

tinguished" to enter parliament. The House of Commons could thus include "the very elite of the country."[49]

The "natural tendency of representative government, as of modern civilization," Mill proclaimed, was "towards collective mediocrity." Only by giving a voice to "the instructed minority" could this tendency be overcome. What was necessary was "a social support, a *point d'appui,* for individual resistance" to the ruling power. The "instructed minority" would provide such a support under Hare's system. Although this elite would not have more seats than their numbers entitled them to, it could exert a moral influence and provide democracy with not only an "occasional Pericles," but a "habitual group of superior and guiding minds.[50]

Hare's scheme, Mill wrote to a friend in 1859, would be "in the best sense of the word, Conservative, as well as, also in the best sense, liberal and democratic." Both parties ought therefore to join in support of it; only people like Bright, "the mere demagogue and courtier of the majority," were its natural opponents."[51] The "Demos itself," Mill believed, wanted to be protected against its own errors. Radical parlimentary speeches on this question "very much disgusted me," he declared. The "demagogues" did not dare admit the smallest doubt that the majority was infallible. Mill wanted to convince "the dress-coated democrats" not to be "plus royalistes que le roi."[52] During the parliamentary consideration in 1866 of a Reform Bill, Mill warned a liberal-minded peer against "the democrats of the old one-sided school" such as

49. J. S. Mill, "Bentham" (1838), *Collected Works* 10: 109; "Representative Government," pp. 450–52, 456.

50. Ibid., pp. 457, 459–60.

51. Mill to Edwin Chadwick, 20 December 1859, *LL*, pp. 654–55.

52. Mill to Max Kyllmann, 15 February 1865, *LL*, pp. 997–98. Mill thought that the Liberal M.P. Charles Buxton had muddied the waters several months earlier by calling for an additional vote for men who owned a certain amount of property. Mill opposed this, but was sympathetic to giving a second vote "by right of education" (p. 998).

John Bright, who would damn the Hare principle as "an aristocratic contrivance." But it would appear that the working classes were better prepared to accept Bright's view of the question than Mill's.[53]

In 1868, the Democratic party in the United States proposed in their platform that the government pay off the Civil War debt in "greenbacks," depreciated paper currency. Such a proceeding seemed immoral to many Americans, among them a Bostonian friend of Mill's who asked him to write a short article on the subject for publication in an American paper. Mill agreed, convinced that this act on the part of the federal government would besmirch the reputation of democratic institutions. That a suggestion so vicious as virtual repudiation of debt could be advanced was clearly a consequence of the tyranny of a majority, in this case not bourgeois but proletarian. Defrauding public creditors by payment of "a vast quantity of paper depreciated to worthlessness by excessive issue" would be "the most unfortunate event for the morality of the world," Mill declared.

In his article, completed some months later, Mill described the proposition in even more vigorous terms, as "one of the heaviest blows" that might be given "to the morality and civilization of the human race." Mill was persuaded that this judgment was not hyperbole. If men could not trust one another's promises, society would be reduced to savagery. This was particularly important where money contracts were at issue, and the State was a party to the engagement. If the government might defraud, all men would believe they could also do so. The detractors of democratic government had long maintained that it would in practice mean a return to barbarism, Mill observed. America must not imitate the medieval despots of Europe who had earned the hatred of their peoples by debasing the coinage. Mill was

53. Mill to Earl Grey, 21 May 1860, *LL*, pp. 1169–70; Mill to J. E. Cairnes, 4 December 1868, *LL*, pp. 1507–08.

confident, however, that the American government would live up to its promises and not pay its debt in depreciated currency.[54]

The issue was complicated and remained so. In the early 1840s Mill and certain of his friends had worried about an actual repudiation of state debts in America, an act about whose immorality there could be no doubt.[55] In 1868, the case was the more subtle one of inflated currency. In such an instance, some might argue, any course adopted by government would tend to favor one class over another, and therefore immorality was merely in the eye of the beholder. Similarly, certain recent economists, among them Keynes, have approved of twentieth-century democracies issuing excess paper money to meet their employment and welfare goals and thereby fueling a continuously inflating economy. Mill understood that democracies would often be tempted, as in 1868, to part from the path of virtue, and he forecast disastrous consequences if they did so.

In the early letters between Mill and Comte, a misunderstanding had arisen about the reasons for Mill's having foregone a career in parliament. Comte had congratulated his English admirer on rejecting "sterile parliamentary battles" in order to devote himself to the development of doctrine. The parliamentary system rested upon a negative metaphysics, Comte declared, and the political routine would "imperceptibly debase superior men," not only by overwhelming them with detail but also by obliging them to follow a life of compromise. As is well known, Mill had followed his father into the East India Company, rising to the post of examiner. Mill tried to explain to Comte that his position at the East India Company made it necessary to refrain from an active political life. For his part, Mill confessed, he had often been tempted to turn to politics and to secure a parliamentary

54. Mill to C. E. Norton, 18 March and 24 September 1868, *LL*, pp. 1376, 1443–45, 1448.

55. See Mill to Sarah Austin, 11 March 1842, *EL*, p. 506.

seat, to focus public attention on new ideas. Indeed, if not for his employment, he would have seen it as his duty to do so.[56]

After Mill retired from the East India Company in 1858, he received offers from Liberals in a number of constituencies asking him to become their candidate. Finally, early in 1865, he agreed to stand for the seat at Westminster. Mill set certain conditions before accepting, among them that he would not pledge himself to party regularity. His object in seeking a seat, he declared, would be to promote his own ideas, whether or not they enjoyed the support of his constituents or his party. Mill clearly intended not to make the political compromises that debased superior men.[57]

In parliament, Mill followed the line he had charted and defended his special opinions regardless of the views of either the Liberal party or the Radical section with which he was usually in sympathy. For example, he continued to oppose the ballot and to support Hare's system. He even succeeded in persuading the initially skeptical John Bright as well as seventy-one other M.P.'s to vote with him to grant women the franchise. In the House of Commons, Mill found himself on two further occasions taking a stand sharply differing from what he at the time described as "advanced liberal opinion." In one instance, he wished the country to take up again the belligerent right to seize enemy goods in neutral ships, a right that liberal England had abandoned as immoral a decade earlier. In another, he opposed the abolition of capital punishment.[58] On both these occasions,

56. Comte to Mill, 20 November 1841, and 17 January 1842, *Lettres inédites*, pp. 8–9, 18–19; Mill to Comte, 18 December 1841, ibid., pp. 11–12.

57. See Packe, *Life of Mill*, pp. 446–51. In the course of Mill's speech to a workingman meeting outlining his views, a billboard quoting his statement that "the lower classes, though mostly habitual liars, are ashamed of lying" was raised. Had he written that sentence, he was asked? When Mill unhesitatingly replied that he had, the workingmen rose and cheered. See *Autobiography*, p. 199.

58. Ibid., p. 200.

Mill saw himself countering the tendencies of a weak-willed, commercial, modern democratic society and providing a basis for a virtuous one.

From their beginnings as a distinct group, the Radicals were the party of fiscal retrenchment and peace. Wars were expensive undertakings which, moreover, dislocated the usual patterns of trade, bringing losses to merchants and manufacturers. The military-minded, feudal aristocracy might delight in armed conflict, the Radicals argued, but the pacifist commercial class saw it as an outmoded and highly injurious survival of a barbaric past. Cobden and Bright had denounced the Crimean War, which other liberals, including Mill, had supported. They favored a policy of isolation and absolute nonintervention in the affairs of other countries as the surest method of keeping taxes low and preserving peace.

Mill's views were more Palmerstonian than they were those of "advanced" liberalism. In an 1859 article he had spoken out forcefully against what he regarded as a craven policy that looked only to mercantile profit and had argued in favor of one that would harness British power to aid the causes of liberty and national self-determination wherever a people was ready to rise up in defense of its rights.[59] In parliament in 1867, Mill was to raise the principle in a way that dramatically displayed his differences with the Radicals.

The question was to focus on England's need to reclaim the traditional belligerent rights at sea that she had abandoned in the 1850s. It had been a shock to world opinion that Great Britain had voluntarily suspended these rights during the Crimean War, with widespread approval at home.[60] In the Declaration of Paris at the conclusion of the war in 1856, England had agreed

59. See J. S. Mill, "A Few Words on Non Intervention," in *Dissertations and Discussions* 3: 153–78.

60. Olive Anderson, *A Liberal State at War: English Politics and Economics during the Crimean War* (London, 1967), pp. 16–18, 248–74.

to establish permanently the right of neutral ships to carry enemy goods. In the absence of a sizeable army, the right to capture enemy goods at sea, even aboard neutral vessels, had been Britain's only effective reply to the military superiority of the continental powers. But the liberal commercial classes were now convinced that such a maritime strategy would interfere with the profits of a cosmopolitan international economy. "Enlightened" opinion in England, the premier liberal nation in Europe, had come to the conclusion that the principle "free ships make free goods" was more in conformity with a modern and progressive epoch than the old rule, which the majority of the public increasingly saw as an immoral and illiberal application of the right of the stronger at sea.

Liberal opinion was almost unanimously favorable to this new view. Not only Radical pacifists like Cobden and Bright, on the left wing of the movement, but also the Peelite spokesmen for commercial interests, and even the more traditional Whigs—even Palmerston—cheered this course, which, in the words of the *Edinburgh Review,* would establish "a partial commercial peace in the midst of a political war."[61] There were at first but few objections to the new policy, with virtually none coming from the liberal side. In February 1855, however, while the war with Russia was still in progress, the Liberal barrister and future attorney general R. P. Collier did protest, asking whether it was to be said "that they would take every measure for the purpose of prosecuting the war with vigour, except one, which was likely to injure their commercial interests?" If this were so, Collier declared, the English "were rightly called a nation of shopkeepers, and they had better stay at home." In response to the last phrase, the isolationist and pacifist John Bright shouted, "Hear, hear!"[62]

61. [Henry Reeve], "The Orders in Council on Trade during War," *Edinburgh Review,* vol. C, no. 203 (July 1854): 221. See also the parliamentary debate in which Mill's long-time associate, Sir William Molesworth, maintained a similar position. *Parliamentary Debates* (Commons), 3d ser., vol. 134 (4 July 1854): 1091–1138. (Hereafter, *PD.*)

62. *PD* (Commons), 3d ser., vol. 136, (20 February 1855): 1670.

Twelve years later, in 1867, Mill took up Collier's position in a speech to the House of Commons. By this time, the party of advanced liberalism was pressing the government to go beyond the 1856 Declaration. The Radicals wished to extend immunity to all private property at sea, even that carried by enemy ships, as well as to abolish the right of commercial blockade. In contrast, Mill argued that Britain must reclaim her traditional right to wage war against the commerce of her enemies. The surrender of 1856, he insisted, had left the country not only exposed to invasion, but condemned to impotence, unable to respond even when "great international iniquities" were "perpetrated before our eyes." It was not on the "narrow grounds" of patriotism alone that Mill urged Britain to "resume that natural weapon which has been the main bulwark of our power and safety in past national emergencies": it was rather because the safety and "even the power" of England were "valuable to the freedom of the world" and "to the truest and most permanent interests of every civilized people." The resumption of Britain's traditional right of capture at sea, Mill warned, was essential to counter-balance the military might of the continental despotisms, which would otherwise be able to conquer and divide the entire world, utterly destroying every semblance of liberty.[63] Was not liberty more important than a comfortable peace and mercantile profits?

Liberals in both parties were horrified at Mill's position. Most Tories agreed with him. Lord Stanley, the Conservative foreign secretary at the time, however, belonged to the liberal wing of his party and was, like the Cobdenite Radicals, an isolationist. In presenting the foreign office's reply, Stanley agreed

63. *PD* (Commons), 3d ser., vol. 189 (5 August 1867): 878–80. Karl Marx saw the issue much as Mill did. By means of the old maritime system, Britain had been able to defend the liberty of Europe against Tsarist despotism, Marx wrote to a friend in 1870; when England subscribed to the 1856 Declaration, "England *disarmed herself*." Marx blamed this foolish act on "the bourgeois imbecility" of the Liberals. See Karl Marx to Dr. Kugelmann, 13 December 1870, Karl Marx, *On Revolution,* ed. S. K. Padover (New York, 1971), pp. 390–91.

that England could now no longer effectively respond to provocation by other powers. However, he argued, "the power to intervene effectually is a temptation to do so." Therefore, if England had been kept by the 1856 Declaration "from mixing ourselves up with Continental complications with which we had nothing to do," the foreign secretary was prepared to regard that as a very good thing.[64]

Peace was the highest aim of a commercial society, which consequently neglected even preparations necessary for its self defense. Liberal England, for example, prided itself on its freedom from the systems of conscription and military training that prevailed on the Continent. Englishmen saw this as a sign not only of their rejection of war and commitment to individual voluntarism, but also, Mill observed, of their commonsensical wish to employ their energies in more profitable pursuits. On this issue as well, Mill stood apart. In corresponding with friends after he had left Parliament, he praised the Swiss system, whose adoption by England he saw as "a question of life & death." For Mill, "the perfection of a military system" was to have no standing army but rather the training of all able-bodied men. Such a system was superior to a force based on volunteers, which would soon acquire the "professional military spirit" of a standing army and might become an "instrument of despotism."[65] In this, almost alone among Victorians, Mill represented the views of the defenders of civic virtue from the Florentine thinkers of the Renaissance to the British and American Whigs of the seventeenth and eighteenth centuries.[66]

64. *PD* (Commons), 3d ser., vol. 189 (5 August 1867): 886. Unhappy with the forceful Disraeli policy on Russo-Turkish affairs a decade later, Lord Stanley (who had by then succeeded to the title of the earl of Derby) would resign as Tory foreign secretary and subsequently join the Liberal party.

65. Mill to Cliffe Leslie, 5 February 1871, *LL*, pp. 1805–06; Mill to E. Chadwick, 2 January 1871, *LL*, p. 1792.

66. This tradition has been traced in J. A. Pocock, *The Machiavellian Moment: Florentine Political Thought and the Atlantic Republican Tradition* (Princeton, 1975).

In 1860, five years before he entered parliament, Mill had anticipated the reasoning of his position on capital punishment for murder in a letter to Florence Nightingale. In a book she had written for the instruction of artisans, Miss Nightingale had followed the argument of the Owenites and had inferred from the doctrine of necessity that there ought to be neither punishment nor blame for a crime, only reformatory discipline. For Mill, however, retaliation for injuries "consciously or intentionally done" was a natural consequence of wrongdoing. Punishment was the only way of making any impression upon many criminals and was thus the only way to begin to reform them, as well as to deter others. A resentment of evil, he held, was entirely proper: though wrongdoing might be explained, it could not therefore be excused. Doing ill was properly "an object of aversion," and if there ceased to be a strong desire to punish crime, Mill warned, the consequence would be the loss of all sense of right and wrong.[67]

When Mill served in the House of Commons, two occasions spurred him to demand the traditional legal retaliation for murder, the execution of the murderer. In the first, the great body of Radicals stood with him; in the second, they were opposed. This contrast could only confirm Mill's views concerning the deleterious effects of modern civilization.

The first incident emerged from events that took place on the Caribbean island of Jamaica. In October 1865, Edward Eyre, the British governor of the colony, had brutally suppressed an uprising of the black peasantry with killing, torturing, and burning. Eyre took advantage of the martial law declared in an outlying parish to secure the illegal execution of a personal and political enemy, a mulatto member of the Jamaica House of Assembly. When news of these events arrived in England, the nonconformist missionary societies and parliamentary Radicals formed the Jamaica Committee to secure the indictment of Eyre and his chief military

67. Mill to Florence Nightingale, 4 October 1860, *LL*, pp. 711–12.

associates for murder. The committee named Mill as its chairman. In what he was later to describe as "the best of my speeches in parliament," Mill called for the prosecution of Eyre in order to protect England against the "tyrannical violence" of martial law. Furthermore, he argued, it was "indispensable that he who takes the lives of others under this discretion should know that he risks his own." After three years Mill was forced to give up the effort, since one grand jury after another declined to indict Eyre or the other perpetrators of the atrocities.[68]

The second incident took place in early April 1868, when a Radical M.P. brought a bill to abolish capital punishment before the House of Commons. The Radicals had long championed such a move, for Miss Nightingale's views were widely shared in philanthropic circles. If the imperfections of social arrangements were the chief causes of crime, these people believed, it was unjust, indeed hypocritical, of society to exact a penalty for wrongdoing. In the course of the 1850s and 1860s, the members of parliament who represented "progressive" views pressed, with noteworthy success, to lighten punishments, to make the lot of the prisoner easier, and to facilitate early parole. And accompanying these efforts was a movement to end capital punishment, substituting imprisonment for life.

On this occasion, Mill spoke in opposition to those he called "the philanthropists." They had assuredly been right to rid the law of the death penalty too often imposed in the past for lesser crimes. However, in Mill's view, there was no call to remove it as punishment for murder, "the greatest crime known to the law." For the hardened murderer, there was but one appropriate penalty: "solemnly to blot him out from the fellowship of mankind and from the catalogue of the living." Execution was certainly the most "impressive" and the "least cruel" method for society to deal with so heinous a crime. It was fallacious to deny, as the

68. See discussion in the *Autobiography*, pp. 207–10; see also Bernard Semmel, *Jamaican Blood and Victorian Conscience*.

Radicals did, that capital punishment deterred, for we only knew of those whom it had not deterred. Equally mistaken was the dread of mistakenly executing an innocent person, for the English rules of evidence were "even too favorable" to the accused.[69]

Mill hoped that "the mania" for "paring down all our punishments" had "reached its limits," for there was a possibility of ending "any effectual punishment" whatsoever. Penal servitude was becoming "almost nominal," given the light sentences, the comfort of the prisons, and the ease of parole. The "ludicrously inadequate" punishments, even for atrocious assaults, were "almost an encouragement to crime." Mill called for more severe sentences, particularly in the case of crimes most offensive "to the moral sentiments of the community."[70]

If the aim of the philanthropists to abolish the death penalty were successful, Mill concluded, it would be "a fatal victory." The Radicals would have achieved their triumph—"if they will forgive me for saying so"—by "an enervation, an effeminacy, in the general mind of the country." Was it not effeminacy to be more horrified of executing a man than of depriving him of his liberty? Was death "the greatest of all earthly ills?" If in the past men had thought too little of death, the danger in contemporary society was that they thought too much of it. The most meaningful and emphatic way to show our regard for human life was to support the rule "that he who violates that right in another forfeits it for himself."[71] This was the principle Mill had proclaimed in the case of Governor Eyre. He again defended it as an indispensable requirement of civilized life.

Liberals were disheartened both by the failure of juries to indict Eyre and by Mill's support of capital punishment. Mill's friend the French socialist Louis Blanc wrote in 1868 to commiserate with him on Eyre's apparent immunity from prosecution

69. *PD* (Commons), 3d ser., vol. 191, 21 April 1868: 1047–48, 1050, 1053.

70. Ibid., pp. 1054–55.

71. Ibid., pp. 1051–53.

and, at the same time, to express his disapproval of Mill's opposition to the Radical motion to abolish the death penalty. On the failure to indict Eyre, Mill replied that he had not expected better of the middle-class juries. Except among the working class, he observed unhappily, one could not find an "honest or energetic" reaction to crimes of this sort. On capital punishment, he noted that "our principles are the same, we only differ on their application."[72]

But such a difference, though Mill was too gentlemanly to suggest it to his friend, went to the heart of the matter. For Mill, it was necessary in all cases of murder to punish the crime by execution. But while "advanced liberal opinion" was prepared to execute a murderer whom they saw as an agent of aristocratic government, it permitted middle-class guilt and sentimentality to debase the standard of virtue in other cases.

Was the modern state doomed to suffer the characteristic defects of a commercial and democratic society, or could men *will* a virtuous government into existence? To what extent were the forms of government under which men lived a matter of choice, and to what extent were they a spontaneous, organic growth, a product of the long-time customs and unconscious habits and instincts of a people? Mill had no doubt that even those who believed that we might establish government by conscious design could still not imagine that a people could successfully operate institutions unsuited to its social and economic circumstances. Nor were those who spoke of governments as organisms proceeding from unconscious instincts "the political fatalists" they pretended to be. Men had a range of possibilities from which to choose. Though there were "very strict limits to human power," it was important to remember that the will could play an effective role in affairs.[73] Thus did Mill once again confront his essential problem and solve it characteristically.

72. Mill to Louis Blanc, 20 June 1868, *LL*, pp. 1416–17.
73. Mill, "Representative Government," pp. 375–76, 380–81.

At bottom, Mill argued in his "Considerations on Representative Government" in 1861, good government depended not so much on constitutional forms as on the "virtue and intelligence" of members of society. The aim of a sound system of representation was not only to bring "the general standard of intelligence and honesty" of the community to bear upon government but to make certain that "the individual intellect and virtue of its wisest members" had a "greater influence" than they would otherwise. Hare's scheme was Mill's method of reconciling the conflicting principles of democratic participation and competence.[74] The best governmental mechanisms were useless, however, if those who controlled them were corrupt, lacking in self control, or ignorant, or if the people were indifferent, passive, undisciplined, selfish, or stupid. For peoples in a state of savagery, good government might mean a quasi despotism that would instruct them in "the indispensable virtue" of obedience and habituate them to the necessity of continuous, unexciting labor. "All real civilization is at this price," Mill declared. Once a people was able to act on general instructions instead of responding solely to the threat of an overseer's blows, it might progress to a government of "parental despotism," like those of the Peruvian Incas and of the Jesuits in Paraguay, or that projected by the Saint-Simonian socialists. But the overriding aim of such a government must be to increase the "mental liberty and individuality" of citizens, to further their virtue and intelligence. When people had achieved self discipline, then they were fully prepared to enjoy liberty.[75]

74. Ibid., pp. 390, 392, 359–67, and 453–65 passim; also the discussion in D. F. Thompson, *John Stuart Mill and Representative Government,* pp. 103–06 especially.

75. Mill, "Representative Government," pp. 394–96. See Alan Ryan's comparison of Mill's participation or self-development model of government, which would improve the quality of citizens and make progress possible, with James Mill's market model. The elder Mill would have been content with the establishment of "a permanent but honest bureaucracy," Ryan observes (p. 110). Alan Ryan, "Two Concepts of Politics and Democracy: James and John Stuart Mill," in *Machiavelli and the Nature of Political Thought,* ed. M. Fleisher, pp. 76–113. The role of the French liberal Doctrinaires (Royer-Collard, Guizot,

The great danger in modern society was that citizens would give their attention to commercial interests or to amusement, that is, to material or sensual happiness, and would withdraw from an active participation in government. A people that left its affairs to the state, Mill argued, was akin to one that left them to Providence, accepting whatever happened "when disagreeable, as visitations of Nature." When such a state of affairs came to pass, "the era of national decline" had arrived and as such often entailed conquest and enslavement by a despot or by a neighboring barbaric people who had retained "with their savage rudeness the energies of freedom." To ward off such evils, a society must be "self-*protecting,*" and "self-*dependent.*" It must favor active virtue, rather than passive submission. "In proportion as success in life is seen or believed to be the fruit of fatality or accident and not of exertion," Mill observed, "in that same ratio does envy develop itself as a point of national character."[76]

Mill looked forward to the application of this active virtue in perfecting not only "outward circumstances" but also "man's inward nature." Contentment was a virtue only if it bespoke indifference to mere material improvement and was accompanied by a striving for spiritual improvement and an unselfish interest in helping others. Passivity—"inactivity, unaspiringness, absence of desire"—was the state of the majority of the race and was fatal to improvement. Despots, however, favored passivity as an aid to their dominion and regarded the "virtues of self-help and self-government" as incompatible with their authority.[77]

Modern civilization made it unnecessary to witness or to experience pain, Mill had observed in 1840; consequently the

---

Barante) as well as that of Tocqueville in providing the sociological foundations for Mill's views on the moral value of political participation has been explored in Larry Siedentop, "Two Liberal Traditions," in *The Idea of Freedom: Essays in Honour of Isaiah Berlin,* ed. Alan Ryan, pp. 170–74.

76. Mill, "Representative Government," pp. 401, 404, 406–08.

77. Ibid., pp. 409–10.

richer classes, in contrast to the higher orders in the ancient or early modern worlds, had little of the heroic in their characters. The heroism whose decline Mill bemoaned in contemporary commercial society consisted "in being ready, for a worthy object, to do and to suffer, but especially to do, what is painful or disagreeable." When it was necessary "not to bear pain but to seek it," civilized men failed: "They cannot undergo labour, they cannot brook ridicule, they cannot brave evil tongues: they have not hardihood to say an unpleasant thing to any one whom they are in the habit of seeing, or to face . . . the coldness of some little coterie which surrounds them." Mill felt such "torpidity and cowardice" was the product of a commercial civilization and called upon "a system of cultivation adapted to counteract it."[78]

Mill approved of Tocqueville's stress on the study of Greek and Roman literature in a democracy, since the classical writings portrayed, in the ancient military and agricultural communities, the virtues that modern commercial society sadly lacked. The writings of the ancients displayed human beings on "a grander scale": "if a lower average of virtue, more striking examples of it; fewer small goodnesses, but more greatness, and appreciation of greatness." Moreover, the Greek and Roman writers exhibited and inspired "high conceptions of the capabilities of human nature." An aristocracy chose the path of virtue because of pride, Mill remarked; a democracy did so because of self interest. While the aristocrat stressed the beauty of virtue in itself, the virtuous democrat spoke of honesty being the best policy and of the ways in which the common good affected each individual.[79]

Mill raised the standard of progress and order, and declared both dependent on virtue. Though conservatives praised order and liberals progress (or improvement), for Mill the two were closely connected. The virtues required for order were "industry,

78. Mill, "Civilization," pp. 131–32.

79. Mill, "De Tocqueville on Democracy in America" (1840), pp. 195n, 184–85.

integrity, justice, and prudence." These were precisely what was required for improvement, though for this purpose, he argued, they must exist to a greater degree. In fact, was not "the growth of these virtues in the community, in itself the greatest of improvements?" Similarly, the qualities regarded as most necessary for progress—"mental activity, enterprise, and courage"—were also those required for order. Though the police were considered an institution for the maintenance of order, what could possibly be more useful to progress—to an increased production, which was progress in "its most familiar and vulgarest aspect"—than the security of life and property?[80]

There were indeed times when progress seemed to undermine virtue and order. "Thus there may be progress in wealth, while there is deterioration in virtue." However, when virtue was sacrificed to the increase of wealth, other forms of progress were also sacrificed, and to a greater extent. For virtue was essential not only to order but even more to progress. "Things left to take care of themselves inevitably decay," Mill declared.[81]

Even without the hope of improvement, life would be "an unceasing struggle" against deterioration. This, in fact, was how the ancients conceived of all politics. The only remedy for the "natural tendency" of men and society toward degeneration was "good institutions virtuously administered." Mill saw an "ever-flowing current of human affairs towards the worse, consisting of all the follies, all the vices, all the negligences, indolences, and supinenesses of mankind." Only the efforts of men of virtue—some "constantly, and others by fits"—kept the powerful tide of degeneration "from sweeping all before it." If these exertions lessened, not only would there be no improvement, but there would be deterioration, which "once begun, would proceed with increasing rapidity" and become "more and more difficult to

80. Mill, "Representative Government," pp. 385–86.
81. Ibid., pp. 387, 386.

check," until civilized society returned to a state of barbarism from which almost nothing "short of superhuman power" could bring about a new move to improvement.[82]

82. Ibid., p. 388.

FOUR

Historical Necessity and Virtue

THE HISTORIAN THOMAS CARLYLE, MILL'S FRIEND AND mentor in the 1830s, is known for his position that the heroes of religion, politics, and letters were the prime makers of history, a view suggesting an important role for the individual will. Yet from his early years, the Scotsman had shared the vision of the German philosophers of history like Herder and Hegel of an immanent course of historical development in which the future was "definitely shaped, predetermined and inevitable," as he observed in his 1831 essay "On History." How did the historian resolve this contradiction? While Carlyle saw the strength of will of such figures as Cromwell and Frederick the Great as sometimes decisive forces in the shaping of events, his concern with great men, as he had written to Goethe a couple of years earlier, was a *practical* means of "singling out from the mass"—in which every event was the product of all other past or contemporary events—a mass "which is too vast and confused for me to shape into History, the main summits."[1]

This strategy for writing history had a philosophical basis. The traditional political historian had dwelled only on the necessities of physical well-being. The "true Good," however, the

1. See Carlyle, "On Heroes and Hero-Worship," *Works* 5; "On History," *Works* 27: 83; Carlyle to Goethe, 31 August 1830, *Collected Letters*, 5: 153.

real clue to "the soul and destiny of man" and one of the greatest forces in history, Carlyle insisted in agreement with the German idealists, was not the outward but the inward, spiritual life of man—a clue the historian could most readily pursue in the biographies of the great.[2]

In historical philosophy as in other matters, the influence of the Saint-Simonians moved Carlyle in much the same direction. When the Saint-Simonian Gustave d'Eichthal had attended Hegel's lectures at Berlin in 1824, he enthusiastically reported the resemblance of Hegel's and Saint-Simon's historical theories.[3] Both philosophers had insisted upon the dominion of historical necessity, in which history led men to a predetermined goal; both looked to the specially endowed and the specially motivated to act as the instruments of what was historically necessary.

After reading one of Carlyle's early essays, Eichthal sent the Scottish writer a parcel of doctrinal tracts; Carlyle was much impressed. In the course of an exchange of letters that followed, Carlyle distinguished the historical views held in common by the Germans and the Saint-Simonians from those of the "Radical or Utilitarian Unbelievers, for whom *Soul* is synonymous with *Stomach,*" although he granted that some of the Utilitarians were honest and therefore worthy of some hope. What may have been in the Scotsman's mind on this occasion were articles that Mill had published anonymously a few months earlier in *The Spirit of the Age*, in which Carlyle had perceived a mystical influence,[4] by which term he probably meant an outlook akin to that shared by the German idealists and the Saint-Simonians.

In the years ahead, Carlyle and Mill sometimes discussed

2. Carlyle, "On History," p. 88; also pp. 83–87.

3. See F. A. Hayek, *The Counter-Revolution of Science* (New York, 1964), p. 193.

4. See Carlyle to Jane Carlyle, 6 August 1830, *Collected Letters* 5: 133; Carlyle to Eichthal, 9 August 1830 and 17 May 1831, ibid., pp. 136–37, 280; Carlyle to Jane Carlyle, 21 January 1831, ibid., p. 216.

historical questions. For example, in an 1833 letter Carlyle wrote of the ethical views of the French historian Thiers as being those of might making right, though Carlyle did not commit himself on the subject at this time.[5] In reply, Mill attributed Thiers's position to an aspect of the German philosophers' "historical fatalism" that annihilated "all moral distinctions except success and not success."[6] But while Mill shared much of the historical determinism of Carlyle and of the Germans and Saint-Simonians, his conception of the part played by the individual and free will in history was a very different one. For Carlyle, as we have seen, the will of the strong operated as an instrument of a necessitarian history. For Mill, history was an arena in which an individual will might act in however limited a way as a *counter* to the powerful drives of necessity.

The highest stage of historical writing, Mill was to observe in the early 1840s, was the construction of "a science of history," which he described as "a progressive chain of causes and effects." The great task of the science of history was to discover the laws of development and thereby to determine the future state of society. This was an enterprise both Tocqueville and Comte had attempted, but Mill saw other historians, among them Michelet and Guizot, as well as the German philosophers Herder, Kant, and Hegel, as having led the way. The science of history had not yet seen its Newton, but Mill believed that its Kepler was the contemporary French historian and statesman Guizot. In Guizot's history, there was "a consistency, a coherence, a comprehensiveness," and "what the Germans would call many-sidedness." Guizot also possessed an underlying theory of "a progressive unfolding of the capabilities of humanity" directed to "a *destination,* as it were, of humanity." Guizot had not exaggerated the influence of any one cause, nor did he write as if the "virtue or the vices" of individuals or of accident on the one hand, or the general

5. See Carlyle to Mill, 12 January 1833, *Collected Letters* 6: 303.
6. Mill to Carlyle, 2 February 1833, *EL*, p. 139.

circumstances of society on the other, were in complete control of events. Rather, he had demonstrated "how they both co-operate, and react upon one another."[7] This was also Mill's view of the interaction of necessity and free will, and of material happiness and virtue, in history.

James Mill, a historian whose first considerable enterprise was a study of India, had taught his son to see history as the story of the inexorable advance of liberty, with John Stuart himself as an actor in that struggle and progress. At the age of eleven, the younger Mill undertook to write a work on Roman government, a narrative of the struggles between patricians and plebeians, in which he defended the plebeian cause. When at sixteen the young man first read a history of the French Revolution, he was astonished to discover that democratic principles had once been the creed of the French nation. Indeed, as he was later to write, "the most transcendent glory I was capable of conceiving, was that of figuring, successful or unsuccessful, as a Girondist in an English Convention." In the 1820s, Mill determined to write a history of the French Revolution and began to collect materials which he was later to turn over to Carlyle for the Scotsman's great work.[8]

In the late 1820s, after Mill had emerged from the most difficult time of his mental crisis, T. B. Macaulay published three articles on James Mill's *Essays on Government.* In these pieces, Macaulay dismissed the conclusions that the elder Mill had deduced

7. Mill, "Michelet's History of France" (1844), in *Dissertations and Discussions: Political, Philosophical, and Historical,* p. 129; "Guizot's Essays and Lectures on History" (1845), in ibid., p. 222; "Michelet," p. 134; "Guizot," pp. 218, 221; "Michelet," pp. 134–35.

8. *Autobiography*, pp. 9–10, 44–45, 92; see also Mill to Charles Comte, 25 January 1828, *EL*, pp. 21–22. For a discussion of Mill's thinking concerning the French Revolution and his views on historical change, see Edward Alexander, "The Principles of Permanence and Progression in the Thought of J. S. Mill," in *Centenary Conference,* pp. 126–42.

from such general principles as the laws of psychology. Certain "propensities of human nature" were assumed by James, and from these assumptions "the whole science of politics is synthetically deduced!"[9] Macaulay acidly observed. Macaulay particularly decried James Mill's premise that human behavior was determined only by the animal appetites and his failure to take into account "tastes and propensities" that belonged to man as a rational and imaginative being. Men were complex, under the sway of many and frequently conflicting motives. Macaulay charged that James Mill had chosen "to look only at one-half of human nature" and declared that the view that history was driven exclusively by animal appetites was as laughable as the study of phrenology.[10] While offended by Macaulay's "unbecoming" tone, John Stuart believed several of his criticisms correct; indeed, his father's premises were "really too narrow."[11]

Macaulay's critique left the younger Mill open to the more complex opinions on history of the Saint-Simonians, who were then making converts in France and Germany as well as England.[12] We recall that it was Comte's synthesis of Saint-Simonian doctrine, written in 1824 in the master's name, which had made somewhat more precise and consistent the flashes of insight scattered through the writings of Saint-Simon, though Comte was later churlishly to insist that he owed nothing substantial to the older man.[13] In

9. T. B. Macaulay, "Mill's Essay on Government: Utilitarian Logic and Politics" (1829), in *Utilitarian Logic and Politics: James Mill's "Essay on Government," Macaulay's Critique and the Ensuing Debate,* ed. J. Lively and J. Rees, p. 101. See also John Clive, *Macaulay, The Shaping of the Historian* (New York, 1973), pp. 126–30.

10. Macaulay, "Mill's Essay on Government," pp. 105, 108, 129.

11. *Autobiography*, p. 111; see also J. H. Burns, "The Light of Reason: Philosophical History in the Two Mills," in *Centenary Conference,* pp. 3–20.

12. See, for example, E. M. Butler, *The Saint-Simonian Religion in Germany* (London, 1926).

13. For Comte's relationship to Saint-Simon, see Henri Gouhier's definitive *La Jeunesse d'Auguste Comte et la formation du positivisme,* particularly vol. 3, *Auguste Comte et Saint-Simon.*

the months that followed their initial meeting, Mill and Eichthal undertook in their correspondence a discussion of the sect's historical doctrines.[14]

Eichthal, good evangelist that he was, took every opportunity to press the gospel and sent to Mill as he had to Carlyle a number of the group's publications, but the Englishman thought them shallow, except for Comte's synthesis. At first reading, Mill was "seduced by the plausibility of his manner"; on reflection, however, he concluded that the parts in which Comte had criticized dominant opinion were sounder than those in which he had elaborated his own: "It abounds indeed, with many very acute remarks though all of them of a kind which the progress of events is suggesting at this moment to all minds, which are *au niveau du siècle* throughout Europe."[15] Comte and the Saint-Simonians, in Mill's eyes, were articulating what Mill would later call "the spirit of the age."

One of the most perceptive and influential social theorists of the nineteenth century, Comte sought historical explanations not in providential interventions but in the conditions of three stages of history. There was a theological, a metaphysical, and a positivist stage through which every branch of knowledge had necessarily to pass. Mathematics, astronomy, physics, chemistry, and biology, he demonstrated, had already proceeded through the first two stages and had entered the positive or scientific stage; only the study of society had not become truly scientific. A pioneer social analyst, Comte understood that collective entities were more readily accessible to the observer in search of sociological laws than were the discrete, individual elements which formed them; he perceived a delicate network of interrelationships between historical agents, a change in any one of which would produce

14. See B. M. Ratcliffe and W. H. Chaloner, eds., *A French Sociologist Looks at Britain: Gustave d'Eichthal and British Society in 1828*, pp. 131–33, 137–40 especially.

15. Mill to Eichthal, 8 October 1829, *EL*, p. 35.

corresponding changes in all others. In surveying history, he saw a steady, irresistible progress at all times, a view that led him to reject the anticlerical obtuseness of the eighteenth-century historians and to praise the medieval church for its path-breaking role, particularly given the limitations of society at that time. Indeed, as a necessitarian Comte held that the state of society at any stage was as perfect as conditions permitted.

The Comtian view of historical development had a special influence on Victorian liberals because of the French thinker's conviction that the military regime of feudalism would inevitably, and soon, be displaced by the industrial order. This social and political transformation would accompany the ousting of theological and metaphysical ways of looking at the world by positive, scientific ones. The idea of irresistible progress, which Comte had derived from Turgot and Condorcet and which became a leading motif of his system, could not but be attractive to those who saw themselves as the beneficiaries of this change.

For Comte, historical advance was powered by the conflict between spiritual and temporal forces, which had occurred most obviously in Comte's ideal period, the Middle Ages. There were two kinds of epochs: a critical or negative epoch, a transitional period dominated by philosophy and marked by egoism, anarchy, and war; and an organic or constructive epoch like that of medieval Europe, dominated by religion and marked by association, obedience, and devotion. The present era, Comte declared, was a negative one in which the proletariat was exploited by the chiefs of industry; it would be replaced by an organic era of harmonious association. He envisioned a future society, whose seeds he saw in the present one, in which a patriciate of the leading bankers and industrialists would possess temporal power, employing it in the interest of increasing production, while the scientists and artists would exercise spiritual authority to keep the patriciate faithful to the common good. In this positivist utopia, materially content and free of conflict, all men would abandon their selfish interests in favor of those of humanity as a whole.[16]

Mill was attracted to many of Comte's ideas—to his conception of stages of development, for example, and to his view of the role played by the conflict between a spiritual and temporal power—but from the beginning he objected to Comte's doctrinaire necessitarianism. Like so many French writers, Mill declared (repeating the criticisms that Macaulay had so recently launched against James Mill), Comte was so content with "this power of systematizing" that he neglected to compare his conclusions with the facts. "M. Comte is an exceedingly clear and methodical writer," Mill continued, "most agreeable in stile [*sic*], and concatenates so well, that one is apt to mistake the perfect coherence and logical consistency of his system, for truth." Such writers "deduce politics like mathematics from a set of axioms & definitions," but "in politics & the social science," unlike mathematics, "error seldom arises from our assuming premises which are not true, but generally from our overlooking other truths which limit, & modify the effect of the former." Comte suffered greatly from this defect, which was in fact what made it possible to give his structure the appearance of a "compact & systematic" science.[17]

Moreover, just as Macaulay had protested the Benthamites' effort to hang all institutions on the peg of self-interest, so Mill found particular fault with Comte's (and Saint-Simon's) view that government existed for but one end. In the ancient and medieval world, according to the positivist thinker, this goal had been conquest; in the modern world, it was the purely economic one of production. "Are conquest & production, the only two

16. See Auguste Comte, *The Positive Philosophy of Auguste Comte,* ed. Harriet Martineau, vol. 2; for a briefer account, see Frank E. Manuel, *The Prophets of Paris*, pp. 251–96. See also J. L. Talmon, *Political Messianism*, pp. 35–124.

17. Mill to Eichthal, 8 October 1829, *EL*, pp. 35–36.

conceivable purposes that human beings can combine for?" Mill inquired of Eichthal in 1829. The "highest & most important" of the ends for which government existed was "the improvement of man himself as a moral and intelligent being," a category the Frenchman had entirely neglected. Had Comte been born in England where the "idol 'production'" had been worshipped for a century, Mill insisted, he would see how such an attitude had warped and corrupted all spheres of life.[18]

Nor was there just one law of development, Mill declared in this early correspondence with Eichthal. England and France were proceeding along two different paths, and neither would pass through the state in which the other found itself. It was the lower animals "which have only one law, that of their instinct," while "the order of the development of man's faculties" was "as various as the situations in which he is placed." "It is melancholy to observe," Mill continued, "how a man like M. Comte has had all his views of history warped & distorted by the necessity of proving that civilisation has but one law, & that a law of progressive advancement; how it blinds him to all the merits of the Greeks & Romans (& the demerits of the middle ages) because there was improvement in some things at such periods, he thinks there must have been so in all: why not allow that while mankind advanced in some things, they went back in others?" And why did Comte's listing of social systems not include that possessed by England? There were many good insights in Comte, but the disciples of Saint-Simon, having established a sect, had swallowed the bad with the useful.[19] Englishmen distrusted any "comprehensive doctrine," Mill warned Eichthal; they would resist Saint-Simonianism because they were suspicious of systems. Mill advised the English members of the sect not to press their full doctrine, but only to try to determine "the stage through which, in the

18. Ibid., pp. 36–37.
19. Ibid., pp. 37–38.

progress of civilization, our country has next to pass, and to endeavour to facilitate the transition & render it safe & healthy." Men of good sense should work to alter gradually opinions and institutions that stood in the way of improvement.[20]

Mill could not accept that development proceeded "by a sort of fatality or necessity" in one invariable order and that "we must be always either standing still, or advancing, or retrograding." Different men and nations, Mill was convinced, although at comparable stages of development, traveled by different routes and were "different in character." Though somewhat impressed by the Comtian historical vision, he wished to proceed cautiously.[21]

When Mill published his articles entitled *The Spirit of the Age* in 1831, he sent them to Eichthal, hoping that the Frenchman would find in them some sign of a Saint-Simonian approach to history, though he could not offer himself fully as a proselyte to their views. In the first of these pieces, Mill wrote of the present as a time of "moral and political transition," a term he had substituted for Saint-Simon's and Comte's "critical period." Since each age contained "the germ of all future ages as surely as the acorn contains the future forest, a knowledge of our own age is the fountain of prophecy—the only key to the history of posterity," Mill declared; if a man truly wished to influence his times, it was of the greatest practical importance that he properly understand the spirit of his age. In the present era of transition, men had become convinced that the old system was outmoded, and they would no longer rally to traditional standards and loyalties. In fact, men now had "no strong or deep-rooted convictions at all"; an "intellectual anarchy" reigned, hardly a healthy state of affairs. Mill looked forward to the reestablishment of a "natural state" like Comte's organic period of the Middle Ages, where both

20. Mill to Eichthal, 9 February 1830, *EL*, p. 48.
21. Mill to Eichthal, 7 November 1829, *EL*, p. 43.

worldly and spiritual power would be exercised by those fittest to hold it.[22]

"Human nature must proceed step by step, in politics as well as in physics," Mill declared. It would be as foolish, for example, to blame the people of the Middle Ages for not having seen the usefulness of universal suffrage and demanded it of their rulers, as to scold the ancients for not having invented the steamboat. The Catholic clergy were in fact the "fittest persons" who "*could* have possessed" an "undisputed authority in matters of conscience and belief" during medieval times. It had been their mission to curb "the unruly passions" and to teach men to postpone immediate gratification in order to secure a "distant end." The clergy, often the sons of the peasantry, had preached equality and the spiritual virtues. But their ascendancy had been undermined: "Mankind outgrew their religion, and that, too, at a period when they had not yet outgrown their government."[23]

Mill saw three grand sources of moral influence: superior wisdom and virtue, religious power, and worldly power, which, in 1831 as in medieval times, he observed, meant the possession of wealth. If all those possessing influence were in agreement, men had a firm, almost unanimous, confidence in received doctrines. This was the condition of Mill's "natural state" as it had existed in the ancient republics and in medieval Europe, and as it at this time existed in the United States. When the Catholic religion lost its ascendancy in England, its moral power had been inherited by the wealthy and united to their worldly power. Access to the wealthy classes by men of ability was possible, and the circumstances necessary to a natural, organic society were present for a time. But that moment had passed. By 1830 the government of the wealthy consisted of "an irresponsible few" and was subject to many abuses. While the idea of the superior capacity of the

22. Mill to Eichthal, March 1831, *EL*, pp. 70–71; Mill, *The Spirit of the Age*, ed. F. A. Hayek (Chicago, 1942), pp. 16, 4, 7–8, 12, 32–38.

23. Ibid., pp. 47–48, 79–81.

upper classes was "a broken spell," Mill concluded, the present possessors of temporal power—the landed aristocracy and the monied classes—still retained sufficient influence to block opinions with which they disagreed. They had to be "divested" of this monopoly of power before "the most virtuous and best instructed of the nation" could "acquire that ascendancy over the opinions and feelings of the rest, by which alone England can emerge from this crisis of transition, and enter once again into a natural state of society."[24]

In two articles on Comte published in 1862, some years after the death of the French positivist, Mill continued in his enthusiastic approval of the Saint-Simonian or Comtian view of historical development, despite his disenchantment with Comte's opinions on politics and society. Social dynamics, the laws of social progress that described the filiation of one stage of social development to another, was the field of Comte's "most eminent speculations": Mill felt unable in so brief an essay "to give even a faint conception of the extraordinary merits of this historical analysis." Those who doubted that the philosophy of history could be made a science, governed by "invariable laws of sequence" instead of by the intervention of a divine Providence, should read Comte's works.[25]

Comte's interest had been the properly scientific one of wishing to predict events, Mill continued; he was not concerned, as were metaphysical writers, with inmost nature or origin but rather with sequences and coexistences. Given this, a reader of the positivist thinker's writings on social dynamics might with reason have anticipated, following "so profound and comprehensive" an examination of past human progress "of which the future can only be a prolongation," that Comte would have attempted to construct a "scientific connexion between his theoretical explanation of the past progress of society, and his proposals for future im-

24. Ibid., pp. 60–61, 63–65, 38, 86–88, 90, 92–93.
25. Mill, "Auguste Comte and Positivism," *Collected Works* 10: 315, 318.

provement." But while Tocqueville, Mill observed, had projected into the future the necessary progress toward equality which he had observed in the past, Comte's proposals for the future were not, "as we might expect, recommended as that towards which human society has been tending and working through the whole of history." Indeed, Mill concluded, the French positivist's recommendations rested as fully on grounds of utility as had those of the ahistorical Bentham.[26]

Comte's final utopian stage of historical development was consequently a product of positivist faith. His projection of the future depicted the only means by which the forces that he (and Tocqueville, as we shall see) believed would soon prevail might be managed to produce a society similar to that of the Middle Ages. Yet critical parts of Comte's forecast were persuasive, for Mill at times appeared convinced that they might well be realized.

Comte Alexis de Tocqueville's *Democracy in America* was widely praised in both England and America,[27] and Mill became one of its early admirers. Tocqueville met Mill on a visit to England in 1835; the two men began a correspondence and were warmed to find they agreed on the essentials of political philosophy.[28]

"I love liberty by taste," Tocqueville declared in writing to Mill, "equality by instinct and reason"—a useful attitude given the Frenchman's view of the inevitability of democracy.[29] As a liberal and a Catholic, Tocqueville recoiled from the vision of historical necessity that in various guises was shared by so many

26. Ibid., pp. 293, 324–25.

27. For Tocqueville and his relations with England and Englishmen, see Seymour Drescher's *Tocqueville and England.*

28. Joseph Hamburger sees the two men as possessing rather different views in his "Mill and Tocqueville on Liberty," in *Centenary Conference,* pp. 111–25.

29. Tocqueville to Mill, June and 12 September 1835, *Correspondance anglaise,* pp. 293–94, 297.

advanced thinkers of the Continent. On the critical question of the coming of democracy, however, he appeared a determinist. Tocqueville dated the movement toward equality from the beginnings of civilization and sketched its steady advance: every age had contributed something to this progress. The increase of wealth and knowledge in most recent times had multiplied the strength of the many at the expense of the few:

> The gradual development of the equality of conditions is therefore a providential fact, and possesses all the characteristics of a Divine decree: it is universal, it is durable, it constantly eludes all human interference, and all events as well as all men contribute to its progress. . . . It is not necessary that God himself should speak, in order to disclose to us the unquestionable signs of his will.[30]

Mill fully agreed that the coming of democracy was irresistible. In a review of Tocqueville's first volume in 1835, he declared it "an established truth, on the proof of which it is no longer necessary to insist, that the progress of democracy neither can nor ought to be stopped." Again like Tocqueville, Mill was persuaded that "a progress, which has continued with uninterrupted steadiness for so many centuries" must proceed until "all artificial inequalities" disappear, leaving only "the natural and inevitable effects of the protection of property." "We have it not in our power to choose between democracy and aristocracy," Mill observed, echoing the French political theorist, "Necessity and Providence have decided that for us."[31]

What can we make of Mill's and Tocqueville's use of words like "necessity," "Providence," "not in our power to choose," and "Divine decree"? Were they merely a rhetorical appeal to their countrymen to accept the coming of an egalitarian society? Perhaps. Certainly both thinkers were convinced that given contemporary realities it was hopeless to contest the interest of the

30. Quoted in Mill, "De Tocqueville on Democracy" (1840), p. 161.
31. Mill, "De Tocqueville on Democracy" (1835), pp. 50–51, 56.

masses in equality; to oppose democracy was to give up the possibility of guiding the many to a sound polity. Yet more was at issue, for both thinkers were seeking to discover the laws of historical development. French readers, Mill remarked, were accustomed to Tocqueville's kind of historical reasoning, but the English public had "less faith" in "irresistible tendencies." Englishmen were "less accustomed to link together the events of history in a connected chain"; for them, "the proposition will hardly seem to be sufficiently made out." In Mill's view, such skepticism about historical theory was a mark of the backwardness of English opinion.[32]

But neither Mill nor Tocqueville was a mechanical determinist. Neither saw *all* events as under the aegis of a providential decree or of a historical necessity. Each, indeed, was convinced that the actions of individuals, groups, and nations could help to shape the "tendencies" of historical development. Though democracy was a certainty, virtue still had a role to play. In reviewing Tocqueville's second volume in the fall of 1840, Mill again declared that "the progress and ultimate ascendancy" of democracy had the character of "a law of nature," that it was "an inevitable result of the tendencies of a progressive civilization." On this occasion, Mill (following Tocqueville) left some scope for the exercise of a freely willed virtue, cautioning that this might be a democracy either of "equal freedom" as in America or of "equal servitude," a condition into which France was in danger of falling.[33]

In the last years of his life, Tocqueville engaged in an exchange of letters on historical necessity with the Comte de Gobineau. A French archaeologist of some distinction, Gobineau in 1853 had begun the publication of a multivolume *Essai sur l'inégalité des races humaines*. The *Essai* asserted that the chief factor in

32. Mill, "De Tocqueville on Democracy" (1840), p. 159.
33. Ibid., pp. 158–59.

the history of mankind was race and argued that the Nordic races were superior to all others. Gobineau's views were welcomed in Germany, though largely ignored by the author's own countrymen. The archaeologist's long-time friend Tocqueville was horrified: the liberal historian and political theorist believed, as he wrote to Gobineau, such doctrines to be "probably quite false" and "certainly very pernicious."[34]

Tocqueville protested not merely the archaeologist's opinions concerning race but more particularly his belief in historical necessity. Tocqueville saw such a view as a threat to political liberty. "Your doctrine is rather a sort of fatalism," he wrote to Gobineau, "of predestination if you wish but, at any rate, very different from that of St. Augustine, from the Jansenists, and from the Calvinists"—though he noted that "the very last are closest to your doctrines"—"since you tie predestination and matter closely together." Tocqueville described Gobineau's doctrine of races "losing or acquiring through an infusion of new blood social capacities which they have not previously had" as a "predestination" that was "a close relative of the purest materialism." From a practical standpoint, moreover, this was a dangerous theory to put into the hands of the masses. Among the consequences would be "a vast limitation, if not a complete abolition, of human liberty." Gobineau's doctrine, Tocqueville suggested, had the ugly effect of persuading those who lived in conditions of barbarism or slavery that they could do nothing to better their position: their racial characteristics had doomed them to a "permanent inequality." However, the differences between individuals, Tocqueville argued, much as had Mill in his correspondence with Comte in the 1840s, were the result of "thousands of different causes," none of them "insuperable." History would not be clarified by the precept of race, he insisted. Rather, he urged a return to the traditional

34. Tocqueville to Gobineau, 17 November 1853, in Alexis de Tocqueville, *"The European Revolution" & Correspondence with Gobineau*, p. 227.

effort "to find the cause of human events in the influence of certain men, of certain emotions, of certain thoughts, and of certain beliefs." Tocqueville claimed by way of example that Julius Caesar would have believed the Britons suited only to live humbly under Roman rule. But "courage, energy, honesty, farsightedness, and common sense," not race, were the true causes of the prosperity of empires as of individuals. Tocqueville concluded that "the destiny of men, whether of individuals or of nations, depends on what they want to be."[35]

Tocqueville was concerned about whether men in a democracy would continue to value liberty. Though it would be more difficult to maintain freedom in egalitarian societies than in certain of the aristocratic societies of the past, he conceded, "I shall never think it impossible," and "I pray to God lest He inspire me with the idea that one might well despair of trying." Gobineau believed that mankind by its physical nature was destined for slavery; "to me," Tocqueville countered, "human societies, like persons, become something worthwhile only through their use of liberty." God had created the human race and had endowed it with aspirations toward freedom and dignity. He had placed mankind "at the head of all visible creation" and had not intended it to become, as Gobineau had argued, a "bastardized flock of sheep" that was to be delivered "without future and without hope to a small number of shepherds." While Gobineau tended to dismiss men as irredeemable, Tocqueville saw hope in "a better upbringing" which "could repair the wrongs done by their miseducation" through an appeal to "their natural decency and common sense." "In brief," he concluded, "I wish to treat them like human beings."[36]

Mill had earlier agreed with Tocqueville's rejection of the fatality of race. The French historian Jules Michelet had seen in the Germanic tribes a species of loyalty to their chieftains and to one another that was characteristic of their race and had made

35. Ibid., pp. 227, 229, 227–229.
36. Tocqueville to Gobineau, 30 July 1856, ibid., pp. 309–10.

them victorious over the Celts, who were prevented from forming an effective union by their racial passion for equality. Mill preferred to explain such differences by "diversity of position" rather than by "diversity of character in the Races." If the Celts, like the Germans, had been composed of small groups maintaining military dominion over a larger body of subjects, they too would have developed qualities of loyalty. All in all, Mill thought Michelet's view of the matter "contestable," though "suggestive of thought." Michelet had also speculated about the influence of the "geographical peculiarities" of the various French provinces upon their populations. Mill was ready to acknowledge the possibility that "in a rude age the fatalities of race and geographical position are absolute"; but with progress, he insisted, "human forethought and purpose" as embodied in a common culture and institutions largely diminished such differences. Yet despite such apparently fatalistic opinions, Mill observed approvingly, Michelet remained, like Mill and Tocqueville, "a strenuous asserter of the power of mind over matter, of will over spontaneous propensities, culture over nature."[37]

In the fall of 1857, Henry Reeve, the editor of the *Edinburgh Review* and also a long-time correspondent of Alexis de Tocqueville and the translator of his study of American democracy, had urged the French historian and political thinker to read the first volume of Henry Thomas Buckle's *History of Civilization in England.* Reeve cautioned Tocqueville, however, that the book included some "quite abominable doctrines." The following spring, Reeve called Tocqueville's attention to the *Edinburgh's* article on Buckle's *History*, and again urged him to read the work despite Buckle's frequent wrongheadedness. Tocqueville had heard Buckle highly praised by such friends of his as Mrs. Grote and the liberal economist Nassau Senior and his wife. He read the article, but

37. Mill, "Michelet," pp. 147–50.

wished to know before buying the book whether he had got its measure. From what he had heard and read, Tocqueville wrote to Reeve, he thought he perceived "the spirit in which it is written":

> On the continent, at present, books which have for their purpose or which would have as their consequence the restricting or expunging of the idea of human liberty are published with regularity. The Germans in particular do their best to prove that in men as in horses one need only substitute one blood for another in order to obtain different sensations and ideas. There has recently appeared in France a four-volume work which make these fine discoveries known to us.

Tocqueville of course was referring to Gobineau's *Essai*. He continued:

> Mr. Buckle, although he has a different point of view, seems to me to belong to the same school. This time it is not race that tyrannizes over the human will, but certain anterior facts. From both directions, they end up at *the machine*. That such systems possess a certain following on the continent, where a violent reaction against liberty prevails, does not astonish me. We find ourselves with the philosophy appropriate to our institutions. But that a book with such a tendency enjoys so great a vogue in England does astonish and distress me.

Tocqueville was clearly persuaded that an energetic, enterprising England ought not to be attracted to such a passive and fatalistic doctrine; yet liberal Englishmen had taken up Buckle's *History* with enthusiasm. Reeve agreed, noting "with real regret that so distinguished a mind [as Buckle's] should lend itself to a doctrine so contrary to all that endows the human race with glory."[38]

Buckle was born in Kent in 1821, the son of a well-to-do

38. Reeve to Tocqueville, 13 October 1857 and 26 April 1858, *Correspondance anglaise,* pp. 246, 262; Tocqueville to Reeve, 16 June 1858, ibid., p. 267; Reeve to Tocqueville, 21 June 1858, ibid., p. 268.

London merchant. His mother feared for his health and kept him from school to avoid overtaxing him, but she subjected the youngster to regular attendance at Calvinistic sermons.[39] After his return from a journey to the Continent in 1841, he became a convert to the Radicalism and skepticism that prevailed in advanced intellectual circles and immersed himself in reading in his considerable private library (ultimately twenty-two thousand volumes) for as long as ten hours a day, in preparation for writing a work which would embody his newfound opinions. Buckle's *History* was to unite the deterministic residue of an early exposure to Calvinism, which he continued to regard as the religion closest to liberal and democratic ideals, a religious skepticism, and a devotion to science, which in positivist fashion he believed would soon replace theology in its position of intellectual authority. The work was to be not only a eulogy of the scientific advances of the preceding two centuries, which in itself commended it to the public, but also a demonstration of how the principles of science might be applied to the writing of history.

In response to an inquiry in 1853 concerning the purpose of the work upon which he was then engaged, Buckle declared in the best Comtian and Millite manner (Mill had written in very similar terms in his *Logic*), "I have long been convinced that the progress of every people is regulated by principles—or, as they are called, Laws—as regular as those which govern the physical world. To discover these laws is the object of my work." He intended to survey the "moral, intellectual and legislative

39. For the details of Buckle's life, see G. St. Aubyn, *A Victorian Eminence: The Life and Works of Henry Thomas Buckle* (London, 1958); also A. H. Huth, *The Life and Writings of Henry Thomas Buckle,* which is still useful. The fullest treatment of Buckle's ideas is J. M. Robertson, *Buckle and his Critics: A Study in Sociology,* a lively defense of the historian. See also the introduction to Henry Thomas Buckle, *On Scotland and the Scotch Intellect,* ed. H. J. Hanham (Chicago, 1970), pp. xiii–xxxvi; and Bernard Semmel, "H. T. Buckle: The Liberal Faith and the Science of History," *British Journal of Sociology* 17, no. 3 (September 1976): 370–86.

peculiarities" of the great countries of the West and to account for them by displaying "certain relations between the various stages through which each people have progressively passed." He would demonstrate that events were not the consequence of pure chance—for him, the primitive conception which had developed into the doctrine of free will—or of supernatural intervention. Rather, there was a necessary connection, a chain linking every event to an antecedent, a concept he thought akin to the theological one of predestination. He was confident that if all the antecedents of the mind of an individual were known, one could predict his behavior. History was the "fruit of a double action": "Nature with its laws, acting upon the mind, with its own laws, and the mind modifying nature."[40]

Buckle's intellectual hero was Mill; he was the "perfect intellect" who combined theory and practice so successfully that he towered above thinkers like Plato, Aristotle, Bacon, or Newton.[41] The message borne by Mill's *Logic* had been persuasive: the public desired to see "principles" induced from a mass of evidence sufficient to satisfy, or perhaps to stultify, the critical faculties. Darwin, an admirer of Buckle's *History*, inquired into and was much impressed by the historian's system of collecting facts, which resembled his own.[42] Other evidences of Mill's influence were to be found in Buckle's abhorrence of a protective paternalism, which became a leading theme of the *History*, and in his views on logic.

Buckle's work became a favorite of the intellectual classes of France, Germany, and particularly and perhaps surprisingly Russia, where liberals desperately wished to believe as Buckle did that a liberal, bourgeois regime was the inevitable destination

40. Quoted in Huth, *Buckle*, pp. 61–62.

41. Henry Thomas Buckle, "Mill on Liberty," in *Miscellaneous and Posthumous Works of Henry Thomas Buckle*, ed. Helen Taylor 1: 23–25.

42. See Sir Francis Darwin, *The Life and Letters of Charles Darwin* (London, 1881), 2: 386.

of all societies.[43] Mill, we know, could not be content with the simplistic position that English commercial and industrial society was the final goal of history. Yet it almost seemed as if Buckle had deliberately sought to write the kind of history Mill himself might have produced, except for the historian's view of historical necessity.

Variations in climate, food, soil, and the general aspect of nature, Buckle asserted in his second chapter, accounted for the leading differences among nations. The historian observed that if a climate and soil provided a cheap food—such as rice in India or potatoes in Ireland—this would encourage a rapid increase in population and more claimants to a fixed wage fund; the result would be low wages and a greater inequality in the distribution of wealth and political power. Most of western Europe had escaped this snare. Where the fearful aspects of nature—volcanoes, earthquakes, hurricanes, plagues—predominated, as in earthquake-prone Spain and Italy, superstition and the plastic arts were supreme while the sciences lagged, and the preeminent method of thinking was a backward deductive logic. In England, with its natural advantages, analysis, skepticism, and reason had triumphed, and the inductive logic of the sciences had generally prevailed.[44]

For Buckle, mental progress was twofold: moral progress which concerned duties, and intellectual progress which concerned the accumulation of knowledge. The historian had found no evidence to suggest that man's intellectual capacity as such or the essential dicta of morality had improved over the millennia; knowledge, on the other hand, was continually growing, and was for him the decisive element in mankind's progress. The Spanish inquisitors, for example, were men of impeccable morals,

43. For Buckle's popularity in Russia, see D. M. Wallace, *Russia* (London, 1877), pp. 167–68, 534.

44. See Henry Thomas Buckle, *History of Civilization in England* 1: 23, 47, 50–59, 85–93, 109–120.

yet they had done incalculable harm because of their ignorance. Wars and intolerance constituted for Buckle the two great plagues of civilization: both had diminished with the increase of knowledge, not as a result of any improvement in morals. The advance in knowledge, moreover, had increased both the authority and the resources of the intellectual classes, by whom Buckle meant the bourgeoisie, consequently diminishing the authority and resources of the military classes. It had been the middle class which had furthered religious reforms in the sixteenth century, had waged political rebellion on behalf of liberty in the seventeenth, and in the nineteenth had established a supremacy of public opinion to which even despots were amenable.[45]

The history of English civilization was his prime subject, Buckle observed, because England represented the ideal of normal historical development in which the "laws of progress" might best be observed. Comte had thought England eccentric, indeed unique, and viewed French history as more typical, and Mill had agreed. Buckle, however, felt France had been too subject to foreign influences, from which England was protected by the Channel, and too much under the sway of meddlesome governmental intervention, which he described as the "spirit of Protection." This spirit, established in the reign of Louis XIV and exhibited in the French admiration for centralized government, trade restrictions, and monopolies and for a paternal state and a strong church, was a serious obstacle to the progress of civilization. The French required an education in "the feeling of independence," not of "veneration"; "pliant and submissive," they followed an external standard, not the "internal standard" which Englishmen obeyed. England consequently had all the benefits of order and liberty. Buckle saw the Reform Bill of 1832 and the 1846 abolition of the Corn Laws as the most important acts ever passed by a parliament, for representative democracy and governmental noninterference were the essential principles of progress.[46]

45. Ibid., pp. 125–31, 134–39, 161–63.
46. Ibid., pp. 168–70; Mill to Comte, 6 May 1842, *Lettres inédites*, pp.

For Buckle, following the model of the philosophes of the Enlightenment, religion was everywhere the enemy of progress; his second volume, published in 1861, a year before his death, depicted the reactionary role of the church in Spain and Scotland as in France. Unfavorable aspects of nature like earthquakes, combined with the religious wars against the Moslems, had engrained superstition in the Spanish national consciousness, encouraging veneration for the monarch and inculcation of a military ethos. In Scotland, loyalty to the Crown was weak but superstition was as powerful as in Spain, since a bigoted and intolerant clergy had long exercised considerable authority.[47]

Buckle was prepared to formulate a historical law that the intellectual condition of a period or a country might be gauged by the extent to which the inductive or deductive methods predominated. In Spain and Scotland, deductive logic had prevailed. The eighteenth-century Scottish philosophers like Hume and Adam Smith had displayed "bold and inquisitive" minds, but had failed to counter ecclesiastical authority because their method of reasoning was not an antitheological induction but deduction. The critical features of England's history had been the rise of the "spirit of doubt" and the triumph and diffusion of reason and inductive logic, more accessible to the average man and more useful in undermining superstition.[48]

The English middle-class reading public avidly seized on the new work, so flattering to itself and to the nation; American liberals also greeted it favorably. One overseas admirer, the New England reformer Theodore Parker, saw the *History* as the most

54–56; Buckle, *History of Civilization* 1: 171, 438–39 (also chaps. 10–11), 486 198–200. One writer saw Buckle's view of history as consisting of the story of an intellectual anti–Corn Law agitation: just as corn had to be freed from the insidious protection of government, so intellectual life had to be freed from that of the churches. See A. W. Benn, *History of English Rationalism in the Nineteenth Century* (London, 1906), pp. 175–87; see also his "Buckle and the Economics of Knowledge" (1880), in *Revaluations: Historical and Ideal* (London, 1909).

47. Buckle, *History of Civilization* 2: 2–7, 11–14, 27–29, 125–26.

48. Ibid., pp. 323–31, 341–49, 365–68, 405, 455–58.

important book written in English since Bacon's *Novum Organum* and Newton's *Principia*. In his memoirs, the Radical John Morley was to observe that "whatever may be decided on his worth either as a philosopher or scholar," Buckle's "system with its panoply of detail" must have "powerfully appealed to some thing or other in the public mind." For Morley, the *History* had satisfied the interest in an explanation of natural or social phenomena "by general laws, at the expense of special providence." Nearly forty years later, in 1894, Bernard Shaw wrote to a friend that there were only a few books in the century that had made "any permanent mark," and "I should certainly mention Marx and Buckle among the first."[49]

Many contemporary reviewers, however, saw serious faults in the work. Some commented on the numerous errors of fact and interpretation: for example, Spain and Italy were not particularly earthquake prone, and Adam Smith had employed the inductive method brilliantly.[50] Moreover, like all makers of systems, Buckle had been too ready to set aside any fact that might upset his tidy analyses. But what most struck Buckle's critics was his treatment of the issue of free will and determinism in history. Buckle was perhaps the first practicing historian to grasp the usefulness of statistics. In this he followed the lead of Comte and the Belgian statistician Quételet, who had sought to prove the regularity of mental phenomena by examining governmental statistics concerning certain moral questions. For example, both Quételet and Buckle saw in the regular occurrence of such crimes as murder and suicide proof that these phenomena were a consequence not of personal aberrations but of the general condition of society.[51] To maintain such a position, Buckle was obliged

49. J. Weiss, *The Life and Correspondence of Theodore Parker* (Boston, 1865), 1: 333–34; John Morley, *Recollections* 1: 14; Shaw to A. J. Marriott, 28 October 1894, *Bernard Shaw: Collected Letters, 1847–1897*, ed. Dan H. Lawrence (New York, 1965), p. 456.

50. [J. F. Stephen], *Edinburgh Review* 107 (April 1858): 467.

51. Buckle, *History of Civilization* 1: 17–26. See also F. H. Hankins, *Adolphe Quételet as Statistician* (New York, 1908).

not only to subordinate the historical role of great men, but virtually to do away with the part played by particular circumstances and by accident in historical events.

Though the public adored the work and lionized its author, most reviewers were unsympathetic to such a conception of scientific history. The jurist and political writer James Fitzjames Stephen took offense not only at Buckle's Voltairean antagonism to religion, but also at his deterministic denial of individual freedom. (This was the article that Reeve had recommended to Tocqueville's attention.) The noted barrister W. Frederick Pollock was unhappy at Buckle's having made men "mere cogs" of a "huge machine" and launched a devastating assault upon his statistical method. When the second volume of the *History* was published, Reeve offered moral Providence as the guardian of "the order of the world" in opposition to Buckle's "system of averages": every event was the result of an infinite number of causes that might be perceived by "the Power of Omniscience alone," Reeve concluded. Lord Acton, then a relative fledgling as a historian, found Buckle's statistical system fallacious: the true historian took the individual as a moral being for his subject, not a machinelike abstraction from a statistical mass.[52]

The Radical *Westminster Review* observed that Buckle's proposition that knowledge was progressive by nature and had been "the one force" controlling social and political change for millennia carried with it the presumption that this impulse would continue indefinitely into the future. "Such a hope would amount to a faith"—"a political faith" that would "inspire the party of

52. *Edinburgh Review* 107 (April 1858): article 7, p. 71; [W. Frederick Pollock], *Quarterly Review* 104, no. 207 (July 1858): 42, 44–48; [Henry Reeve], *Edinburgh Review* 114, no. 231 (July 1861): 184, 211; see Lord Acton, *Historical Essays & Studies*, ed. J. N. Figgis and R. V. Lawrence (London, 1907), pp. 305–43. The article declared that Gobineau's thesis that the progress and decline of civilization depended on racial purity was "founded on most various and conscientious research, and an abundance of appropriate learning." Gobineau's work "strongly contrasted with the dishonest affectation of knowledge by which Mr. Buckle deludes his readers."

Progress with that far-sighted confidence in their cause which itself would accelerate their victory." Yet the Radical reviewer was conscious of the "formidable" character of passion "allied to Power" and warned that the "ignorance and fanaticism" of the "unenlightened mass" were still cause for anxiety. "What security have we that the sleeping volcano of Passion will not flame forth with irresistible violence?" "Such is the rival theory, or ordinary view of European history, in place of which Mr. Buckle substitutes his irresistible advance of knowledge." Apparently Justin Macarthy, whose later article on Buckle's second volume in the *Westminster Review* Mill found most perceptive, was more hopeful on this score. An educated people could not relapse into ignorance, Macarthy asserted; there could no more be "a reaction from free-trade back again into protection" than one "from railways back to mail-coaches."[53]

Years later, the historian W. E. H. Lecky, who had once described himself as Buckle's disciple, suggested that Buckle's "master error" had been to underrate the importance of chance and of individuals in history. Lecky saw in this the reason for the collapse of Buckle's reputation, adding that while Carlyle may have exaggerated in seeing great men as the prime agents of history, Buckle had erred in "leaving out the men and women" altogether.[54] Lecky believed Buckle unfortunate in having written at a time when "advanced liberal thinkers" saw circumstances and experience in virtually complete command over the individual, leaving no room for the "innate, transmitted, or hereditary." Caught up in this intellectual scheme, Buckle had even denied the possibility of hereditary insanity. Lecky observed that the publication of Darwin's *Origin of Species* in 1859 made "the

53. *Westminster Review,* n.s. 12 (October 1857): 395–97; see Mill to John Chapman, 12 July 1861, *LL*, p. 732; [Justin Macarthy], *Westminster Review* 76, n.s. 20 (July 1861): 193.

54. Quoted in E. Lecky, *A Memoir of the Right Hon. William Edward Hartpole Lecky* (London, 1909), p. 106.

supreme importance of inborn and hereditary tendencies" central to English thinking.[55]

Buckle greatly respected Mill, as we know, and believed that his *History* had followed the lines of Mill's philosophical and methodological views. In 1855, when a friend asked his advice concerning books she might take with her while traveling abroad, Buckle recommended both Mill's *Principles of Political Economy* and his *System of Logic*. Writing to another woman friend in early 1859, Buckle urged her to read "John Mill's new book on 'Liberty,'" which was "full of wisdom." He described "how it roused me" when "I was stagnating at my old work."[56] The inspiration for Buckle's "spirit of protection" was clearly to be found in Mill's *Principles*,[57] and his views on logic stemmed as certainly from the *System of Logic*. In a letter in 1859, Buckle wrote of Mill's "profound views" on the difference between induction and deduction; they were "far in advance of the public mind." The historian thought that he had probably done "some service in popularizing them."[58]

Yet Buckle had failed to meet many of Mill's criteria for good history. In his 1840 essay on Coleridge, Mill had been critical of the historical writings of the French rationalists of the eighteenth century. The German idealist school, Mill had observed, had uncovered the importance in long-lived societies of loyalty to "*something* which is settled, something permanent, and not to be called in question," whether a common religión, laws, the principle of nationality, or the state itself. More important, the German school did not ignore, as had the eighteenth-century Enlightenment, "the culture of the inward man as the problem

55. W. E. H. Lecky, *Historical and Political Essays* (London, n.d.), pp. 100–02.

56. Huth, *Buckle,* pp. 89, 245.

57. See Mill, *Principles of Political Economy* 2: 758–62. Also Buckle, "Mill on Liberty," pp. 35–37.

58. See letter quoted in Huth, *Buckle,* p. 262.

of problems." How could they, since this would have been incompatible with their belief in Christianity and their recognition of the prime part it had played in the progress of civilization?[59] On both these important scores, Buckle's *History* had failed. Buckle was a mechanist, not a humanist liberal. In the manner of Voltaire and Condorcet, Buckle had excoriated the ethos of loyalty and nationality praised by the Germans as belonging to an inferior stage of development. The churches, religion itself, were the enemies of progress; the "culture of the inward man" was for him meaningless mysticism.

Nonetheless, Mill was prepared to welcome Buckle's *History*, although with important qualifications. In the 1862 edition of his *Logic*, he observed that Buckle had been the first to have "flung down this great principle [of general historical laws] together with many striking exemplifications of it, into the arena of public discussion." Buckle had moreover "most clearly and triumphantly brought out" by statistical demonstrations the existence of "regularity *en masse,* combined with the extreme of irregularity in the cases composing the mass," thus surmounting the philosophical difficulties of the problem of free will and determinism. To see matters in this way, Mill stressed, was not to accept the "overruling fatality" frequently implied by a doctrine of necessity. But Buckle had been careless in his use of words, and consequently the English public believed him to have pronounced in favor of fatalism; unfortunately, Mill noted, the pages of the *History* frequently supported this view.[60]

Mill perceived a fatalism in Buckle's contention that the moral qualities were secondary to the intellectual ones. The historian's argument that the increase of knowledge rather than the improvement of morals had motored the progress of civilization, since moral qualities were capable of but small improvement,

59. Mill, "Coleridge," 133–34, 140.
60. Mill, *System of Logic,* pp. 931–33, 934–35.

had discomforted many English liberals who saw Christianity slighted. If Buckle's statistics had been drawn from longer periods and wider geographical areas, Mill argued, greater variations in the moral element would certainly have appeared. Mill's own hopes, as we know, depended on the further development of moral qualities, the increase of virtue. Along similar lines, Mill complained that while "general causes count for much," Buckle did not understand the sometimes decisive importance of individuals in history as demonstrated in Grote's *History of Greece*.[61]

Buckle's untimely death in 1862 "grieved me deeply," Mill wrote to a friend; some months later, he pronounced Buckle's death "a great loss." Despite its overly grand generalizations, the *History* had popularized important ideas and had spurred an interest in applying "general principles to the explanation and prediction of social facts." If he had lived longer, Mill believed, Buckle would have come to understand that the moral element in man was as capable of improvement as the intellectual and would have cast aside the errors which led his readers to comprehend "the doctrine of the invariability of natural laws as identical with fatalism."[62]

This might have come to pass: in his replies to critics, Buckle again stressed that although free will might be evident in the behavior of individuals, history was concerned with "the dynamics of masses" which could be described only by statistics. Individuals might wish to marry because of personal considerations, for example, but this was merely "the *proximate* cause." Science sought "the most *remote* cause, or the highest generalization," in this case the physical laws of sustenance. The intellect was therefore decisive among "the remote and Primary causes" of society's progress, whereas the proximate, moral factor was probably decisive

61. Ibid., pp. 934–35, 941–42.

62. Mill to Henry Fawcett, 21 July 1862, *LL*, p. 786; Mill to H. S. Chapman, 24 February 1863, *LL*, pp. 844–45; Mill, "Auguste Comte and Positivism," *Collected Works* 10: 322.

for the individual.[63] But like Mill, though more secretively, Buckle also sought a compromise that would leave room for free will in a deterministic system. In an early, unnoticed footnote in his *History*,[64] he had quoted a long passage of Kant's in which, as he wrote to a friend in 1857, the German philosopher "vindicates *transcendentally* the freedom which he destroys *logically*." While he defended this proposition, Buckle was concerned that it might expose him to charges of mysticism and of trafficking with the idealist "opposition," as he once described the German philosophers. He asked his correspondent to burn his letter![65] That his confusion on these questions probably went beyond purely intellectual considerations is further suggested by the fact that in his last years, after the death of his mother, to whom he had been devoted, the "rationalist" Buckle turned to spiritualism.[66]

There was a demand for philosophies of history, the novelist and clergyman Charles Kingsley, a long-time disciple of Carlyle, observed in his inaugural address as regius professor of modern history at Cambridge in 1860. Kingsley was not opposed to historical theory as such; indeed, he welcomed "such startling speculations as those on the influence of climate, soil, [and] scenery on national character" that had "lately excited so much controversy." "They give us hope of order," he declared. The interest in inductive science had "awakened this appetite," and the French historians had stimulated it further, "till the more order and sequence we find in the facts of the past, the more we wish to find." And was it not the goal of science to discover the order of the universe? Was the history of human development an exception to the logic upon which all science was based?[67]

63. Quoted in Huth, *Buckle,* pp. 126–29.

64. Buckle, *History of Civilization* 1: 26–28n.

65. See Huth, *Buckle,* pp. 110, 120–21.

66. See the curious concluding passages in Buckle's "Mill on Liberty," pp. 65–69.

67. Charles Kingsley, *The Limits of Exact Science as Applied to History,* pp. 9, 70, 12–13.

But there was a decisive difference between the positions of Kingsley and Mill on the one hand, and of Comte and Buckle on the other, despite Mill's great sympathy with the latter. Comte's description of the historical process had a political as much as a scientific purpose; his social dynamics was a faith, carefully designed to assure positivists of the inevitable coming of the utopia he had envisioned. Similarly, Buckle had invoked historical necessitarianism to exalt the society of contemporary England as the achievement of humanity's highest goals. In our time, the Marxist view of history has served similar ends. Mill was ready to accept Comte's social dynamics as a highly persuasive hypothesis but never as a political faith, and he probably had Buckle's vision of the perfection of a free-market society in mind when he implicitly criticized the historian for thinking "any practical rule or doctrine" in politics was "universal and absolute."[68]

Kingsley suggested in his inaugural address that the so-called scientific historians had carelessly employed, as if to "blink the whole of the world-old argument between necessity and free will," such ambiguous words as "invariable, continual, immutable, inevitable, irresistible." Was it irresistible or inevitable that the spinning jenny which supplied employment for millions in Lancashire had also helped to extend slavery in the American South? These determinist historians ignored the unforeseeable follies and irrationalities of mankind which made it difficult to use statistics for purposes of prediction. They did not see that human destiny was not "always decided by majorities," that there was "a demonic element" in human nature which defied "all law, and all induction," witnessed by such events as the Anabaptist war, the French Revolution, or the Crusades.[69]

There was more than one echo of Carlyle in Kingsley's

68. Mill, "Auguste Comte and Positivism," p. 323. For his part, Buckle described Mill's opinions on distribution as "blots" upon the escutcheon of "that very great man," examples of Benthamite meddling. See Huth, *Buckle,* pp. 387–88.

69. Kingsley, *Limits of Exact Science,* pp. 18, 52, 32–34.

address. "We shall not be inclined here [at Cambridge], I trust," he observed, "to explain (as some one tried to lately) the Crusades" by a theory of "overstocked labour-markets on the Continent." Instead of saying that "the history of mankind is the history of its masses, it would be more true" to say that it was "the history of its great men." In the present state of social science, Kingsley urged, it would be better to stick to facts, hoping that if we could master them, "some rays of inductive light will be vouchsafed to us from Him who truly comprehends mankind." Both the English laissez-faire political economists and the French socialists had described man as a creature of his circumstances, the regius professor remarked, but this was not true. Man was a free agent. Certainly students of history ought to learn political economy: the laws which governed "the supply of the first necessaries of life are, after all, the first which should be learnt, and the last which should be ignored." But the chief lessons to be learned were "not statistical, but moral." "If human folly has been a disturbing force for evil," Kingsley observed, "surely human reason has been a disturbing force for good." "The true subjective history of man" was "the history not of his thought, but of his conscience." Morals did not depend on thought, he continued, but thought on morals.[70]

It was at this point in his address that the regius professor surprisingly invoked on his side of the argument, not on Buckle's or Comte's, "our greatest living political economist" John Stuart Mill. Mill had pleaded in his recently published essay *On Liberty* "for the self-determining power of the individual, and for his right to use that power."[71] This was how the Coleridgean and Carlylean Kingsley had understood the message of the tract. The "self-determining power of the individual" might serve as a counter to historical necessity.

70. Ibid., pp. 9, 44, 50, 38–39, 42–43, 35, 55.
71. Ibid., p. 40.

But Mill agreed with Buckle, and with Comte before him, that individuals played a more critical role in the earlier stages of history than subsequently. While insisting that there was still room for individual free will in history, Mill saw this area of freedom narrowing: though "the course of affairs never ceases to be susceptible of alteration both by accidents and by personal qualities," Mill declared, civilization as it progresses "deviates less from a certain and preappointed track." A science of history was becoming more and more possible.[72] What place would there be for virtue and for liberty if progress increasingly diminished the importance of individuals in the shaping of human affairs? This, as we shall see, was the problem underlying Mill's tract *On Liberty* and, though less prominently, *Utilitarianism* as well.

72. Mill, *System of Logic,* p. 942.

FIVE

Logic, Liberty, and the Pursuit of Happiness

ONE OF THE CLASSIC PROBLEMS OF TRADITIONAL logic with which Mill was much concerned was the distinction between metaphysical liberty and necessity. His *System of Logic*, we recall, had tried to solve this question by distinguishing between necessity defined as the dependence of every event upon some earlier cause and as a quasi-religious fatality. In the sphere of history and politics, he made a place for personal responsibility through the exercise of individual free will and looked to virtue as a counter to the strong forces within the historical process that were moving men to a mechanical conformity and uniformity. Mill thus shared in the ambivalent faith in both liberty and necessity established on the contradiction that Alfred North Whitehead was to find so prevalent. The consequent confusions in Mill's thought caused the loyal Benthamite George Grote, a special admirer of the *Logic* and a logician himself, to express misgivings about his friend Mill's "persistence in the true faith" of utilitarianism.[1]

Although another friend, Alexander Bain, saw Mill as "first of all a Logician, and next a social philosopher or Politician" and thought he had a talent "for the abstract and the logical, out of all proportion to his hold of the concrete, and the poetical,"[2]

1. Quoted in Bain, *John Stuart Mill,* pp. 83–84.
2. Ibid., pp. 117, 142.

the logician and political economist W. S. Jevons differed sharply and in some respects correctly from this view. During the last dozen years of his life, Jevons waged an intellectual vendetta against Mill, whose reputation stood in the way of Jevons's professional claims.[3] Jevons had been raised a liberal of the Benthamite school. Bentham, author of another classic of logic, the once-celebrated *Book of Fallacies*, had been a more consistent reasoner than Mill and did not hesitate to take the felicific calculus to its logical conclusions; like him, Jevons was an uncompromising logician. His formulation of the new marginalism had been developed as a logical extension of the Benthamite felicific calculus, as the term "marginal utility" clearly displayed. In his *Theory of Political Economy*, published in 1871, Jevons observed, "I have attempted to treat Political Economy as a Calculus of Pleasure and Pain." He had set out to determine precise mathematical notions of "indefinitely small amounts of pleasures and pain" and to base his theory of value on these minute degrees of utility. Jevons may well have believed that Mill's failure to come to a similar view of the subject had been due in no small part to his having been, as Jevons was to write in 1877, "really a bad logician."[4]

Although Mill thought himself "a bulwark of the Utilitarian Morality," Jevons complained that he had "unconsciously" converted the ideas of Bentham and Paley into something very different, most particularly in his *Utilitarianism*. Indeed, there were significant instances, Jevons continued, in which "the view which he professes to uphold is the direct opposite of what he really upholds." He particularly noted that while Mill "clearly reprobates the doctrine of Free Will, and expressly places himself

3. See W. Stanley Jevons to Leon Walras, 14 February 1875, *Letters and Journal of W. Stanley Jevons,* ed. by Harriet Ann Jevons, p. 332.

4. W. S. Jevons, *The Theory of Political Economy* (1871; reprint, London, 1942) pp. vi–viii; Jevons to Walras, 28 February 1877, *Letters and Journal of Jevons,* p. 366 (see also Jevons to H. S. Foxwell, 7 February 1875, p. 331, and pp. 329, 342–43, 349, and 409).

in the camp of Necessity," he not only objected to "the name of Necessity," but explained "it away so ingeniously, that he unintentionally converts it into Free Will"! "Mill's mind was essentially illogical," Jevons concluded: "in one way or another Mill's intellect was wrecked." The marginal economist speculated that this may have been the result of "the ruthless training" his father had imposed upon him in childhood.[5]

But another explanation stemming from Mill's early education was more likely than Jevons's. The utilitarian philosophy had posited that men *must* by their nature always prefer pleasure to pain, yet James Mill had instructed his son *voluntarily* to choose virtue over material or sensual happiness. Mill may well have been spoiled for the task of developing the economics of marginal utility by his father's contradictory injunctions that he follow the pleasure philosophy of Epicurus and Bentham and at the same time choose, like Hercules, the virtue of the Stoics. In almost all Mill's writings from the 1830s through the 1860s, there was a recurring motif of the conflict between material happiness as the goal to which future society should aspire, and liberty that could be preserved only by virtue.

In 1838 Mill wrote "Bentham," an essay as distinctly unfriendly to the utilitarian as his earlier anonymous piece had been and a marked contrast to his sympathetic critique of Coleridge two years later. Since his father had died in 1836, nothing now prevented Mill from signing his analysis of the inadequacies of Benthamism. In this essay Mill described Bentham as one of the school of "negative, or destructive" philosophers, a group that included Voltaire and Hume, thinkers who easily perceived what was false but often failed to know what was true. If Bentham's philosophy had few inconsistencies, it was also narrow and inadequate, revealing no understanding of "the most natural and

5. W. S. Jevons, "John Stuart Mill's Philosophy Tested," in *Pure Logic and Other Minor Works,* pp. 200–01, 203, 201.

strongest feelings of human nature." The idea of man, "that most complex being," as "capable of pursuing spiritual perfection as an end" was entirely foreign to him. He had failed to recognize "the existence of conscience" as distinct from philanthropy or self-interest and had been unaware of "self-respect" or "*honour*, and personal dignity."[6]

At bottom, Bentham had not understood "the power of making our volitions effectual"; he had not perceived the central importance of what Mill called "that grand duty of man," self-development. For Bentham there had been but three sanctions that worked to keep harmony among men, each following his own interests: a political sanction, made effective by legal rewards and penalties; a religious sanction, which moved believers by divine rewards and penalties; and a popular or moral sanction, "operating through the pains and pleasures arising from the favour or disfavour of our fellow-creatures." Such a view of the world, despite its apparent practicality, was to Mill hardly adequate. It was just as well for humanity, he observed, that Bentham had turned his attention to jurisprudence rather than to ethics, since his ethical system did not even consider the need "to aid individuals in the formation of their own character." Bentham's sanctions regulated only *outward* behavior. Without "self-education," the "training, by the human being himself, of his affections and will" which taught a man to govern his *inward* life, how was it possible to regulate "the nicer shades of human behaviour," such as those involved in "sexual relations, or those of the family in general"? All this had been "a blank in Bentham's system."[7]

But Mill also found a grave flaw in Bentham's jurisprudence. In stressing the popular or moral sanction, in placing confidence in the numerical majority as protection against abuses of governmental authority, the utilitarian philosopher had taken a fatal

6. Mill, "Bentham," pp. 79, 91, 95–96.
7. Ibid., pp. 96, 97–98.

step. Was it always good, Mill inquired, for men to be placed under the absolute authority of a majority? Whatever body had political power would seek control over opinions and sentiments that differed from the norm it had set, if not by legal penalties then "by the persecution of society." To give any one "set of partialities, passions and prejudices" absolute power without attempting to correct or counterbalance it would leave society without "a shelter for freedom of thought and individuality of character." Was it, Mill again demanded, "the proper condition of man, in all ages and nations, to be under the despotism of Public Opinion?"[8]

Thus as early as 1838 Mill had defined the political conclusion toward which in his view Benthamite principles tended: Bentham's great intellectual crime was to have devised, perhaps unwittingly, a plan for liberticide. He had devoted his ingenuity to constructing methods "for rivetting the yoke of public opinion closer and closer round the necks of all public functionaries," excluding the influence of a minority's or even of an individual official's idea of right. When all society's forces acted in but one direction, Mill warned, the rights of individuals were "in extreme peril."[9] Later, having become familiar with Auguste Comte and his ideas, Mill saw the utopia constructed by the French positivist as a deliberate attempt to achieve the liberticide society toward which the Benthamites were less consciously and less explicitly moving.

Mill's friends Bain and Grote had been kept informed of his intimacy with Auguste Comte in the 1840s. From the beginning, Bain was to observe, Grote had had misgivings about "the grand theories" of the French school of sociological history, noting particularly the mistakes and distortions of fact in Comte's volumes. Grote had also been quick to recognize that Comte's perception of historical development welcomed the introduction of "a new despotism over the individual." The "repression of

8. Ibid., pp. 106–08.
9. Ibid., p. 108.

liberty by a new machinery touched his [Grote's] acutest sensibility," Bain observed, and he "would not take any comfort" from Bain's often repeated suggestion "that there was little danger of any such system ever being in force."[10] Unlike Grote, Mill was sympathetic to "the grand theories" of the French philosophers of history. He therefore had all the more reason to fear the new despotism, being convinced as well that Comte's vision of the future was far from improbable.

The French thinker's antagonism to liberty had already been fully set down in the *Cours de philosophie positive*, to whose methodology and social dynamics Mill was devoted. In the *Cours*, Comte had denounced metaphysical doctrine as the great adversary of progress and order. The metaphysical school had translated its hostility to the order of the theological system into a view of government as "the enemy of society," a position that had proved useful, indeed essential, to the undermining of the old regime, but that constituted the greatest obstacle to the building of a new one. Such metaphysical doctrines as "the right of free inquiry, or the dogma of unbounded liberty of conscience" had led to anarchy. Liberty of conscience, Comte continued, was already impossible in areas like astronomy; soon it would be impossible in social questions as well, for order was incompatible with a free inquiry that encouraged endless discussion of the foundations of society. Another destructive dogma of metaphysical politics was the belief in equality. Comte argued that moral and intellectual inequalities were even more marked than physical ones and that the gap increased rather than diminished with the progress of civilization. Still another metaphysical dogma rooted in liberty of conscience was a belief in the sovereignty of the people, which condemned the superior few to rule by the inferior many and transferred to peoples the divine right of kings. These doctrines had been proclaimed as absolute rights by "a sort of religious

10. Bain, *John Stuart Mill,* pp. 70–71, 74–75.

consecration," leading the French positivist to observe that liberalism was "a Christianity more and more attenuated."[11]

Comte saw the English system, caught in an unstable position between the old and the new, as the perfect embodiment of metaphysical thinking. England's parliamentary government was the product of special local conditions and depended on Protestantism for its spiritual base; its inevitable end was not far off. It certainly could not constitute a solution to the crisis of modern society. Positivists could only scoff at the most advanced branch of the metaphysical school which maintained it could civilize Tahiti by "a wholesale importation of Protestantism and a Parliamentary System." The French had fortunately escaped "the treacherous stage of Protestantism" and had passed from the Catholic to "the fully revolutionary stage." Nevertheless, they were not exempt from the intellectual anarchy that belonged to a "prolonged exercise of the absolute right of free individual inquiry" and resulted in a universal decline of public and private morality.

Mankind could more easily resign itself to the inevitable if it knew the true laws of progress and historical development, Comte declared. But the only idea of progress disseminated by the revolutionary school was "the continuous extension of liberty." The Frenchman proclaimed "true liberty" as "a rational submission" to "the laws of nature, in release from all arbitrary personal dictation." So long as political decisions were referred to "Will, divine or human"—to laws passed by legislatures as instruments of the popular will instead of to invariable and necessary natural laws—liberty would remain "illusory and precarious." The task of the positivist school was to substitute "the empire of genuine convictions for that of arbitrary will," and in this way to "put an end to the absolute liberty of the revolutionary school."[12]

11. Comte, *The Positive Philosophy of Auguste Comte,* ed. Harriet Martineau, pp. 2–4, 11–15, 17.

12. Ibid., pp. 22–23, 37, 25, 39.

Mill was particularly disturbed that Comte had demoted to the category of the metaphysical "the first of all the articles in the liberal creed," the right of liberty of conscience. As he suggested in his full treatment of Comte's ideas in 1862, Comte's opinion on this issue was the clue to all his politics. Mill saw all the leading principles of liberalism, whatever their origins, as sound positive doctrine, scientific inferences from the laws of human nature and historical circumstances. While agreeing with Comte that in practical life men of lesser abilities had to be subordinated to those of greater, Mill insisted that when properly educated, and permitted "to find their places for themselves," people would "spontaneously class themselves in a manner much more conformable to their unequal or dissimilar aptitudes, than governments or social institutions are likely to do it for them." Moreover, Mill defended direct participation in government not as a natural right but as the best means to the perfection of civic virtue.[13]

Nor was Mill content with Comte's allocation of temporal and spiritual powers. Temporal power in the positivist utopia would be exercised by a dictatorship of three bankers who would act in conformity with the interest of all, under the moral and spiritual supervision of a high priest of humanity. Comte's notion of the duties of spiritual power—"obtruding" upon all persons throughout their lives "the paramount claims of the general interest" and "guiding men's opinions and enlightening and warning their consciences"—appalled Mill. He was horrified at the "frightful aberrations" Comte had predicted would be "the last and highest result of the evolution of Humanity."[14]

Mill did agree with Comte that doctrines that enjoyed the virtually unanimous approval of the specialist experts should and would be generally accepted by society, as they already were in certain of the sciences. He argued, however, as he had in his earlier correspondence with Comte, that it was not necessary to

13. Mill, "Auguste Comte and Positivism," pp. 301, 303–04.
14. Ibid., pp. 313, 351.

organize power to make certain that only the most eminent thinkers would prevail. With the attainment of unanimity, intellectual ascendancy would come spontaneously. While individuals belonging to "the speculative class" might in fact informally perform this function, to entrust it to an organized body, as Comte wished, would make for just such "a spiritual despotism" as had existed in the Middle Ages. Indeed Mill was persuaded that this was "what Comte really contemplated."[15]

Like Bentham, Comte wished to impose conformity not by legal sanctions but by the pressure of public opinion. Individual "Liberty and spontaneity" formed no part of their ideal. The French thinker viewed liberty with "as great jealousy as any scholastic pedagogue, or ecclesiastical director of consciences," Mill declared. In Comte's future society, "every particular of conduct, public or private, is to be open to the public eye, and to be kept, by the power of opinion, in the course which the Spiritual corporation shall judge to be the most right." Comte had in fact organized "an elaborate system for the total suppression of all independent thought."[16]

Comte had not desired an increase in mental power or knowledge, but merely "submission and obedience." The positivist had even suggested that the study of astronomy be limited to the interrelationships of earth, sun, and moon, since all other parts of the science could bring no significant benefit to humanity. He had called for a similar paring of the other sciences because only those parts that helped to form a foundation for his positivist sociology were necessary! The theory of the sciences, as far as he was concerned, had been completed. Mill was convinced that Comte had "gradually acquired a real hatred" for scientific and intellectual pursuits and had come to regard "all abstraction and all reasoning as morally dangerous." The positivist, wishing all to have a systematized view of the world, had deprecated the

15. Ibid., p. 314.
16. Ibid., pp. 327, 351.

"pedantic anxiety" for complete proof, which he described as a mark of "distrust, if not hostility, to the sacerdotal order," referring to the spiritual priesthood of his future society. (This had also been Comte's view of Mill's resistance to phrenology on the grounds that it had been insufficiently proven.) Comte had even planned to burn all books except the hundred titles in his positivist library![17] Submission had been for him a prime virtue: all learning was to be accepted on the authority of the teacher, and the spirit of inquiry was to be discouraged. For Mill, a man obsessed with the discovery of truth in every field, this was unacceptable, indeed reprehensible.

Comte's portrait of the positivist society of the future was an elaboration of the conformist horror that had long been Mill's nightmare, and he determined to write a tract alerting the public to the enemies of liberty. In Mill's words, the French positivist had boasted that in his utopia "human life may be made equally, and even more, regular than the courses of the stars." We recall that Mill's fear of a Comtian society had first been associated with the positivist's view of a fixed hierarchy of the sexes and of the classes; Mill had pronounced this outlook "contrary to human liberty," making every life "inexorably closed against all change."[18] Worse yet, Mill had long believed, the overall tendency of a commercial and egalitarian civilization was toward the realization of just such a society.

In 1855, Mill wrote to his wife Harriet from Rome of his intention to write an essay on liberty. There was a growing need for a work on this question, he observed, for "opinion tends to encroach more & more on liberty, & almost all the projects of social reformers in these days are really *liberticide*—Comte, particularly so."[19] The visions of the future advanced by social re-

17. Ibid., pp. 352, 354–57.
18. Ibid., p. 366; Mill to J. P. Nichol, 30 September 1848, *EL*, p. 739.
19. John Stuart to Harriet Mill, 15 January 1855, *LL*, p. 294.

formers, Bentham as well as Comte among them, spurred the writing of *On Liberty*.

In *On Liberty*, as we noted earlier, Mill praised three periods of ferment in Europe that had "stirred up" the minds of all classes and had raised the most ordinary persons "to something of the dignity of thinking beings." The first immediately followed the Reformation; the second, though limited to a continental elite, was the late eighteenth-century Enlightenment; and the third, even briefer in duration, was "the intellectual fermentation" of the Germany of Goethe and Fichte. Though producing widely different philosophies, the three were alike in that in each "the yoke of authority" and an "old mental despotism had been thrown off." "The impulse given at these three periods," Mill declared, "has made Europe what it now is."[20]

On Liberty must itself be understood as the product of these three historical impulses. In the essay, Mill paid special tribute to Protestantism for championing "the right of the individual against society" on "grounds of principle" in its proclamation of "freedom of conscience as an indefeasible right." This Protestant liberty to seek one's own salvation, Mill observed, could and did exist and even prosper in societies in which political liberty was unknown.[21] Of course in his views on economics and psychology Mill was the intellectual heir of the Enlightenment, a conscientious disciple of his father's philosophy. This was in good part why Comte's positivism, modeled on the physical sciences and derived from such thinkers as Condorcet and Saint-Simon in its vision of historical progress, attracted Mill, and why he had come to believe that a society much like that of Comte's organic period was in the offing. In *On Liberty*, Mill observed that such a development threatened to establish "(though by moral more than by legal appliances) a despotism of society over the indi-

20. Mill, *On Liberty,* p. 243.

21. Ibid., p. 232; see also Mill, "Auguste Comte and Positivism," p. 321.

vidual."[22] He sought to adopt the views of the period of German "intellectual fermentation" as the most effective means of preserving individual freedom in the future.

The support German philosophy gave to liberty was the principal theme of Mill's best-known tract. At the time of his friendship with Carlyle, Mill had become a Germanophile of the type frequently encountered among European intellectuals whose eyes had recently been opened by Madame de Staël to the new philosophical and literary movements across the Rhine. After completing the essay, Mill insisted in a letter to a friend on the Continent that Germany, while deficient in political liberty, possessed both moral and intellectual liberty, and that consequently "my little book is . . . as little needed in Germany as it is much here." He repeated these views in other letters.[23] Living under the petty despotisms of their duchies and principalities, the German philosophers had exalted the freedom of self-realization, which was clearly akin to the Protestant insistence on a believer's right to seek his own salvation, and similarly feasible even in the absence of political liberty.

The conflict between philosophical liberty and necessity, between free will and determinism, was critical to the argument of *On Liberty*, in keeping with the central role it played in Mill's thought. Curiously, however, the very first sentence of the tract explicitly denied any intention of discussing this metaphysical question. "The subject of this Essay is not the so-called Liberty of the Will so unfortunately opposed to the misnamed doctrine of Philosophical Necessity," Mill insisted.[24] But why begin a tract on "civil or social liberty" with this unnecessary disavowal?

22. Mill, *On Liberty,* p. 227. Comte's work on politics was "a monumental warning" of what might happen when men lost sight of "the value of Liberty and of Individuality"; see *Autobiography*, p. 149.

23. Mill to Arnold Ruge, 2 March 1859, *LL*, 2: 598; see also, for example, Mill to Theodore Gomperz, 5 October 1857, *LL*, p. 539, and Mill to Pasquale Villari, 9 March 1858, *LL*, p. 550.

24. Mill, *On Liberty*, p. 217.

There was no reason to think that a reader would otherwise be confused by the title or by a straightforward statement of the subject. We need not ask why Mill saw an opposition between "so-called" free will and "misnamed" necessity as unfortunate, for we have seen that this conflict profoundly marked his life and thought.

In the *Autobiography*, Mill described the ideas of the Coleridgians, the German thinkers, and Carlyle as containing "much truth" which was "veiled" by "transcendental and mystical phraseology." He hoped to express these truths in "terms which would be intelligible and not repulsive to those on my own side in philosophy."[25] This is what he did when he wrote *On Liberty*. In this essay, Mill translated his earlier metaphysical and religious crisis into the terms of political philosophy, following the pattern he had established in his *System of Logic*. He presented the argument, moreover, so as to make it converge with his earlier defense of free will. This time he made the historically necessary organic period of the Comtists fill the role formerly played by metaphysical determinism, while the German liberty of self-development, the principal theme of the essay, played the role of free will, just as it had in his *Logic* thirty years earlier.

On Liberty was consequently not merely (as it has been generally regarded) a defense of "negative" freedom, the liberty of the individual from the restraining authority of the state or society sought by classic nineteenth-century liberalism. The essay was also, and primarily, a plea for positive liberty, for the sense of participation and self-realization in the idea of freedom associated with the German thinkers. Mill was to resort to this concept of liberty as best suited to counter Comte's priestly despotism as well as Bentham's utilitarian state in their very similar efforts to use the force of public opinion to mold everyone into conformity. Mill hoped to place the ultimate spiritual power in neither a

25. *Autobiography*, p. 172.

positivist priesthood nor a utilitarian bureaucracy, but, in line with the intuitive morality of the German idealists, in the conscience of the individual. This would be essential if the structure of common moral values characteristic of an organic period, which Mill on the whole welcomed, was not to degenerate into social despotism. In this way, a virtuous society could remain a free society.

Mill's essay was introduced by an epigraph from the German philosopher Wilhelm von Humboldt (not his scientist brother, Alexander), an unambiguous announcement that this was to be no mere tract on freedom of speech or toleration. "The grand, leading principle, towards which every argument unfolded in these pages directly converges," he quoted Humboldt, "is the absolute and essential importance of human development in its richest diversity."[26] Nor did Humboldt, the friend of Goethe and Schiller, stand alone in Germany: "The doctrine of the rights of individuality, and the claim of the moral nature to develop itself in its own way, was pushed by a whole school of German authors even to exaggeration," Mill added, making particular mention of Goethe's views on "the right and duty of self-development" and of the writings of Fichte.[27]

Specifically, Mill announced that he would consider "the nature and limits of the power which can be legitimately exercised by society over the individual," already an important question and, given "the stage of progress" which the advanced societies were entering, soon to become "the vital question of the future."

26. Mill, *On Liberty*, p. 215. See Wilhelm von Humboldt, *The Limits of State Action*, ed. J. W. Burrow and *Humanist Without Portfolio: An Anthology of the Writings of Wilhelm von Humboldt*, trans. Marianne Cowan. See also Paul R. Sweet, *Wilhelm von Humboldt: A Biography*, vol. 1; W. F. Bruford, *The German Tradition of Self-Cultivation: Bildung from Humboldt to Thomas Mann*; and Lawrence Krieger, *The German Idea of Freedom* (Boston, 1957), chap. 8. For a comparison of Mill and Humboldt, see R. Leroux, "Guillaume de Humboldt et John Stuart Mill," *Etudes germaniques* 6 (1951): 262–74 and 7 (1952): 81–87.

27. *Autobiography*, p. 179.

What particularly characterized this future stage was the growth of democracy and with it, the possible "tyranny of the majority." Mill was concerned less with the tyranny of "political functionaries" than with that of society itself. "Society can and does execute its own mandates," he observed, and "practises a social tyranny more formidable than many kinds of political oppression." What we would increasingly require in the future would be protection against "the tyranny of the prevailing opinion and feeling" which might act "to fetter the development, and if possible, prevent the formation, of any individuality."[28] This was the danger against which Mill had warned his countrymen almost a generation earlier when he perceived commercial and egalitarian civilization as the enemy of virtue.

Mill sought to protect "individual spontaneity" against "external control" except insofar as such behavior might harm others. Of course, the state had no right to interfere to protect an individual against his own behavior. Mill did not defend this position by an appeal to "abstract right, as a thing independent of utility"; utility continued to be "the ultimate appeal" on ethical questions, but for Mill this was utility "in the largest sense, grounded on the permanent interests of man as a progressive being." There were nonetheless cases where a person might be compelled—either by the state or by public opinion—to act for the benefit of others: for example, to give evidence in court, to share in the common defense, or to act to prevent injury from being inflicted on another. In other instances such compulsion would not be desirable. By what philosophical criterion did Mill distinguish between these cases? The appeal was to be directed to conscience. "The conscience of the agent himself," Mill declared, "should step into the vacant judgment seat." The "appropriate region of human liberty," he suggested in the best Kantian manner, included first of all "the inward domain of consciousness; demanding liberty

28. Mill, *On Liberty*, pp. 217, 219–20.

of conscience, in the most comprehensive sense." A proper Benthamite might well shy from this utility "in the largest sense," so close to the concept of natural rights, as well as from the invocation of individual conscience as the standard of judgment.[29]

For Mill, as for the school of Goethe and Fichte, and of Coleridge, Carlyle, and Emerson, "individuality is one of the leading essentials of well-being," and "individual spontaneity" deserved every encouragement; in defending this view, Mill turned for support both to Humboldt and to Coleridge's disciple John Sterling, his friend and Carlyle's. There were "few persons, out of Germany," Mill declared, who "even comprehend the meaning" of Humboldt's doctrine that "the end of man, or that which is prescribed by the eternal or immutable dictates of reason, and not suggested by vague and transient desires, is the highest and most harmonious development of his powers to a complete and consistent whole." Every person, Humboldt had written, and Mill wholeheartedly agreed, had to aim at "individuality of power and development." To attain this, "freedom, and a variety of situations" were necessary, and from these came the "individual vigor and manifold diversity" that combined to producc "originality." "At present," Mill observed, "individuals are lost in the crowd" (a phrase that had first appeared in his 1836 essay "Civilization"); "society has now fairly got the better of individuality." Even in what they did for pleasure, people thought first of conformity. Mill called for, in Sterling's words, a revival of "'Pagan self-assertion,'" which he held was as much an element of "human worth" as "'Christian self-denial.'" Only where individuality, that is, individual development, was encouraged could genius

29. Ibid., pp. 223–24, 225. Wollheim has argued against Isaiah Berlin and others that by grounding his view of utility "on the permanent interests of man as a progressive being," Mill avoided any appeal to abstract rights and was able to remain a utilitarian; see Richard Wollheim, "John Stuart Mill and Isaiah Berlin; The Ends of Life and the Preliminaries of Morality," in *The Idea of Freedom: Essays in Honour of Isaiah Berlin*, pp. 254–55.

flourish; without such encouragement, "collective mediocrity" prevailed.[30]

These sections of *On Liberty* bring to mind the writings of Carlyle and Emerson. While he denied that he was countenancing a Carlylean hero worship, Mill nonetheless echoed the Scotsman in his complaint that "the greatness of England is now all collective." "It was men of another stamp than this that made England what it has been," he observed, "and men of another stamp will be necessary to prevent its decline." Mill was once more calling for a revival of individual virtue. If the "collective mediocrity" of public opinion succeeded in extirpating individuality, England would have emulated the Chinese, who "have succeeded beyond all hope in what English philanthropists are so industriously working at—in making a people all alike.[31]

Far from making negative liberty an absolute end, as such critics as Fitzjames Stephen and Matthew Arnold were to allege, Mill felt that the pressure of public opinion, though not of law, could exercise in certain matters an entirely justifiable supervision over private conduct. We know that he yearned for a time when "the moral and intellectual ascendancy, once exercised by priests," would "pass into the hands of philosophers," and when "convictions as to what was right and wrong, useful and pernicious" would be "deeply graven on the feelings by early education and general unanimity of sentiments." Men might be induced to be virtuous. Even in this tract on individual liberty, Mill did not neglect the advantages of the coming organic period. It would be a time when "the self-regarding virtues" would rank second to the social ones, and he urged public opinion to a "great increase of disinterested exertion to promote the good of others." "Human beings owe to each other help to distinguish the better from the worse," he wrote, "and encouragement to choose the former and avoid the latter." Among other necessary intrusions on the individual,

30. Mill, *On Liberty*, pp. 261, 268, 264, 266, 268.
31. Ibid., pp. 269, 272–73.

Mill would grant the state the right not only to compel men to educate their children, but to deny them the liberty of marrying if they were not in a position to support a family. All this is hardly the defense of a merely negative liberty, though that is how Mill's essay is generally understood. We have Mill's own word, both in the tract and in his autobiography, that *On Liberty* was the exposition of a "single truth," the importance of diversity as the fruit of the liberty of self-realization: "the importance, to man and society, of a large variety in types of character," and of "giving full freedom to human nature to expand itself in innumerable and conflicting directions"—yet without losing sight of the prior moral claims of society. Mill's primary theme was a positive liberty.[32]

The doctrine of positive liberty has had more than one evaluation. Among the Germans, the doctrine of positive liberty began as that of individual freedom, though it was to end—almost inescapably, one political theorist seems to suggest—as something quite different, even in the writings of its most individualist exponents, Kant and Fichte. Positive liberty, having become embodied in a supraindividual entity—a nation, race, class, or party—became an opponent to negative, individual liberty, and the rhetoric of positive liberty became a mask for despotism in the name of expanded freedom.[33] Carlyle, similarly, moved from the self-realization of *Sartor Resartus* to an authoritarian hero worship, alienating Mill. In America, the destination of the doctrine of self-realization was very different: though it remained

32. *Autobiography*, pp. 148, 116–17; Mill, *On Liberty*, pp. 277, 301–02, 304; *Autobiography*, p. 177. For a perceptive and stimulating discussion of the distinction between negative and positive liberty, see Isaiah Berlin, *Four Essays on Liberty,* pp. 118–72. C. B. Macpherson has presented an interesting critique of Berlin's essay in his *Democratic Theory*, pp. 95–119. Like Berlin, Macpherson sees *On Liberty* as the classic statement of negative liberty. While approving of what he calls a positive "developmental liberty," Macpherson does not describe this concept in the idealist, individualist, noncoercive terms of the "self-development" that is the heart of Mill's essay and of his view of virtue.

33. See Berlin, *Four Essays,* especially pp. 152–54, 164–72.

on the whole a doctrine of freedom in the writings of Emerson and other New Englanders, the anarchist, self-worshipping tendencies of transcendentalism became clearly pronounced in the writings of Thoreau.[34] These self-indulgent, narcissistic qualities were also found in the Bloomsbury liberalism of early twentieth-century England. But Mill characteristically no more moved positive liberty to a collectivist conclusion than he did either positive or negative liberty to an anarchist one.

In 1859, in a review of a collection of Mill's essays, the Unitarian theologian James Martineau inquired, "Was he not surely destined by his high sympathies with heroic forms of character, to give the hereditary doctrine a nobler interpretation?" Martineau remarked that Mill had made an effort in the 1830s "to escape from party one-sidedness," from a Benthamite necessitarianism, but suggested that he had somehow failed to realize this early promise. The fault lay in Mill's refusal to acknowledge a priori truths or an "inner moral rule." Mill had limited his knowledge to experience, "yet not without glances of thought,—pathetic in their very anger,—towards the dark horizon of necessity and nescience around." The following year, after the publication of *On Liberty*, Martineau wrote an essay in which he contrasted the two Humboldt brothers, Alexander, who in affirming his lack of faith proclaimed himself to be of "the religion of all men of science," and his brother Wilhelm, a believer in a divine government.[35] Of course, Martineau approved of the opinions of the believing brother and could not have helped observing that in *On Liberty* Mill had based his views on those of Wilhelm rather than Alexander. Following Wilhelm in his appeal to self-assertion and conscience, Mill had striven to pierce "the dark

34. See Quentin Anderson, *The Imperial Self: An Essay in American Literary and Cultural History*.

35. James Martineau, "John Stuart Mill's Philosophy," in *Essays, Reviews, and Addresses* 3: 491–92, 494; "Nature and God," in ibid., pp. 143–44.

horizon of necessity" and to establish his ethics on an inner moral rule.

Charles Kingsley, a Carlylean and no political friend to Mill, saw *On Liberty* on a table at the shop of Mill's publisher soon after its appearance. He sat down and read it through and before leaving the bookstore remarked that it had made him "a clearer-headed, braver-minded man on the spot."[36] In his inaugural address as regius professor of history at Cambridge the following year, mentioned above, Kingsley observed that in the tract Mill had voiced a plea "unequalled" in modern times "for the self-determining power of the individual, and for his right to use that power."[37] Kingsley, a disciple of Coleridge and the Christian socialist F. D. Maurice, as well as of Carlyle, responded enthusiastically to what was for him a familiar call in behalf of the positive liberty long preached by his mentors, by the German philosophers, and by the Christian theologians of the nineteenth century.

Mill's *Three Essays on Religion* were published by his stepdaughter about a year after his death. Somewhat surprisingly, he appeared in these essays to be a man who had sought to salvage as much as he could from traditional faith. Mill held forth the hope that God possibly, even probably, did exist and the conviction that the immortality of the soul was a concept no rigorous thinker could absolutely deny. Moreover, he accepted Jesus as a model of human excellence, carefully excluding from consideration those portions of the Gospels that might inspire doubt in a nineteenth-century liberal. In his effort to unite faith and reason, Mill was prepared to accept a Deity who was beneficent and omniscient, but since apparently unable to prevent the existence of evil, not omnipotent—a compromise that resembled his efforts to reconcile free will and determinism. (Like James

36. Quoted in Bain, *John Stuart Mill,* p. 112. See also Fanny Kingsley, *Charles Kingsley: His Letters and Memories of His Life* (London, 1877) 2: 294.

37. Kingsley, *Limits of Exact Science,* p. 40.

Martineau in his sermon proclaiming his conversion to free will in the 1830s, Mill could not accept the God of the necessitarians, who was "the author of sin and suffering.") These opinions shocked a number of his admirers, most notably Alexander Bain[38] and John Morley, who took their late mentor severely to task. Morley feared that Mill's arguments were likely to serve as "the springs of a new and mischievous reaction towards supernaturalism" and particularly noted the "incongruity in the author's final appeal to a mystic sentiment."[39]

Mill had in 1852 defended utility against the faulty logic of Whewell's intuitionist attack, we recall, while laying claim to virtue on behalf of a properly conceived utilitarianism. Nearly a decade later, in his *Utilitarianism*, Mill confronted the choice of Hercules anew, and attempted to justify this claim. In the argument that aroused Jevons's doubts, Mill somewhat awkwardly reasoned his way from accepting pleasure as the greatest good to erecting a virtue that transcended the lower pleasures and became the most important element of happiness. Once more, Mill appeared to be a Stoic rather than an Epicurean: as sensual or material happiness per se almost vanished as his prime desideratum, Virtue, Duty, and Truth became his chief injunctions. In this essay, virtue and its associated qualities filled the role played by self-development in *On Liberty*, that of opponent to the necessitarian forces encouraging men to sloth and animal pleasure.

Since the time of Epicurus, Mill observed, many philosophers

38. J. S. Mill, *Three Essays on Religion* (1874), in *Collected Works* 10: 434–50, 426–28, 460–67, 416–17, 423, 451–59; Drummond and Upton, *Life and Letters of Martineau* 2: 272; Bain, *John Stuart Mill*, pp. 158, 134–36, 139.

39. See [John Morley], "Mr. Mill's Three Essays on Religion," *Fortnightly Review* 22 (1 November 1874): 637 and 23 (1 January 1875): 103–31. See also Robert Carr, "The Religious Thought of John Stuart Mill: A Study in Reluctant Scepticism," *Journal of the History of Ideas* 23 (1962): 475–95; and Karl W. Britton, "John Stuart Mill on Christianity," *Centenary Conference*, pp. 21–34.

had felt that if pleasure were the standard of morals, men would become like swine. But this view placed human nature "in a degrading light." Human beings had "faculties more elevated than the animal appetites" and "once made conscious of them, do not regard anything as happiness which does not include their gratification." While noting that the Epicurean philosophers had generally assigned to intellectual pleasures, moral sentiments, and the imagination a "much higher value" than to "mere sensation," the justification for this ranking had been made on grounds of "greater permanency, safety, uncostliness, &c." It was necessary to invoke not only circumstantial advantages but, more important, the "intrinsic nature" of the higher pleasures. (Bentham would have denounced this approach as an appeal to a fictional abstraction, and Comte might well have declared it pure metaphysics.) Mill asserted that the Epicureans had not argued the matter satisfactorily because of the severe limitations of their philosophy; to do so, "many Stoic as well as Christian elements" would have to have been included in the proof.[40]

For Mill, to recognize that some kinds of pleasure were "more desirable and more valuable than others" was entirely compatible with the principle of utility. One might judge one pleasure to be of a higher quality than another if it were decidedly preferred by those who had experienced both. Certainly those who had known intellectual pleasures did value them above all others. "Few human creatures would consent to be changed into any of the lower animals," even "for a promise of the fullest allowance of a beast's pleasures." At core, men possessed "a sense of dignity," a feeling that Mill had accused Bentham of ignoring. "It is better to be a human being dissatisfied, than a pig satisfied," he observed, paraphrasing a maxim of ancient philosophy. Together with the importance of a sense of dignity, Mill stressed "the love of liberty and personal independence" (likewise neglected by

40. J. S. Mill, *Utilitarianism* (1861), *Collected Works* 10: 210–11.

Bentham)—"an appeal to which was with the Stoics one of the most effective means for inculcation of it."[41]

Mill contrasted his view of happiness and his standard of "nobleness of character" with those set forth by Carlyle. The Scotsman had doubted any right to happiness and had urged "the lesson of Entsagen or renunciation," a view clearly akin to the Christian doctrine of self-mortification to which Mill took sharp exception. For Mill, nobility of character was a readiness to give up individual pleasure voluntarily for the happiness of others. The true utilitarian standard, he reminded his readers, was not the greatest happiness of the individual but that of the entire community. While decrying the yielding of happiness for any other reason as "no more deserving of admiration than the ascetic mounted on his pillar," Mill urged "all honour to those who can abnegate for themselves the personal enjoyment of life, when by such renunciation they contribute worthily to increase the amount of happiness in the world." This was "the highest virtue which can be found in man." This had been the virtue, he declared, of "many a Stoic in the worst times of the Roman Empire."[42]

Mill sought to persuade his readers that so noble and unselfish a philosophy as the Stoics proposed was still able to direct the lives of great masses in modern society. How could such a moral system be implanted? The principle of utility, like other systems of morals, would be inculcated and enforced by external sanctions—"the hope of favour and the fear of displeasure" from fellow citizens or from God—but more importantly by "the internal sanction of duty," and by a "pain, more or less intense, attendant on violation of duty." This was "the essence of Conscience," and this "subjective feeling in our own minds" constituted "the ultimate sanction . . . of all morality." Mill said much the same thing in his essay *On Liberty*. He did not believe that those who saw this conscious sense of moral obligation as "a transcendental fact," that is, as innate or divinely implanted, were more likely to obey

41. Ibid., pp. 211–12.
42. Ibid., pp. 214, 217–18.

its dictates than those who, like himself, saw it as "entirely subjective, having its seat in human consciousness only."[43]

Mill preached a virtue "desired disinterestedly, for itself," because, he argued (perhaps too loosely), all properly founded virtue promoted the general happiness. Virtue "as a psychological fact" might even be a good in itself to an individual, "without looking to any end beyond it." Indeed, taking up the language of the theologians, Mill declared that without such a view of virtue, "the mind is not in a right state, not in a state conformable to Utility, not in the state most conducive to the general happiness." We must love virtue even if it did not in an individual case produce the "other desirable consequences which it tends to produce."[44] It was hardly sound Benthamite doctrine to suggest that virtue was to be desired for itself, even if in a particular case it produced unhappiness.

For Mill, truth had also achieved the status of immanence. Though it might be expedient to lie to avoid a difficulty, any "deviation from truth" weakened "the trustworthiness of human assertion" upon which "all present social well-being" rested. The "insufficiency" of truth was the principal obstacle to the progress of "civilization, virtue, everything on which human happiness on the largest scale depends." "We feel that the violation, for a present advantage, of a rule of such transcendent expediency, is not expedient," he argued. Truth, then, was a rule of "transcendent expediency" and might be invoked as an ultimate principle, as was a generalized virtue in this essay, and just as individual liberty had been justified in *On Liberty* by utility "in the largest sense," "grounded on the permanent interests of man as a progressive being."[45] Idealist philosophers might attack Benthamism as being mere expediency rather than a doctrine based on principle; that charge would not fit Mill's version of utilitarianism.

Mill's doctrine was clearly not a philosophy for swine or a

43. Ibid., pp. 228–29.
44. Ibid., p. 235.
45. Ibid., p. 223; Mill, *On Liberty*, p. 224.

doctrine of selfishness, charges which had been brought against the Benthamites as they had been against the ancient Epicureans. The moral philosophy of *Utilitarianism* was at bottom the Stoic-Christian creed of virtue. A just society, Mill argued, would rely on the "person of confirmed virtue" who was prepared to ignore immediate pleasures. Nor did Mill think this view of virtue "a departure from the Happiness principle." Many elements made up the aggregate of happiness; for those who loved it, virtue was "desired and cherished, not as a means to happiness, but as a part of their happiness." The "will to be virtuous" could, he believed, be "implanted or awakened" by making a person desire virtue because he saw it could give the highest form of pleasure. It would be the "habit of virtue" upon which society must rely to defend personal liberty or property as well as other legal and moral rights.[46] Once again, Mill had made the choice of Hercules.

Was not Mill's vision of virtue much like Comte's "altruism"? Comte wished to educate men to live for others (vivre pour autrui). Mill urged the readers of *Utilitarianism* to examine Comte's system of politics and morals to convince themselves that a society ruled by the positivist religion of humanity, one of service to others, could in fact be efficiently realized. But under Comte's system, he warned, "human freedom and individuality" would be in serious danger. Nonetheless, in this tract Mill certainly appeared to be recommending a faith dedicated like that of the French thinker to "the service of humanity."[47]

Mill wished to protect the individual against the inculcation of Comte's extreme view of virtue, which would injure rather than promote the general happiness. To believe in "the Infinite nature of Duty," as did Comte, was a magnificent conception, Mill observed in an article a few years later, and it possessed a

46. Mill, *Utilitarianism*, pp. 235, 238–39.
47. Ibid., p. 232.

great capacity for inspiring service and achievement. However, Mill argued that the French thinker had made a fundamental mistake in the "rule of life" he had fashioned for his religion. In calling for "altruism" (a word Comte had coined) to conquer egoism, the positivist asked the individual to repress the satisfaction of all his personal desires other than the brute necessities. As a phrenologist, Comte had even looked forward to the atrophying from disuse of the cerebral organs associated with egoism. Mill did not object to the proposition that egoism ought to be instructed to yield to certain general interests, but he could not accept this wish "to deaden the personal passions and propensities" and to condemn and mortify all personal indulgences. Following Novalis's description of Spinoza as a God-intoxicated man, Mill described Comte as "a morality-intoxicated man." In common with other French thinkers, though in a much more extreme form, Comte had sought a kind of "unity" or harmony by which life might be somehow "systematized." When "personal propensities" predominated, that unity, never actually attainable, could not even be approximated. It was therefore necessary to subordinate these propensities, in Mill's words, to "the social feelings, which may be made to act in a uniform direction by a common system of convictions." For Mill, "the *fons errorum*" of Comte's doctrines was this "inordinate demand for 'unity' and 'systematization.'"[48]

Might it be argued that any system, logically pursued, was illiberal? This was especially the case when the issue was happiness. "May it not be the fact," Mill inquired, "that mankind, who after all are made up of single human beings, obtain a greater sum of happiness when each pursues his own [ends], under the rules and conditions required by the good of the rest than when each makes the good of the rest his only subject, and allows himself no personal pleasure not indispensable to the preservation of his faculties?" "The regimen of a blockaded town should be

48. Mill, "Auguste Comte and Positivism," pp. 335–36.

cheerfully submitted to when high purposes require it," he added, "but is it the ideal perfection of human existence?" Comte had apparently felt that all men should model themselves after him. "It would never do [for him] to suppose that there could be more than one road to happiness, or more than one ingredient in it," Mill observed.[49]

For his part, Mill put forward an ideal of life that stressed "personal enjoyments" while it educated individuals to wish to share them with others. People who disinterestedly tried to promote the general good, as did Mill's men of habitual virtue, were certainly worthy of praise—so long as such behavior was spontaneous, "so long as they are in no way compelled to this conduct by any external pressure." For "the notion of a happiness for all, procured by the self-sacrifice of each . . . is a contradiction." Mill wished to leave room for the "sympathetic encouragement" that made "self-devotion pleasant, not that of making everything else painful." One might encourage service to others by "natural rewards," rather than burden the pursuit of our own interests and inclinations "by visiting it with the reproaches of others and of our own conscience."[50]

Comte had desired that men should not merely be ready to set aside personal interests in favor of the general good, but should regard following personal inclinations as inherently wicked, as a confession that their lives were not in "complete unity." The positivist ought, in the manner of the Catholic church, to have distinguished between the commonly accepted standard of moral obligation, which widened with society's progress and which alone was necessary for salvation, and the higher standard that marked the saint. Instead, like "extreme Calvinists," Comte had damned all who were not saints.[51] Mill saw his man of habitual

49. Ibid., p. 337.
50. Ibid., p. 338.
51. Ibid., pp. 337, 338.

virtue as saintlike, on the model of the Stoic republicans of ancient Rome, but he was too practical—and too unsystematic—to conceive that all men could or need become saints.

In 1867, the poet and essayist Matthew Arnold published his *Culture and Anarchy,* a tract that repeated the humanist themes of Carlyle's "Signs of the Times" nearly forty years earlier. Arnold's enemies, like Carlyle's, had put their faith in a mechanical and material civilization and had sought greatness in wealth rather than in moral improvement. Early in the work, Arnold took issue with the Radical leader John Bright and the barrister Frederic Harrison, Comte's English disciple, for their denigration of classical culture, which he believed resembled true Christianity in seeking to cultivate the perfection of the inner man and to establish it on a social and not merely an individual basis. Arnold recollected having read in Bentham's *Deontology* that Socrates and Plato had been speaking "nonsense under the pretence of teaching wisdom and morality"; from that moment, he declared, he was delivered from "the bondage of Bentham" and "the fanaticism of his adherents." Culture was the enemy of the "system-makers and systems." "Men like Comte or the late Mr. Buckle, or Mr. Mill," he observed, were the enemies of culture and the advocates of moral anarchy.[52]

The gospel of the modern liberal, Arnold continued, was that of "doing as one likes," while culture aimed at shaping each individual as closely as possible into what was beautiful and good in accordance with a spiritual standard of perfection. Following the ancient Greek ideal, culture wished to subdue "the great obvious faults of our animality." The modern liberal idea of freedom without restraint posed the danger of drifting toward a dangerous anarchy. Arnold sought to persuade his countrymen that the proper rule was not to do what one wished, but to do

52. Matthew Arnold, *Culture and Anarchy*, pp. 53–54.

what right reason ordained. He saw the ideal state as "the organ of our collective best self, of our national right reason."[53]

Arnold was clearly wrong in pillorying Mill as an enemy of culture and an advocate of a new moral anarchy. Nor was Mill a system maker; indeed, he opposed system making, as we have seen. Despite certain marks of a mechanical liberalism, which led observers astray, then as now—his associationist psychology, for instance, and his political economy—Mill, like Arnold, was a humanist dedicated to achieving the inner perfection of man. Like Arnold, he enjoined men to call upon their best selves and to practice virtue.

Arnold thought well of Wilhelm von Humboldt, "one of the most beautiful souls that ever existed," and approved of his message that (in Arnold's words) "one's business in life was first to perfect oneself by all the means in one's power," and then to create a society with a numerous aristocracy of talent and character. These of course were Mill's goals as well. But Arnold believed that Humboldt's outlook was not appropriate for the England of his day, whose people tended not so much to overdependence on the state, as to unrestrained individualism.[54] Six years later, the Benthamite James Fitzjames Stephen likewise insisted that fears of the social tyranny of public opinion trampling on individuality and diversity were foolish, though he had argued rather differently around the time Mill's essay first appeared.[55] Individuality and even eccentricity flourished in England as never before, Stephen

53. Ibid., pp. 45, 79; for Arnold on virtue and the general good, see pp. 90–91 and 104 especially. For a perceptive comparison of Arnold and Mill, see Edward Alexander, *Matthew Arnold and John Stuart Mill.*

54. Arnold, *Culture and Anarchy*, pp. 105–06.

55. In 1858, a year before the publication of *On Liberty*, Stephen had written a review of Buckle's *History* in which he acknowledged the difficulty of freely discussing certain questions in England, particularly those concerning religion and morals: "Intellectual cowardice is the only form of that vice which is at all common in this country, but it prevails to a lamentable degree. Most writers are so nervous about the tendencies of their books, and the social penalties of unorthodox opinions are so severe, and are exacted in so unsparing a manner, that philosophy, criticism, and science itself too often speak among us in ambiguous

argued in 1872;[56] other liberals, Macaulay among them, had earlier voiced this view.[57] If this was the case, what purpose could Mill's essay serve except as an invitation to moral anarchy?

In his autobiography, Mill acknowledged that superficially England did not appear to need the lesson offered in *On Liberty*. Fears that "the inevitable growth of social equality and of the government of public opinion" would impose "an oppressive yoke of uniformity in opinion and practice" might well seem fanciful to those who saw only the present situation. A readiness to listen to new views was characteristic of periods of transition, when old ideas were unsettled. The message of *On Liberty* was not for such a time. But Mill had been primarily concerned with long-range tendencies. In the coming organic period, "some particular body of doctrine" would dominate public opinion and would organize "social institutions and modes of action conformably to itself." The new creed would soon acquire the "power of compression" exercised by the dominant views of other organic periods, unless men became aware that such "noxious power" could not be exercised "without stunting and dwarfing human nature." It would be when the new organic period arrived that "the teachings of the 'Liberty' will have their greatest value," and Mill was persuaded "that they will retain that value a long time."[58] Far from issuing a call to anarchy and libertinism, Mill

whispers what ought to be proclaimed from the house tops. There are many of Mr. Buckle's speculations with which we do not agree, but we admire the courage with which he propounds them." See [James Fitzjames Stephen], *Edinburgh Review* 107 (April 1858): article 7, p. 471.

56. James Fitzjames Stephen, *Liberty, Equality, Fraternity*. This was the first thoroughgoing critique of *On Liberty*; see discussion in Himmelfarb, *On Liberty and Liberalism,* pp. 161–65. As a consistent utilitarian, Stephen, like Jevons, saw *On Liberty* as a product of a "sentimental mood" and of Mill's desertion from "the proper principles of rigidity and ferocity in which he was brought up." See Leslie Stephen, *The Life of Sir James Fitzjames Stephen* (London, 1895), p. 308.

57. See G. O. Trevelyan, *The Life and Letters of Lord Macaulay* (London, 1923), 2: 671.

58. *Autobiography*, pp. 177–78.

wished to preserve a gleam of inner freedom in the repressive climate of the coming organic society. At the close of Europe's previous organic period, Protestantism had enjoined the positive freedom and duty of the individual strenuously to seek personal salvation. The German romantics and idealists had called for the positive freedom of self-realization as a defense against petty despots and officious bureaucracies. Similarly, the pursuit of positive liberty would prove useful against a future tyranny of public opinion molded by priests of humanity or by bureaucrats.

Mill was certainly no party to Bentham's crude dismissal of the humanist tradition. Some thirty years before Arnold's attack, we recall, Mill had condemned Bentham for his rejection of liberty and the "law of nature, social compact, &c." as "fictive abstractions," mere "sacramental expressions," and for having described a moral sense or right reason as nonsense. While Bentham's speculations were "eminently systematic and consistent," he had observed, the utilitarian philosopher had understood only half the truth. For Bentham had neglected the "individual personality" and had failed both to recognize man as "capable of pursuing spiritual perfection" and to perceive "the existence of conscience" as distinct from philanthropy or self-interest. Nor had Bentham understood "that grand duty of man," self-formation and self-realization.[59] Mill had observed that the mechanical order that derived from the felicific calculus was Bentham's highest, almost his only, concern. The utilitarian had had little experience of life and lacked sympathy for the wide range of human emotions; he had never known passion, adversity, or sickness. "He knew no dejection, no heaviness of heart. He never felt life a sore and weary burthen. He was a boy to the last." Nor had he ever experienced the "daemon" of "self-consciousness."[60] Mill knew both dejection and the burden of self-consciousness all too well and had written both *On Liberty* and *Utilitarianism* to provide

59. See chap. 3 and above, this chapter.
60. Mill, "Bentham," p. 92.

liberals with that critical other half of life that Bentham and Comte had neglected.

In the final analysis, Mill was prepared to follow neither of his former mentors, Bentham and Comte, to the logical conclusions of their systems for promoting the welfare of the majority. For Mill, as he had observed in 1838, the power of the majority had to be "tempered by respect for the personality of the individual, and reverence for superiority of cultivated intelligence."[61] In his essays *On Liberty* and *Utilitarianism,* Mill had sought in the self-development expounded by the German idealists a counter to the logic of Bentham and Comte, a remedy to the faults he had perceived in their views decades earlier. He also turned to the Stoic faith of republican Rome, with its adherence to virtue, duty, and truth as transcendent ideals. Clearly, these values were of decisive importance to Mill's conception of a good society.

Mill understood, as the Benthamites and Comtians did not, that in modern, mass society, the best and most benevolently founded *system* would merely confirm the tendency toward liberticide. Perhaps it would be more accurate to say not that the Benthamites and Comtians failed to understand these threats to liberty, but that liberty was not one of their central values. They were dedicated to material happiness, to the general contentment of the masses to whom liberty, honor, and the other abstractions must always come after economic and psychological satisfaction.

Mill, on the other hand, had chosen a road different from that of either Bentham's mechanical utility or Comte's beseiged-city altruism. For him, the genuine welfare of society had to be based on the humanist values of individual personality, personal dignity, and spiritual perfection. Mill had no doubt that the permanent interests of the human race depended first on their following the example of Hercules: he perceived that liberty and a good society could survive only if men were ready to prefer a virtue that could yield the highest and most meaningful happiness over a shortsighted sensual and material pleasure.

61. Ibid., pp. 108–09.

EPILOGUE

Liberalism at the Crossroads

THE GRAND PHILOSOPHICAL PROBLEMS THAT PERMEATED John Stuart Mill's writings had absorbed thinkers for millennia; in 1867, in his rectorial address to the University of St. Andrews, Mill described them as man's relationship to time and space, the connection between matter and spirit, and whether man's will was free or determined.[1] Mill had in fact translated these metaphysical questions into the terms used in the study of individual ethics and society. We may see in his views on God and history and in his stress on the need for both order and progress his perception of man's connection with social time and space. The other two problems were embodied in the choice of Hercules. Hercules' power to choose transferred the problem of free will and determinism from the metaphysical (and scientific) to the social sphere. Similarly, we may see a social and moral translation of the antinomy between spirit and matter in the choice between virtue and happiness.

The Stoic model of Hercules' choice was before Mill to the last; its lessons informed all his thinking. When discussing the

1. Mill, *Inaugural Address*, p. 64. Carlyle, in his "Signs of the Times" in 1829, had described those problems as "the grand secrets of Necessity and Freewill, of the Mind's vital or non-vital dependence on Matter, of our mysterious relations to Time and Space, to God, to the Universe"; see Carlyle, *Works* 27: 64.

thought of the ancients in his later years, he wrote fondly of that moral myth and of its author, Prodicus. In 1853, for example, Mill defended the Sophists against the commonly held view of them as "knaves and profligates," observing that not only might both Socrates and Plato be numbered among them, but that they taught the "morality of the age in its best form"; he cited as proof that "the apologue of the Choice of Hercules was the composition of a Sophist." Again, in 1866 he described that apologue as "one of the most impressive exhortations in ancient literature to a life of labour and self-denial in preference to one of ease and pleasure." On this last occasion, Mill had taken the opportunity in an essay on Plato to reiterate his loyalty to the Socratic virtues which his father had inculcated. He praised Plato's *Gorgias* as inspiring "the cultivation of a disinterested preference of duty for its own sake," "a higher state than that of sacrificing self-preferences to a more distant self-interest," and lauded the Stoics, who had "the glory of being the earliest thinkers who grounded the obligation of morals on the brotherhood . . . of the whole human race."[2] For on the duty that enjoined the subordination of personal interest to that of the community and of humanity as a whole depended genuine progress and the highest happiness.

For Mill, moreover, there was an intimate articulation between the three great problems of social metaphysics—those of free will and determinism, virtue and happiness, and of order and progress—and his solutions to them, an interconnection that gave a decided shape and direction to his ideas, and formed not so much a system as a faith. But this faith was not that of the liberal stereotype of either Mill's time or our own. For Mill was not prepared to see man as innately virtuous, nor progress as inevitable. He believed, as we have seen, in the tendency of all things to decay and, in

2. J. S. Mill, "Grote's History of Greece" (1853), in *Essays on Philosophy and the Classics, Collected Works* 11: 329; "Grote's Plato" (1866), *Collected Works* 11: 391–92, 416, 419.

a posthumously published essay, depicted man in his natural state as a wild animal. Whatever was good about humanity, he declared, was a product not of nature or necessity but of will, not of instinct but "of a victory over instinct." Only after long efforts of education could virtue become a habit. Courage, supposedly a characteristic of savage man, had in fact to be taught, to enable mankind to overcome its natural fearfulness; even the selfish postponement of present for future happiness was "most unnatural to the undisciplined human being." If the self-regarding virtues were not instinctive, certainly neither were the social virtues. Contrary to sentimental writers like Rousseau, Mill insisted that savages were generally liars who had no conception of "truth as a virtue"; similarly artificial was the supposedly natural sentiment of justice.[3]

Yet despite his rejection of the concept of the natural goodness of man, Mill, no less than Matthew Arnold, was in the mainstream of the humanist and liberal tradition in his confidence in human perfectibility, even while he stressed the difficulties of the process. He urged that men and women not resign themselves to their animality. Mankind had the obligation not to follow what were falsely called the dictates of nature but to improve that nature, not to yield to a supposed necessity but to cultivate virtue. We must assume that Providence intended only that which was good, Mill declared, and assist that intention by our freely willed actions. Mill refused, for example, to accept as a purpose of nature or of the Deity that "the strong should prey upon the weak," that "a large proportion of all animals should pass their existence in tormenting and devouring other animals." Such instincts as those that led men to destroy, to dominate others, and to perpetrate cruelties ought not to be indulged, but weakened by lack of use.[4]

3. J. S. Mill, "Nature," *Collected Works* 10: 393–96.

4. Ibid., pp. 396–98. J. M. Robson has discussed Mill's various attempts to distinguish man's sensual or instinctual animality from his rational humanity. He suggests that Mill discriminated between such unpleasant and self-indulgent "tendencies" or "propensities" as pugnacity or cruelty and the unfolding and

The view of Mill as pre-Darwinian in having somehow failed to profit by the revelation of the *Origin of Species* is a common one. But Mill had read both the *Origin* and Herbert Spencer's works on biology and society, which owed much to Darwin's influence. He was prepared to accept Darwin's hypothesis as highly suggestive, but not as proven (which was in fact the case); he certainly did not wish to join Spencer and others who transferred evolutionary theory to human society, seeing it as a revelation of what was natural and therefore inevitable in the life of mankind. If the view of life as a struggle for existence prevailed, he believed that it would rationalize the rule of the strongest and most vicious.[5] Mill had no intention of accepting a social-Darwinian necessity and called upon men to seek virtue in order to frustrate this supposed design of a natural Providence.

Commercial and egalitarian societies in our century, in a much more decided way than in the previous one, have almost entirely given themselves up to necessity and physical happiness. In 1938, John Maynard Keynes, who regarded himself as being in the humanist tradition, saw Bloomsbury liberalism as having "perhaps alone amongst our generation" escaped the influence of Benthamism, which he, much as Carlyle and Arnold earlier, believed to be "the worm which has been gnawing at the insides of modern civilization and is responsible for its present moral decay." Bloomsbury's escape from Benthamism and its "unsurpassable individualism," Keynes wrote, served "to protect the whole lot of us from the final *reductio ad absurdum* of Benthamism known as Marxism." The Cambridge aesthetes of Bloomsbury

generally benign possibilities of man's "capacities." It was to the human capacities for a virtuous altruism and not to the more animal propensities that Mill looked for "the improvement of mankind." J. M. Robson, "Rational Animals and Others," in *Centenary Conference*, pp. 148–54, 159.

5. Mill to Alexander Bain, 11 April 1860 and Mill to H. C. Watson, 30 January 1869, *LL*, pp. 695, 1553–54; Mill to Herbert Spencer, 2 December 1868 and Mill to E. L. Youmans, March 1869, *LL*, pp. 1505, 1570; Mill, "Nature," pp. 398–99.

had regarded Christianity as their principal antagonist in the Edwardian years. By the 1930s their enemies had become Marxism and the Benthamite calculus, with their "over-valuation of the economic criterion" in portraying men as mere creatures of economic necessity, just as other thinkers saw them as the playthings of their sexual drives.[6]

Keynes boasted that Bloomsbury breathed "a purer, sweeter air by far than Freud cum Marx,"[7] the intellectual combine that has dominated the thought of advanced liberals in our time. It is not surprising that a commercial civilization that values material accumulation so highly should convince itself that men will respond to no other motive. The prevalence of such a determinist and materialist outlook, moreover, contains an element of self-fulfillment; men are persuaded to behave as they are told nature intended. A crude Freudianism that uses a sexual criterion as its leading principle for comprehending human behavior has become sometimes the alternative and sometimes the ally to this crude Marxism, for if the tendency of modern commercial society has been to promote self-indulgent pleasure rather than virtue, that pleasure is sensual as well as material, as Mill understood. Here, too, mankind is portrayed as in the grip of powerful natural forces: to attempt to resist them, we are warned, would mean to suffer the penalties of repression. We have turned to a routine of libertinism that jeopardizes not only sexual pleasure but, more important (as Freud himself warned), the fabric of civilized society. (Certainly Freud himself did not see men as mere creatures of the id, of animal instinct,[8] any more than Marx subscribed to

6. Keynes, *Two Memoirs*, pp. 96–97.

7. Ibid., p. 92.

8. Peter Gay has discussed the problem of free will and determinism in Freud's thought in his "Freud and Freedom; On a Fox in Hedgehog's Clothing," in *Idea of Freedom*, ed. Ryan, pp. 41–59. Gay has stressed the importance of choice in Freud's psychology while noting that its range was much narrower than choosers believed (p. 48). The object of psychoanalysis, Gay observed, is "to *enlarge* the area of freedom" by making it possible for the individual to see and to take into account the unconscious, irrational determinants to which he

the mechanical, economic determinism of some who have called themselves his disciples.)[9]

But Keynes, despite his success in avoiding what he described as the "bogus faiths" of a Marxism and a Freudianism that regarded men as the puppets of economic interest or sexual impulses, fell into another and as dangerous a snare: the Bloomsbury circle indulged itself, Keynes declared, in a "disastrously mistaken" view of people as sufficiently "reliable, rational, decent," and ready to embrace objective truth not to require conventional restraints and rules of behavior. In the classic choice described by Prodicus, its members freely chose pleasure, not because they saw themselves under the sway of animal necessity, but because they were willfully narcissistic. This proved a dangerous course. By the late 1930s, Keynes had become convinced that there were "insane and irrational springs of wickedness in most men." In ignoring these and irreverently devaluing the forces that made for order and stability, Bloomsbury, anticipating the liberalism of the middle and late decades of the century, had gone too far. "We were not aware," Keynes wrote, "that civilization was a thin and precarious crust erected by the personality and the will of a very few, and only maintained by rules and conventions skilfully put across and guilefully perserved."[10]

"We were living in the specious present," Keynes continued

---

has been subject. Gay's conclusion was that "Sigmund Freud was a determinist, yet his psychology is a psychology of freedom" (p. 41).

9. Marx had of course contrasted his economic determinism with the idealism of the German philosophers in his and Engels's *The German Ideology* (1846). In this early work, however, they were prepared to see a certain reciprocity, observing that "circumstances make men just as much as men make circumstances." Marx later believed the end of the market system would liberate the power of men to shape their own destinies. See Duncan, *Marx and Mill*, pp. 289–91. For recent Marxist critiques of crude deterministic Marxism, with its rejection of a humanist and moral perspective, see Martin Jay, *The Dialectical Imagination: A History of the Frankfurt School and the Institute of Social Research, 1923–1950* (Boston, 1973); and E. P. Thompson, *The Poverty of Theory and Other Essays* (New York, 1978).

10. Keynes, *Two Memoirs*, pp. 97–99.

in his critical evaluation of Bloomsbury liberalism, "nor had begun to play the game of consequences." Keynes himself, one may argue, was to the end vulnerable to this charge. We may speculate, for example, whether he had conscientiously calculated the consequences of the economic program he proposed. In 1919, Keynes, much like Mill earlier, had denounced the debauching of the currency as a sure way of "overturning the existing basis of society" and engaging "all the hidden forces of economic law on the side of destruction." With the coming of the hard times of the 1930s, however, Keynes responded to a short-range expediency and knowingly urged practical remedies of a directly inflationary character. When warned of grave future difficulties by critics of his policies, difficulties he himself had well understood for several years, the self-acknowledged "immoralist" is supposed to have replied, "in the long run we'll all be dead." As Keynes confessed in his *Memoirs,* Bloomsbury lived "entirely in present experience";[11] in the vanguard of twentieth-century liberalism, he opted for a transitory material happiness at the risk, as he himself believed, of undermining the fabric of society.

If Keynesian economics and crude Marxian and Freudian interpretations of men and history have been among the leading insignia of many contemporary liberals, so has a necessitarian behavioral psychology, whose outstanding representative has been B. F. Skinner. Skinner, a builder of utopias, has seen man as a machine or an animal and has presented this view as a decided scientific advance.[12] He has quoted approvingly the statement of the nineteenth-century Darwinian T. H. Huxley that "if some great power would agree to make me always think what is true and do what is right, on condition of being some sort of clock and wound up each morning before I got out of bed, I should

11. Ibid., p. 95; John Maynard Keynes, *The Economic Consequences of the Peace* (London, 1920), pp. 220–21; Keynes, *Two Memoirs*, p. 96 (see also p. 98).

12. B. F. Skinner, *Beyond Freedom and Dignity*, p. 201 especially.

instantly close with the offer."[13] Skinner's principal target has been "the myth" of autonomous man and the idea of free will that supports it. The chief enemy of a scientific view of behavior, he has written, is "the literature of freedom and dignity." Understandably, John Stuart Mill, despite the links between behaviorism and Mill's associationalism, is his principal villain.[14]

In the best Comtian (or Marxist) manner, Skinner has described the rights to life, liberty, and the pursuit of happiness as historically connected with "the aggrandizement of the individual" at the expense of society. The advocates of freedom and dignity have vaunted man as "a moral hero," possessing "inner virtues" and engaged in a grand "moral struggle," he has noted. Skinner did not wish to encourage such a struggle but "to make life less punishing":[15] like Bloomsbury, he urged men to yield to a sensually gratifying happiness; like Bentham and Comte, he welcomed a future, in the words of the title of his best-known work, "beyond freedom and dignity." A commercial society, as Mill had understood over a century earlier, had little use for either moral or physical heroism and held no value greater than animal contentment.

In the past generation, social scientists—resembling the scientific and technical cadres of Comte's elite—became convinced that their expertise could bring about an era of social and personal happiness. They too believed that they could "make life less punishing," and like Mill's Owenite opponents attributed none

13. Quoted in ibid., p. 66.

14. See, for example, ibid., pp. 20, 32, 61, 70. For a friendly view of Skinner's battle against the humanist tradition, see C. E. Wollner, "Behaviorism and Humanism: B. F. Skinner and the Western Intellectual Tradition," *Review of Existential Psychology and Psychiatry* 14, no. 3 (1975–76): 146–68. The humanist opposition to Skinner among psychologists has been led by Carl R. Rogers; see his "In Retrospect, Forty-Six Years," *American Psychologist* 29, no. 2 (February 1974): 118–19. See also Leonard Krasner, "The Future and the Past in the Behaviorism-Humanism Dialogue," *American Psychologist* 33, no. 9 (September 1978): 799–804.

15. Skinner, *Beyond Freedom and Dignity*, pp. 180, 81.

of man's ills to himself or to the human condition but rather regarded all as consequences of a remediable malfunctioning of society. Psychologists, employing the wisdom of the behaviorists or of the psychoanalysts, would inaugurate a time of personal contentment; sociologists believed they could disentangle class and racial conflicts; Keynesian economists, despite their master's doubts concerning Benthamism, were certain they could produce the greatest material happiness for the greatest number. The effect of much of this was to foster a new paternalism—to promote an increased dependence upon the state instead of the individual independence and self-dependence that Mill had urged. The personal and social problems, of course, remain unsolved. We now recognize that social science has failed to realize its hubristic, utopian claims,[16] and find we must look again at Mill's at once more modest and less easily attained solution.

In his autobiography, Mill described as his "philosophy of life" an "anti-self-consciousness theory" he had borrowed from Carlyle. Seeing happiness as "the test of all rules of conduct, and the end of life," Mill considered happy only those who fixed their minds on some goal other than their own happiness—"on the happiness of others," he suggested, "on the improvement of mankind"; this goal might be "some art or pursuit, followed not as a means, but as itself an ideal end." This was the role that the pursuit of virtue was to enact in Mill's own life, and he wished to have this "ideal end" play a similar role in the life of society as a whole. Elsewhere, he observed that the existence of an "ideal nobleness of character, or of a near approach to it, in any abundance, would go further than all things else towards making human life happy." He defined this happiness "both in the comparatively humble sense, of pleasure and freedom from pain, and in the higher meaning, of rendering life, not what it

16. For an account of this failure, see C. E. Lindblom and D. R. Cohen, *Social Science and Social Problem Solving* (New Haven, 1979).

now is almost universally, puerile and insignificant—but such as human beings with highly developed faculties can care to have."[17]

Could Mill's goal of moral improvement for a mass, commercial society, one that would make possible the highest form of happiness, prove realizable? How, moreover, could one instill virtue without destroying liberty? These were the problems that Mill faced and, sometimes uncertainly and ambiguously, moved to solve. The more traditional philosophers of free will had invoked a God-implanted soul as the mechanism of virtue, but we have seen that Mill's answer lay in a man-made conscience. Although possessing a religious sense, Mill was too much in the Enlightenment tradition to make use of supernatural support. He could only urge a moral education based on associationalist principles and thus appeared illogically to call on psychological determinism to inspire a freely willed virtue.

There were other occasions when Mill's views suffered from inner contradictions or displayed one-sidedness instead of their characteristic balance. We have observed, for example, Mill's sometimes uncritical acceptance of Comte's sociology of history;[18] in this Mill found himself caught up in a relatively unstable mix of deterministic and voluntaristic elements that transformed history into an arena for the confrontation between historical necessity and individual virtue. We also recollect his dismissal of evidence that called into question man's innate equality. Yet while biological science could not yet come to definitive conclusions concerning hereditary differences among men, or between men and women, there were no stronger grounds for justifying Mill's exclusively environmentalist position. This environmentalism also provided a field for the exercise of self-development and virtue, though

17. *Autobiography*, p. 106; Mill, *System of Logic*, p. 952.

18. See Karl R. Popper, *The Poverty of Historicism*, where the historical sociology of Comte and Mill appears in the forefront of ideological "historicist" thinking.

no doubt Harriet Taylor's doctrinaire faith in sexual equality played some role in shaping Mill's belief.[19]

Some writers have consequently argued that Mill was an ideologue. For a few years in the late 1820s and early 1830s, when he saw himself as a leader of the young Benthamites, this was probably true in good part.[20] But Mill soon gave up what narrow sectarianism he possessed, as we have observed.[21] From the mid-1830s onward, an abhorrence of any one-sided system—whether that of Bentham, of Coleridge, or of Comte—distinguished his intellectual posture. This is why his rare descents into doctrinaire thinking, as on the questions of equality and of Comte's social dynamics, are matters of special interest. Certainly Mill's pursuit of virtue had none of the authoritarian and sectarian fanaticism historically associated with that goal in men like Robespierre or Savonarola. Mill's virtue, as he stressed in discussing Comte's ideal of "altruism," was not that of a perfection imposed upon men but rather Goethe's goal of self-perfection—not a state-directed, coercive model of development but one of individual self-development leading to self-dependence, and, significantly, diversity in patterns of life.

Mill called on men and women to achieve a positive liberty, to assume the control over their lives necessary to individual self-development and to both order and social progress. He spoke of "the feeling of moral freedom" that came when an individual believed that he could modify his own character if he wished,

19. Harriet Taylor's influence has been stressed most recently, as noted earlier, by Gertrude Himmelfarb in *On Liberty and Liberalism*, pp. 187–207.

20. See, for example, Joseph Hamburger, *Intellectuals in Politics: John Stuart Mill and the Philosophic Radicals*, pp. 1–29, and 276–87 especially. A similar view of the "theoretical extremism" of the Benthamites is taken by William Thomas in *The Philosophic Radicals: Nine Studies in Theory and Practice, 1817–1841* (see especially pp. 445–53). On the other hand, Thomas has observed that "John Mill's education and experiences had made him suspicious of orthodoxy of any sort" (p. 453).

21. See Mill to Lytton Bulwer, 23 November 1836, *EL*, p. 312; and discussion above, in prologue and elsewhere.

that he was master of his habits and temptations. To "render our consciousness of freedom complete," we must have already succeeded in efforts of self-improvement, or else "we are not free." In the 1868 edition of the *Logic*, nine years after the publication of the essay *On Liberty*, Mill added, "And hence it is said with truth, that none but a person of confirmed virtue is completely free."[22]

Mill reconciled positive and negative liberty. He argued that only when an individual was permitted to develop freely, without unnecessary social or political constraints, could he become self-dependent and participate usefully in the life of his society. And he believed that only by promoting the interests of others could a man further his personal development. A life of isolation from society, or one given up entirely to self-interest, diminished individuality and consequently diminished individual liberty.

Mill was convinced that all historical progress was powered by conflict. We recall that he had agreed with Comte on the central role played by the struggle between the spiritual and the temporal powers in having kept medieval Europe from both despotism and stagnation. A Manichaean struggle between good and evil was implicit in his theology, with its benevolent but not omnipotent God. While noting his father's attraction to this religious position, Mill claimed to disown it. Yet he had semi-consciously adopted a social Manichaeanism. For a Manichaean, he wrote, the world was a battleground on which the forces of decay, which relied on instinct, sloth, and the animal necessities, fought continually with those of improvement, which depended on virtue. This was Mill's world. "A virtuous being assumes [for a Manichaean] . . . the exalted character of a fellow-labourer with the Highest, a fellow-combattant in the great strife," Mill declared, "contributing his little, which by the aggregation of many like himself becomes much, towards that progressive ascendancy, and

22. Mill, *System of Logic*, p. 841. See Charles Taylor, "What's Wrong With Negative Liberty," in *Idea of Freedom*, ed. Alan Ryan, p. 177.

ultimately complete triumph of good over evil." "Against the moral tendency of this creed no possible objection can lie," he concluded; it could have "no other than an ennobling effect."[23]

This "ennobling effect" was felt by those who like Hercules at the crossroads had chosen virtue—and so had made possible both liberty and a higher happiness. The elder Mill had instructed his son to make this choice, and in both his writings and his life Mill recommended it to his countrymen, particularly to those who shared his liberal convictions. The story of the choice of Hercules was Mill's personal myth. He sought to make its lesson the public morality of all of society. Like the ancient philosophers whom he admired, and their Christian-Stoic disciples of the Renaissance, as well as the moral philosophers of the Scottish Enlightenment and the humanists Carlyle and Matthew Arnold, Mill understood that a good society could not long survive the eclipse of a freely chosen virtue.

23. See Mill to Comte, 25 February 1842, *Lettres inédites*, pp. 28–29; *Autobiography*, p. 28. Mill, "Utility of Religion" (1874), *Collected Works* 10: 425. Eisenach has seen Mill as pursuing "a kind of religious quest" in his efforts to achieve a better world. See E. J. Eisenach, *Two Worlds of Liberalism: Religion and Politics in Hobbes, Locke, and Mill*, p. 201.

Selected Bibliography

Alexander, Edward. *Matthew Arnold and John Stuart Mill.* New York: Columbia University Press, 1965.

———. "The Principles of Permanence and Progression in the Thought of J. S. Mill." In *James and John Stuart Mill: Papers of the Centenary Conference*, ed. John M. Robson and Michael Laine. Toronto: University of Toronto Press, 1976.

Anderson, Quentin. *The Imperial Self: An Essay in American Literary and Cultural History.* New York: Knopf, 1971.

Annan, Noel. "John Stuart Mill." In *The English Mind,* ed. H. S. Davies and G. Watson. Cambridge: Cambridge University Press, 1964.

Anschutz, R. P. "J. S. Mill, Carlyle, and Mrs. Taylor." *Political Science* 7 (1955): 65–75.

———. *The Philosophy of J. S. Mill.* Oxford: Clarendon Press, 1953.

Arendt, Hannah. *The Life of the Mind.* 2 vols. New York: Harcourt, Brace, 1978.

Arnold, Matthew. *Culture and Anarchy.* 1867. Reprint. New York: Bobbs Merrill, 1971.

Bain, Alexander. *John Stuart Mill, a Criticism: With Personal Recollections.* London: Longmans, 1882.

Baron, Hans. *The Crisis of the Early Italian Renaissance.* Princeton: Princeton University Press, 1966.

Berlin, Isaiah. *Four Essays on Liberty.* Oxford: Oxford University Press, 1969.

Britton, Karl W. *John Stuart Mill.* New York: Dover, 1969.

———. "John Stuart Mill on Christianity." In *James and John Stuart Mill; Papers of the Centenary Conference,* ed. John M. Robson and Michael Laine. Toronto: University of Toronto Press, 1976.

Bruford, W. F. *The German Tradition of Self-Cultivation: Bildung from Humboldt to Thomas Mann.* Cambridge: Cambridge University Press, 1975.

Buckle, Henry Thomas. *A History of Civilization in England.* 2 vols. 1857 and 1861. Reprint. New York: D. Appleton, 1882.

———. *Miscellaneous and Posthumous Works of Henry Thomas Buckle.* Ed. Helen Taylor. 3 vols. London: Longmans, 1872.

Burns, J. H. "The Light of Reason: Philosophical History in the Two Mills." In *James and John Stuart Mill: Papers of the Centenary Conference*, ed. John M. Robson and Michael Laine. Toronto: University of Toronto Press, 1976.

Carlyle, Thomas. *The Collected Letters of Thomas and Jane Welsh Carlyle.* Ed. C. R. Sanders and K. J. Fielding. Durham, N.C.: Duke University Press, 1970–.

———. *The Works of Thomas Carlyle.* Ed. H. D. Traill. New York: Scribner & Sons, 1904.

Carr, Robert. "The Religious Thought of John Stuart Mill: A Study in Reluctant Scepticism." *Journal of the History of Ideas* 23 (1962): 475–95.

Coleridge, Samuel Taylor. *Collected Works of Samuel Taylor Coleridge.* Vol. 1. Ed. Lewis Patton and Peter Mann. Princeton: Princeton University Press, 1971.

———. *Letters of Samuel Taylor Coleridge.* Ed. E. H. Coleridge. Vol. 1. London: Heinemann, 1895.

Comte, Auguste. *Cours de philosophie positive.* Vols. 4–6. Paris: Bachelier, 1830–42.

———. *The Positive Philosophy of Auguste Comte.* Ed. Harriet Martineau. 2 vols. London: Trübner & Co., 1875.

———. *System of Positive Polity.* 4 vols. New York: B. Franklin, 1968.

Coser, Lewis A. *Masters of Sociological Thought: Ideas in Historical and Social Context.* New York: Harcourt, Brace, 1971.

Courtney, William Leonard. *Life of John Stuart Mill.* London: Scott, 1889.

———. *The Metaphysics of John Stuart Mill.* London: Kegan, Paul, 1879.

Cowling, Maurice. *Mill and Liberalism*. Cambridge: Cambridge University Press, 1963.

Cranston, Maurice. *John Stuart Mill*. London: Longmans, Green, 1958.

Cumming, Robert D. *Human Nature and History; A Study of the Development of Liberal Political Thought*. Chicago: University of Chicago Press, 1969.

Drescher, Seymour. *Tocqueville and England*. Cambridge, Mass.: Harvard University Press, 1964.

Drummond, J., and C. B. Upton. *The Life and Letters of James Martineau*. 2 vols. London: Nisbet, 1902.

Duncan, Graeme. *Marx and Mill: Two Views of Social Conflict and Social Harmony*. Cambridge: Cambridge University Press, 1973.

Duncan, Graeme and John Gray. "The Left Against Mill." In *New Essays on John Stuart Mill and Utilitarianism*, ed. W. E. Cooper, K. Nielsen, and S. C. Patten, *Canadian Journal of Philosophy*, supplementary volume 5 (1979).

Eisenach, E. J. *Two worlds of Liberalism: Religion and Politics in Hobbes, Locke, and Mill*. Chicago: University of Chicago Press, 1981.

Feuer, L. S. "John Stuart Mill as a Sociologist: The Unwritten Ethology." In *James and John Stuart Mill: Papers of the Centenary Conference*, ed. John M. Robson and Michael Laine. Toronto: University of Toronto Press, 1976.

Fournier, G. "Influence de Coleridge sur Stuart Mill dans la problème de la liberté et de la necessité." *Revue de philosophie* 21 (1921): 134–51.

Galinsky, G. K. *The Herakles Theme*. Totowa, N.J.: Rowman and Littlefield, 1972.

Gay, Peter. "Freud and Freedom: On a Fox in Hedgehog's Clothing." In *The Idea of Freedom: Essays in Honour of Isaiah Berlin*, ed. Alan Ryan. Oxford: Oxford University Press, 1979.

Gilbert, Felix. *Machiavelli and Guicciardini*. Princeton: Princeton University Press, 1965.

Gildin, Hilail. "Mill's *On Liberty*," In *Ancients and Moderns: Essays on the Tradition of Political Philosophy in Honor of Leo Strauss*, ed. J. Cropsey. New York: Basic Books, 1964.

Gouhier, Henri. *La Jeunesse d'Auguste Comte et la formation du positivisme*. 3 vols. Paris: J. Vrin, 1933–41.

Halévy, Elie. *The Growth of Philosophic Radicalism.* 1928. Reprint. Clifton, N.J.: Augustus Kelley, 1972.

Hamburger, Joseph. *Intellectuals in Politics: John Stuart Mill and the Philosophic Radicals.* New Haven: Yale University Press, 1965.

———. "Mill and Tocqueville on Liberty." In *James and John Stuart Mill: Papers of the Centenary Conference*, ed. John M. Robson and Michael Laine. Toronto: University of Toronto Press, 1976.

Hayek, F. A. *The Constitution of Liberty.* Chicago: Gateway, 1960.

———. *The Road to Serfdom.* 1944. Reprint. London: Routledge & Kegan Paul, 1971.

Himmelfarb, Gertrude, ed. Introduction to *John Stuart Mill: Essays on Politics and Culture.* New York: Doubleday Anchor, 1962.

———. *On Liberty and Liberalism: The Case of John Stuart Mill.* New York: Knopf, 1974.

Humboldt, Wilhelm von. *Humanist without Portfolio: An Anthology of the Writings of Wilhelm von Humboldt.* Trans. Marianne Cowan. Detroit: Wayne State University Press, 1963.

———. *The Limits of State Action.* Ed. J. W. Burrow. Cambridge: Cambridge University Press, 1969.

Huth, A. H. *The Life and Writings of Henry Thomas Buckle.* New York, 1880.

Jevons, W. Stanley. *Letters & Journal of W. Stanley Jevons.* Ed. Harriet Ann Jevons. London: Macmillan, 1886.

———. *Pure Logic and Other Minor Works.* London: Macmillan, 1890.

Keynes, J. M. *Two Memoirs.* New York: A. M. Kelley, 1949.

Kingsley, Charles. *The Limits of Exact Science as Applied to History.* London: Macmillan, 1860.

Leroux, R. "Guillaume de Humboldt et John Stuart Mill." *Etudes germaniques*, 6 (1951): 262–74 and 7 (1952): 81–87.

Letwin, Shirley Robin. *The Pursuit of Certainty: David Hume, Jeremy Bentham, John Stuart Mill, Beatrice Webb.* London: Cambridge University Press, 1965.

Levi, Albert William. "The Value of Freedom: Mill's *Liberty* (1859–1959)." *Ethics* 70 (1959): 37–46.

Lévy-Bruhl, L., ed. *Lettres inédites de J. S. Mill à Auguste Comte.* Paris: Alcan, 1899.

Lindley, Dwight N. "The Saint Simonians, Carlyle and Mill: A Study in the History of Ideas." Ph.D. diss., Columbia University, 1958.

Lindsay, A. D. Introduction to *Utilitarianism, Liberty, and Representative Government,* by J. S. Mill. London: Dent, 1947.

Littré, M. P. E. *Auguste Comte et Stuart Mill.* Paris: Germer-Baillière, 1886.

Lively, J. and J. Rees, eds. *Utilitarian Logic and Politics: James Mill's "Essay on Government," Macaulay's Critique and the Ensuing Debate.* Oxford: Clarendon Press, 1978.

McCloskey, H. J. *John Stuart Mill: A Critical Study.* London: Macmillan, 1971.

Macpherson, C. B. *Democratic Theory: Essays in Retrieval.* Oxford: Clarendon Press, 1973.

———. *The Life and Times of Liberal Democracy.* Oxford: Oxford University Press, 1977.

MacRae, Donald Gunn. *Ideology and Society.* London: Heinemann, 1961.

Manuel, Frank E. *The New World of Henri Saint-Simon.* Cambridge: Harvard University Press, 1956.

———. *The Prophets of Paris.* New York: Harper, 1965.

Martineau, James. "John Stuart Mill." In vol. 3 of *Essays, Reviews, and Addresses.* London: Longmans, 1891.

Mayer, J.-P. *Alexis de Tocqueville: A Biographical Essay in Political Science.* New York: Viking, 1940.

Mazlish, Bruce. *James and John Stuart Mill: Father and Son in the Nineteenth Century.* New York: Basic Books, 1975.

Mill, John Stuart. *Autobiography and Literary Essays.* Vol 1 of *Collected Works.* Ed. J. M. Robson and J. Stillinger. Toronto: University of Toronto Press, 1981.

———. *The Autobiography of John Stuart Mill.* Ed. John Jacob Coss. New York: Columbia University Press, 1924.

———. *Dissertations and Discussions: Political, Philosophical, and Historical.* Vols. 1–2, London: J. W. Parker, 1859; vols. 3–4, London: Longmans, 1867, 1875.

———. *The Earlier Letters of John Stuart Mill, 1812–1848.* Vols 12–13 of *Collected Works.* Ed. Francis E. Mineka. Toronto: University of Toronto Press, 1963.

———. *The Early Draft of John Stuart Mill's Autobiography*. Ed. J. Stillinger. Urbana, Ill.: University of Illinois Press, 1961.

———. *Essays on Economics and Society*. Vols. 4–5 of *Collected Works*. Ed. J. M. Robson. Toronto: University of Toronto Press, 1967.

———. *Essays on Ethics, Religion, and Society*. Vol. 10 of *Collected Works*. Ed. J. M. Robson. Toronto: University of Toronto Press, 1969.

———. *Essays on Philosophy and the Classics*. Vol. 9 of *Collected Works*. Ed. J. M. Robson. Toronto: University of Toronto Press, 1978.

———. *Essays on Politics and Society*. Vols. 18–19 of *Collected Works*. Ed. J. M. Robson. Toronto: University of Toronto Press, 1977.

———. *An Examination of Sir William Hamilton's Philosophy*. Vol. 9 of *Collected Works*. Ed. J. M. Robson. Toronto: University of Toronto Press, 1979.

———. *The Later Letters of John Stuart Mill, 1849–1873*. Vols. 14–17 of *Collected Works*. Ed. F. E. Mineka and D. N. Lindley. Toronto: University of Toronto Press, 1972.

———. *Principles of Political Economy*. Vols. 2–3 of *Collected Works*. Ed. J. M. Robson. Toronto: University of Toronto Press, 1965.

———. *The Subjection of Women*. London: Longmans, Green, 1869.

———. *A System of Logic, Ratiocinative and Inductive*. Vols. 7–8 of *Collected Works*. Ed. J. M. Robson. Toronto: University of Toronto Press, 1974.

Morley, John. "Mr Mill's Three Essays on Religion." *Fortnightly Review* 22 (1 November 1874): 634–51 and 23 (1 January 1875): 103–31.

———. *Recollections*. Vol 1. London: Macmillan, 1917.

Mueller, Iris Wessel. *John Stuart Mill and French Thought*. Urbana: University of Illinois Press, 1956.

Neff, Emery. *Carlyle and Mill: An Introduction to Victorian Thought*. New York: Columbia University Press, 1926.

Packe, Michael St. John. *The Life of John Stuart Mill*. London: Secker and Warburg, 1954.

Pankhurst, R. K. P. *The Saint Simonians, Mill and Carlyle*. London: Sidgwick and Jackson, 1957.

Pappé, H. O. "The English Utilitarians and Athenian Democracy." In *Classical Influences on Western Thought: A. D. 1650–1870*, ed. R. R. Bolgar. Cambridge: Cambridge University Press, 1979.

———. *John Stuart Mill and the Harriet Taylor Myth*. Melbourne: Melbourne University Press, 1960.

Plamenatz, John P. *The English Utilitarians*. Oxford: Blackwell, 1966.

Popper, Karl R. *The Open Society and Its Enemies*. Princeton: Princeton University Press, 1950.

———. *The Poverty of Historicism*. London: Routledge & Kegan Paul, 1957.

Randall, J. H., Jr. *The Career of Philosophy*. 2 vols. New York: Columbia University Press, 1966.

Ratcliffe, B. M. and W. H. Chaloner, eds. *A French Sociologist Looks at Britain: Gustave d'Eichthal and British Society in 1828*. Manchester: Manchester University Press, 1977.

Rees, J. C. *Mill and His Early Critics*. Leicester: Leicester University Press, 1956.

Robertson, J. M. *Buckle and His Critics: A Study in Sociology*. London, 1895.

Robson, John M. *The Improvement of Mankind: The Social and Political Thought of John Stuart Mill*. Toronto: University of Toronto Press, 1968.

———. "Rational Animals and Others." In *James and John Stuart Mill: Papers of the Centenary Conference*, ed. John M. Robson and Michael Laine. Toronto: University of Toronto Press, 1976.

Robson, John M. and Michael Laine, eds. *James and John Stuart Mill: Papers of the Centenary Conference*. Toronto: University of Toronto Press, 1976.

Ryan, Alan, ed. *The Idea of Freedom: Essays in Honour of Isaiah Berlin*. Oxford: Oxford University Press, 1979.

———. *John Stuart Mill*. New York: Pantheon, 1970.

———. "Two Concepts of Politics and Democracy: James and John Stuart Mill." In *Machiavelli and the Nature of Political Thought*, ed. M. Fleisher. New York: Atheneum, 1972.

Schapiro, J. Salwyn. *Liberalism and the Challenge of Fascism*. New York: McGraw-Hill, 1949.

Schneewind, J. B., ed. *Mill: A Collection of Critical Essays*. New York: Doubleday Anchor, 1968.

Schwartz, Pedro. *The New Political Economy of J. S. Mill*. Durham, N.C.: Duke University Press, 1972.

Semmel, Bernard, *Jamaican Blood and Victorian Conscience*. Boston: Houghton Mifflin, 1963.

———. *The Methodist Revolution*. New York: Basic Books, 1973.

Siedentop, Larry. "Two Liberal Traditions." In *The Idea of Freedom: Essays in Honour of Isaiah Berlin,* ed. Alan Ryan. Oxford: Oxford University Press, 1979.

Skinner, B. F. *Beyond Freedom and Dignity*. New York: Knopf, 1972.

Skinner, Quentin. *The Foundations of Modern Political Thought*. Cambridge: Cambridge University Press, 1978.

Spitz, David. "Freedom and Individuality: Mill's *Liberty* in Retrospect." In *Liberty,* ed. C. J. Friedrich. New York: Atherton Press, 1962.

Stephen, James Fitzjames. *Liberty, Equality, Fraternity*. Ed. R. J. White. 1872. Reprint. Cambridge: Cambridge University Press, 1967.

Stephen, Leslie. *The English Utilitarians*. 3 vols. New York: Augustus Kelley, 1968.

Sweet, Paul R. *Wilhelm von Humboldt: A Biography*. Vol. 1. Columbus, Ohio: Ohio State University Press, 1978.

Taine, H. A. *History of English Literature*. 4 vols. Edinburgh: Edmonston and Douglas, 1871.

Taylor, Charles. "What's Wrong with Negative Liberty." In *The Idea of Freedom: Essays in Honour of Isaiah Berlin*, ed. Alan Ryan. Oxford: Oxford University Press, 1979.

Ten, C. L. *Mill on Liberty*. Oxford: Clarendon Press, 1980.

Thomas, William. *The Philosophic Radicals: Nine Studies in Theory and Practice, 1817–1841*. Oxford: Clarendon Press, 1979.

Thompson, D. F. *John Stuart Mill and Representative Government*. Princeton: Princeton University Press, 1976.

Tocqueville, Alexis de. *Correspondance anglaise*. Vol. 2 of *Oeuvres complètes*. Ed. J.-P. Mayer. Paris: Gallimard, 1954.

———. *Democracy in America*. New York: Harper & Row, 1966.

———. *"The European Revolution" & Correspondence with Gobineau*. Garden City, N.Y.: Doubleday Anchor, 1959.

———. *Oeuvres, papiers et correspondances*. Vols. 5 and 6 of *Oeuvres complètes*. Ed. J.-P. Mayer. Paris: Gallimard, 1954.

Viner, Jacob. "Bentham and J. S. Mill: The Utilitarian Background." In *The Long View and the Short*. Glencoe, Ill.: Free Press, 1958.

Whitehead, Alfred North. *Science and the Modern World*. New York: Macmillan, 1925.

Willey, Basil. *Nineteenth Century Studies*. New York: Columbia University Press, 1948.

Wolff, R. P. *The Poverty of Liberalism*. Boston: Beacon Press, 1968.

Wollheim, Richard. "John Stuart Mill and Isaiah Berlin: "The Ends of Life and the Preliminaries of Morality." In *The Idea of Freedom: Essays in Honour of Isaiah Berlin,* ed. Alan Ryan. Oxford: Oxford University Press, 1979.

Young, G. M. *Victorian England: Portrait of An Age*. New York: Doubleday Anchor, 1954.

Index